According to Islamic law, women are entitled to inherit property, to receive a dower at marriage, and to manage their own income. Through an anthropological study of Palestinian women in the Jabal Nablus region of the West Bank, Annelies Moors demonstrates that this is not always the case in practice. In fact, their options vary greatly depending on whether they gain access to property through inheritance, through the dower or through paid labour, and, indeed, on their background and position in society. The narratives of wealthy and poor urban women, and of women in the villages and in the refugee camps, indicate under what circumstances they claim property rights, when they are prevented from doing so, and in which contexts they prefer to give up property in order to gain other advantages. While this is essentially an ethnographic work, the author's use of court records has enabled her to address major historical changes in women's ability to negotiate their rights to property, focusing on the relation between local traditions, international politics and transnational labour migration.

*Cambridge Middle East Studies*

# Women, property and Islam

*Cambridge Middle East Studies 3*

**Cambridge Middle East Studies** has been established to publish books on the nineteenth- and twentieth-century Middle East and North Africa. The aim of the series is to provide new and original interpretations of aspects of Middle Eastern societies and their histories. To achieve disciplinary diversity, books will be solicited from authors writing in a wide range of fields including history, sociology, anthropology, political science and political economy. The emphasis will be on producing books offering an original approach along theoretical and empirical lines. The series is intended for students and academics, but the more accessible and wide-ranging studies will also appeal to the interested general reader.

# Women, property and Islam

*Palestinian experiences, 1920–1990*

Annelies Moors

*University of Amsterdam and University of Leiden*

CAMBRIDGE
UNIVERSITY PRESS

)f the University of Cambridge
itreet, Cambridge CB2 1RP
Y 10011-4211, USA
)ourne 3166, Australia

© Cambridge University Press 1995

First published 1995

Printed in Great Britain at the University Press, Cambridge

*A catalogue record for this book is available from the British Library*

*Library of Congress cataloguing in publication data applied for*

ISBN 0 521 47497 3 hardback
ISBN 0 521 48355 7 paperback

SE

This book is dedicated to the memory of my parents

# Contents

ix

# Acknowledgements

Without the help of my Palestinian friends this book could not have been written. Those who incorporated me into their families, in whose homes I slept, who shared their food with me, and who confided in me, providing me with the words and stories to write, have become part of my own history. I sincerely regret that, in order to protect their privacy, I am not able to thank them by name.

Palestinian institutional support was generously provided by Al-Najah National University and the University of Bir Zeit. The Nablus Shariʿa Court allowed me to work extensively in their archives, while the Tailoring Workers Union and the Committee of Working Women, both in Nablus, assisted me with regard to women garment workers. I am also grateful to the Municipality of Nablus for their help.

Financial support was given, in chronological order, by the University of Amsterdam, the Funds to Promote Emancipatory Research, the Foundation for Social and Cultural Sciences (subsidised by the Netherlands Organisation for Scientific Research), and Leiden University.

For reading earlier drafts of this study when it was still a PhD thesis I am grateful to Kathy Glavanis, Niko Kielstra, Joyce Outshoorn, Rudolph Peters, Joke Schrijvers, Wasif Shadid, Leila Shahid, and Salim Tamari. Nadieh al-Fuqaha is thanked for transcribing numerous tapes and commenting on these, and Lynn Welchman and Judith Tucker for pleasant discussions on the West Bank court material. The comments on my presentation by the trainees of the Women's Resource Centre, started by Sahar Khalifa in Nablus, have been particularly helpful, as were the comments of Pandeli Glavanis following my presentations at the Middle East ERASMUS seminar in Amsterdam.

I would finally like to thank those friends, students, and colleagues who have supported me in completing this study, especially Anna Aalten and Helma Lutz. Most of all I would like to thank my family and especially my parents, who through their own life stories have made me aware of the relations between biography and society, and my husband, Steven Wachlin, who has encouraged me to complete secondary education and has remained supportive of my scholarly endeavours ever since.

# 1 Introduction: women and property

## 1.1 The theme: lessons from the field

It was during my first fieldwork in a West Bank village in 1981 that my attention was drawn to property. I was struck by the restrained eagerness with which elderly rural women told me about the dower gold they had received at marriage and what they had done with it. The anthropological literature on the Middle East which I had read rarely referred to women's access to property and if it did so, then the focus was on women's inheritance rights.[1] Yet when I asked women in the village whether they had received an inheritance share, they seemed somehow ill at ease and emphasised that they had refrained from claiming their rights. Questions abounded. Why did elderly women express pride in the fact that they had bought goats and even land from their dower gold, but show discomfort at the thought of claiming a share in their father's estate?

Talking with women from different walks of life further complicated the issue. A superficial reading of the dower system may lead one to interpret it as a transfer of resources from men to women, a system it would seem to be in women's interest to support. Indeed, many rural women considered the dower as an important institution through which they could acquire property. Yet, younger village women rarely expressed an interest in selling their gold to buy productive property; they would rather invest it in their husband and his house. Urban, educated women commonly recognised the dower as part of their cultural heritage, but tended to downplay the material side of it, dismissing a (high) dower as an archaic practice, degrading to women. They did, however, consider it quite acceptable for women to claim their inheritance share, while many of those who were employed were able to acquire considerable property, such as real estate, through a career in professional work. This raised more questions. With the dower being such a gender-

---

[1] In his anthropological introduction to the Middle East, Eickelman (1989), for instance, pays considerable attention to marriage, but spends no more than a few words on the dower as women's property. For the literature on women's inheritance rights, see chapter 3.

specific institution, why did women differ so much in their attitudes and practices toward it? How did this tie in with the various ways in which they dealt with their inheritance share and with property acquired through paid labour?

If discussions with Palestinian women encouraged me to focus on property, they were not the only source of inspiration. In *Orientalism*, Said (1978) has argued that the tremendous emphasis in Western discourse on the dichotomy between the West and the Orient has been intrinsically linked to projects of domination. As gender issues have been central to debates about Orientalism, writing on women in the Middle East requires a critical reflection upon established scholarly traditions.[2] With the Middle East historically reduced to Islam, there has been a strong tendency to define women from this region as 'Muslim women'. This has not only encouraged a culturalist perspective, but has also tended to underline the homogeneity of women in the region and – because of the negative associations of Islam – their particular subordination.[3]

Discussing women's access to property can help challenge this discourse. Yet, as Abu-Lughod (1990: 104) has pointed out, this very 'arguing against' established stereotypes may well lead to parochialism and discourage theoretical reflection if it becomes the sole *raison d'être* of subsequent work. For instance, women's rights to property ownership in Islamic law have frequently been cited as an indication of the high regard in which Islam holds women. Such an approach may well turn out to be an inversion of the Orientalist discourse; Islam is valued positively, but the culturalist approach, the textual nature of the method, and the conceptualisation of Muslim women as a homogeneous category are not questioned. In this study the way in which the material presented contributes to specific theoretical discussions is referred to in the relevant chapters. Before turning to the multifarious relations of women to property, I will, however, first elaborate on some theoretical notions which inform my approach.

---

[2] See Lazreg (1988) for this discussion in general; Keddie (1979) and Tucker (1983) focus on history; Waines (1982) and Abu-Lughod (1990) concentrate on anthropology. Sayigh (1981), Joseph (1986), and Ahmed (1992) underline how gender issues have been used in political interventions for such divergent aims as to justify state rule, to defend or criticise religion and culture or to argue for social transformation.

[3] Actually the main problem is not so much the label 'Islam' in itself, but the process of differentiating, taking place within the framework of contrast schemes, with the Orient standing in a continually reproduced negative opposition to the West. Just as Western concepts of femininity are divergent, contradictory and historically specific, so too constructions of 'Oriental femininity' are not unitary. Yet here it suffices to point out that the particular subordination of 'Muslim women' is a dominant strand of thought (see Moors 1991a: 116).

## 1.2    The perspective: a note on women and property

*'Subordinated women': owners of property?*

Both in anthropology and in Middle Eastern studies, considerable attention has been paid to women. The centrality of kinship and marriage in anthropology has made it hard to leave women out of the picture, while the fascination with women in Middle Eastern studies has led Sayigh (1981: 258) to refer to a 'woman complex'. The way in which women have been represented is, however, problematic. In the established anthropological discourse women's subordination has commonly been taken for granted. This implies not only that gender asymmetry was not questioned but also that gender differences were often automatically interpreted in terms of gender hierarchy. In the case of the Middle East, this tied in well with the emphasis in Orientalist discourse on the subordinate position of Muslim women.

Such a perspective in itself discourages focusing on women's access to property. While for women on the West Bank marriage presentations have been a major source of property, anthropologists of various persuasions have concentrated on the rights a man acquires in his wife and the presentations offered for her, rather than discussing a woman's rights in her husband or the presentations she herself receives.[4] Some have explained this bias by pointing to how anthropologists up to the 1960s displayed greater interest in bridewealth, lineages and tribal communities than in dowry, households and peasant and urban societies (Schlegel and Eloul 1988: 299). Yet such an explanation is insufficient, as those who have done work on dowry systems have also tended to overlook the importance of dowry as a device for women to acquire property. Goody, for example, whose work I will discuss later, has indeed paid attention to property transferred to women through dowry, yet at the same time he considers a woman's economic dependence on her husband as self-evident. Taking women's subordination as a point of departure impedes a serious discussion of women's access to, and control over, property.

On the other hand, there is also a considerable body of anthropological literature on women and property which does problematise women's subordination. Gender asymmetry has been central in the work of those nineteenth-century thinkers whose interest focused on the relations

---

[4] This is the case in different anthropological traditions which largely neglect 'women as actors'. Radcliffe-Brown pays attention only to the rights men gain over women (see Caplan 1984); Meillassoux defines women as 'the means of reproduction' (see Harris and Young 1981); while for Lévi-Strauss the exchange of women is a structural principle (see MacCormack 1980).

between property rights, marriage forms and the position of women. Twentieth-century critics have largely dismissed this earlier work because of its very limited access to field data and the strongly evolutionist perspective it employed. Yet, the work of Engels (1884) in particular has had a strong impact on feminist studies. Various authors have critically elaborated on his thesis that women's subordination originated in the development of private ownership of the means of production, monogamous marriage and the marginalisation of women from social production.[5]

In various ways, these studies trace the origins of women's subordination to the development of private property ownership and class society. Since in twentieth-century Palestine, most property was already held individually and women had less access to the means of production than men, my questions are different. My interest here is not to trace origins, but rather to look closely at changes in the women–property relation from the 1920s to the late 1980s. Ignoring women's access to property in 'class societies' leaves out issues which are important to women on the West Bank and makes processes of change within such societies invisible. Before discussing these issues, it is necessary to explain some of the concepts used, in particular 'property', 'women' and 'power'.

### Situating property: persons and things

The common sense notion of property as consisting of things or objects owned by persons with specific rights takes for granted a strict separation between 'persons' and 'things'. Yet such a notion is far from universal. Strathern (1984: 164ff.), for instance, has pointed out that where gift exchange rather than commodity exchange is central, such as in Melanesia, there is no separation between 'person' and 'thing', between subject and object; part of the person resides in the exchanged thing. Working in a very different setting, Bourdieu (1979; 1980) has stretched the notion of capital to include not only material means but also membership in social groups and cultural knowledge. Social and cultural capital, such as that embodied in certified education, are forms of 'property' which are personally held and cannot be separated from the person.

Rather than taking the notion of property as the ownership of things by people as point of departure, this study is informed by the work of those who see property as a social relation, a relation between individuals or groups holding rights vis-à-vis each other, which may be expressed in terms of rights of control over things. As Whitehead (1984) has pointed

---

[5] For a critical appraisal of his work see, for instance, various contributions in *Critique of Anthropology* (1977), in Hirshon (1984), and in Sayers *et al.* (1987).

out in her discussion of gender and property, this asks for a shift in focus from property as a material resource to concepts of the person. Taking issue with a materialist strand of thought which sees social relations as grounded in property, Whitehead's work indicates how access to and control over property can be seen as the outcome of gendered power relations.[6] She argues that in kinship or family systems in all societies women are constructed, both legally and actually, as less separable from other people than men, and women's capacity to act in relation to property is always more circumscribed than that of men (1984: 180; 189). Although I do not share her universalism, her focus on gender invites a thorough contextualisation of property, which goes beyond linking the nature of property relations to specific economic systems. Appadurai's work (1986) on commodity exchange has further encouraged such a line of thought. Arguing against distinguishing between things which are commodities and which are not (as has often been done by linking commodities with capitalism), he sees commodities as things in certain situations and underlines the need to look at the commodity potential of all things (1986: 13). Informed by his approach, the emphasis in this study is on the situated nature of property. In the Jabal Nablus region, women's control over property does not depend on the nature of the property involved so much as on the way in which it was acquired. A woman's ability to deal with land for instance, may vary depending on whether she obtained it as part of her father's estate, whether it was given to her as dower, or whether she had bought it from her savings from paid employment.

### Conceptualising women: position and power

Discussing the women–property nexus raises questions not only about what is meant by property but also about how women might be conceptualised. Feminist anthropology started a critique of established anthropological discourse by exposing male bias in the apparently gender-neutral concept of humanity, problematising women's subordination rather than taking it for granted. Considerable emphasis was placed on similarities between women, on a woman's point of view, and on the repressive nature of power; women were by and large regarded as victims of a universal system of male domination.

Such a strong emphasis on sameness and identification can be read as a powerful critique of Orientalism's essentialised cultural difference. Yet, in various ways the theoretical notions implied in such an approach have become disputed. Leacock (1978), for instance, has taken its universalist

---

[6] For an elaborate study of theories about the relations between property and power, see Pels (1986).

assumptions to task and has criticised such a perspective for being ahistorical. Black women have shown how taking sameness as a point of departure often implied a projection of Western women's concerns onto 'other women'. Reducing women's problems to gender issues and the female subject to gender identity, has led to the erasure of other power differentiations, such as race.[7]

The essentialism inherent in universalist perspectives has also become criticised. Rather than accepting 'women' and 'men' as given, feminist studies raised the question of what it means to be a woman (or a man). For anthropologists, emphasis on the constructed nature of gender was first of all an emphasis on its cultural construction (MacCormack and Strathern 1980; Ortner and Whitehead 1981). A further deconstruction of the category 'women' has entailed the recognition of a multiplicity of differences in which no specific difference (be it gender, class, ethnicity or whatever) is granted *a priori* significance. The female subject is then no longer conceptualised as unitary, fixed and with an essence; rather, identity is seen as fragmented, in process, possibly ambiguous and even contradictory (Flax 1987). These notions have been helpful in understanding contradictions in the views women express in regard to property. If giving property to a husband means both upward social mobility *and* greater dependence on the husband, women may express contradictory opinions, depending on whether their frame of reference at the moment of speaking is class or gender. There is, then, no point in looking for women's 'true' or 'authentic' point of view. The aim, rather, becomes to understand their statements within the relevant context.

Yet a focus on meanings, texts and discourses runs the danger of leaving out concrete experiences of individual women and the way in which these are infused with power. In this regard, Alcoff's (1988) elaboration on positionality has been helpful. In her view, the concept of woman is relational in the sense that her identity is relative to a constantly shifting context, yet at the same time she argues for its grounding by concentrating on the differences between women in terms of their daily lived experiences. Among themselves, women have unequal access to power resources, and we need to recognise that gender asymmetry is intertwined with a multitude of power differentials (Alcoff 1988: 433ff.); for instance, in the Jabal Nablus region the dower may be gendered property *par excellence* but it is also interwoven with social inequalities among women.

To discuss positionality it is necessary to deal with power. In anthropology (and other social sciences), perspectives which focus on either systemic power or on individual agency have increasingly given way to a

---

[7] For early critiques see, for instance, hooks (1982); Hull *et al.* (1982); and Amos and Parmar (1984).

'practice perspective' (Ortner 1984) which focuses on both. Such an approach does not consider that structural elements fully determine people's lives, but neither does it give exclusive attention to human agency or endow the acting individual with total freedom of action. The powerful effects which constrain or enable human action are located not only in the economy and politics but also in culture. These systems are constituted through the practices of individuals, which produce, reproduce and transform them. In this way, a practice perspective pays attention to processes of change. Similarly, the concept of positionality does not imply that 'women' are solely determined by the external context; it also acknowledges that women can use the position they are located in to construct meaning and to develop strategies. Focusing on women's situated practices invites us to look at the widely varying strategies women employ in the field of property, without losing sight of the constraints of the system. As such, it stimulates discussing gender without taking its meaning or significance as a point of departure; it calls attention to power, without defining 'Muslim women' *a priori* as victims of 'Islamic social structure' or, in its mirror image, underlining women's capability to act freely.

## 1.3     From fieldwork to text

### Sources and methods: the oral and the written

Anthropological fieldwork is often equated with participant observation. What this means largely depends on the background of the researcher, with 'insiders' becoming observers through developing detachment and distance and 'outsiders' turning into (partial) participants through a process of socialisation.[8] The strength of this method is its dynamic character, the acknowledgement of a 'relation in process' between researcher and researched. Yet the notion of observation tends to emphasise distanciation between subject and object, rather than understanding through communication (see Fabian 1983). In this study, descriptions of an observational nature have largely given way to the words of the women concerned, filtered through my presence and presentation.

If socialising and socialisation involve a continuous and highly fluid process, I also followed two more specific paths to gain insight in the women–property nexus: archival research in the Nablus shariʿa court and topical life story interviews. The archival data, mainly consisting of marriage contracts, divorce registrations and summaries of court cases,

---

[8] The various contributions in Altorki and El-Solh (1988) point to the problem of drawing the line between 'insider' and 'outsider'.

are one of the few contemporary sources available. Whereas these sources cannot be taken to reflect actual social practices, they do document the history of the *registration* of marriages, divorces and court cases. If brides did not always receive the dower written down in the contracts, these contracts are present in sufficiently large numbers to gain insight into the historical trends in dower registrations. While not all repudiations were brought to court, the divorce registers indicate historical changes in the various ways of registering separations. It is true that the summaries of court cases do not reveal all incongruencies between the law and social practices, but these cases do indicate under which circumstances women were willing and able to turn to the court to claim the rights they were not automatically granted.

My main source, however, has been interviews with women from various backgrounds centring around specific aspects of property relations. Inspired by Bertaux (1980), I have opted for the topical life story method. In Bertaux's view, acquiring knowledge is a process, with one story building upon the other. Through a process of 'saturation of knowledge', with new stories increasingly confirming what is already understood, one may become aware of recurrent practices and structural relations (Bertaux 1980: 37). Such life stories are pivotal in gaining insight into the relation between structural power and individual agency. They indicate how the system influences women's access to property, while simultaneously demonstrating how actors cope with these restraints, define their interests and reproduce or transform the system. Topical life stories can, for example, elucidate earlier dower practices – which none of the contemporary written sources revealed – such as women refraining from claiming the full dower in order to strengthen their bargaining position *vis-à-vis* their husbands. But these stories are always constructions in retrospect. What can be discussed depends on many factors, such as later experiences of those interviewed and present-day views on the topics concerned. It also depends on the relation between those interviewed and the anthropologist.

## Fieldwork: methods in practice

As personal relations between researcher and researched are so central in anthropological fieldwork, it is necessary to provide an account of how these relations developed through time so that readers are able to evaluate the material presented. Still, readers ought to keep in mind that the authenticity of such personal accounts always remains in question. If anthropologists are able to write about others because they provide some degree of anonymity, in writing about oneself no such option is available.

Some measure of self-censoring is inevitable, be it for personal, political or cultural reasons.

Given that 'becoming socialised' is such a fluid and unbounded process, I find it hard to delineate the exact period I was engaged in fieldwork. In the early 1970s, I lived for several years in the Middle East, mainly in Syria. My later academic interest in the area was the result of my encounters with women in the Middle East, which stimulated me to take up anthropology. In a sense, then, fieldwork started long before I began my first fieldwork in 1980/81, when I spent about nine months in the Jabal Nablus region. At that time, the focus of my research was on changes in the gender division of labour in the rural areas. Israeli control made renting village accommodation problematic, so together with my husband, who did some teaching at the local Al-Najah National University, I lived in Nablus city. I was, however, able to spend on average three to four days a week in the village on end, lodging with various families. When I returned later for shorter periods of fieldwork, concentrating on the urban context and spending gradually more and more time in one of the refugee camps on the edge of the city, my earlier experiences in the city were very helpful even if these had not constituted 'fieldwork' in the narrow sense of the word. In total, I have spent roughly one year and nine months in the Jabal Nablus region.

The major factors affecting the way in which I was able to do fieldwork were politics and gender. My connections with Al-Najah University opened many doors and gave me credibility in Palestinian circles. The university and other non-governmental institutions, such as hospitals, have given me complete freedom to interview on their premises, while the shariʿa court allowed me to work on court material for considerable stretches of time. I did not, however, approach Israeli institutions in the occupied territories. The (Israeli-run) office of land registration and the labour exchanges (where Palestinian workers from the occupied territories have to apply for permits to work in Israel) may have had interesting data on women's access to land and labour, but well-informed sources strongly discouraged me from approaching them, as it would only draw attention to my presence and yield little result. Also, I was not very eager to do so, as I found it difficult to switch between being socialised in the Palestinian community and dealing, as a foreigner, with the occupational forces.

Gender also influenced the relations I could develop in the field. In a sense, distancing myself from men was almost a condition for developing meaningful relations with women. Although it is true that the practical implications of gender differed according to the setting, with gender segregation in social interaction more strictly adhered to in the villages than in the city or the camps, I chose to work with and through women in all locations. To a large extent this was imperative because of my interest in women's strategies in regard to property. It was, however, also the result of the restraint required in relations between unrelated men and women. Well aware of the doubts people held about Western women's morality, I may have expressed this restraint even more than local women. In as far as I talked to men – and with some of them I did so extensively – this was usually in a formal interview setting; informal talks were largely limited to men closely related to the women I was visiting.

When in December 1987 the intifada began, notions of freedom of movement were transformed. In a way, gender turned out to be an advantage, with the situation for men more dangerous in terms of direct army violence. Still, everyone was effected by the extensive and complete curfews which the army imposed.[9] To some extent I could counteract its effects by renting accommodation where I was able to socialise with many women without having to go onto the streets. Yet as this was also very close to a non-governmental hospital where many of the intifada victims were brought, this meant a continuous and direct confrontation with the army's indiscriminate violence and attempts at totalising power.[10] Once it became clear that the intifada would continue for a considerable period, I did what most people attempted to do, that is to continue with their work in spite of the harsh repression. As research for this study was conducted up to 1989, the impact of the first two years of the intifada on women's access to property is touched upon. It has not become the major focus of this study, however, as its main thrust concerns longer-term processes of historical change. Whenever the ethnographic present is used in this study, it refers to the late 1980s.

To evaluate the topical life stories which are central in this study, something needs to be said about the interactions and conversations on which these are based, and how these were coloured by people's perceptions of me. Since my research questions required interviews with women from divergent socio-economic backgrounds, coming from abroad may have been an advantage. The feelings of the wealthy towards the poor and vice versa were often antagonistic, and it was helpful that I did not occupy

---

[9] During the intifada, I did fieldwork in the summers of 1988 and 1989. Roughly one-quarter of the four and a half months I spent in the Jabal Nablus region was under complete curfew.

[10] Some victims were very young, many were shot in the back and virtually all of them were from the poorer sectors of society. The army did not hesitate to burst into the hospital and to take those wounded with them; and the relatives of those who died had to control their grief in order to hope to avoid attracting the army's attention which would then claim the body in order to prevent a martyr's funeral.

a space in the local class hierarchy and that my own class background was not immediately transparent. 'Being educated', a central aspect of my identity as everyone knew I was involved in academic research, helped my relations with the elite, many of whom were themselves academically trained. And amongst the poor, everyone knew examples of upward social mobility such as a lower-class woman entering university, a situation much closer to my own background.

My relations with individual women differed according to a host of factors, such as age, marital status, employment, personality and politics, yet the major divide I perceived was that of class. That my 'interview relations' with the well-to-do and the poor were so different relates largely to their different concepts of propriety. Urban women from a prominent background would usually allow me an interview at their homes, and often were very open during these interviews, but only in a few cases did anything more than a formal interview relation develop. Most of these topical life story constructs are based on a limited number of interviews, often no more than two. Although at first I thought I ought to try harder, gradually it became evident that restraint and being in control are central elements in the upper-class ideal of womanhood.

My relations with the lower classes, with the women in the camps and the villages, were very different. We would eat together, and they would invite me to sleep in their houses and sometimes to wear their clothing. Through this extensive socialising, many of them attempted to break down barriers between us and to incorporate me into their world. For some of them, I represented contact with relatives abroad, and with my reasonable but far from perfect Arabic I was often taken for a visiting migrant. The greater informality of these contacts and the close relations which developed with many of them meant that what they told me in 'formal interviews' was elaborated upon in many informal talks.

### Writing it up: creating images

In this study, topical life stories are not only a source for gaining insight into social relations, but also a medium for creating images. In anthropology, the emphasis on cultural specificity can have the effect of exoticising others and constructing them as fundamentally different from 'us'. Keesing (1989) convincingly argues that anthropologists tend to select the most exotic cultural texts, and to interpret these in the most exotic ways; those aspects of other cultures which are similar to 'our own' are generally not considered worth writing and publishing about. In the case of the Middle East, this ties in with the Orientalist discourse, which, as

has been argued elsewhere, also underlines difference and creates distance.[11] As a consequence, the literature on this area has paid relatively
little attention to, for instance, the rather mundane concept of the male
provider, which is central in Islamic law and, as it turns out, also in social
practice in the Jabal Nablus region.

Focusing on the experiences of individual women from divergent
backgrounds and in very different positions, I hope to avoid creating an
image of essential difference. In extensively presenting their stories,
rather than seeing them as 'cultural dupes' or victims of their own society,
I intend to convey both their concerns, the way in which their options
have been limited by systemic power, and the strategies they themselves
have developed. Although many of these stories refer to a harsh reality, I
hope that they also bring out women's understanding of their own
situation, and the ways in which they attempt to make the best of it, in
some cases enforcing existing gender asymmetries, in other cases suc-
ceeding in changing the system.

In a sense, their stories are all there is to say; many women described
their own particular situation in terms no social scientist could improve.
Yet gaining insights into historical processes of change requires knowledge of a different sort, the ability to build on the stories of women in
various walks of life and from different generations, knowledge not
immediately available to each individual actor (see Bertaux 1980: 40).
This is what I intend to do in the contexts I provide for these stories. As I
present the stories quite extensively and in detail, even if they are limited
to certain topics, the reader is given an impression of the nature of the
material these contexts are based on. Issues the women raised which did
not fit neatly into the subsequent contextualising paragraphs have not
been erased, but are referred to in later sections or may well escape any of
the contexts. As such they can be a check as to the relevance of the contexts
provided.

In choosing which topical life stories to include in this study, my main
concern has not always been their representativeness; this issue I have
addressed, if necessary, in the accompanying contexts. Rather, I have
opted to include the stories of those women who were most apt at
conveying their concerns, feelings and understandings to me. Writing up
their stories I have attempted to remain as close as possible to their own
words; many of the stories were tape-recorded at least in part. However, I
have taken the liberty to engage in extensive editing as these stories are not
presented for the sake of detailed narrative analysis, but rather to gain
insight in social relations. Moreover, as *topical* life stories they are

---

[11] See Abu-Lughod (1990) about how anthropologists in their quest for the exotic have
created their own Middle East.

explicitly partial and do not hold any claims to comprehensiveness. This then means that these stories are very much my constructs. Still, the women themselves have set the limits within which I have been able to do so; they have made the first selection by choosing to talk to me or not, and by deciding what to tell me.

The set up of this study reflects the terms women themselves employed in discussing property. In the course of the research process, it became evident that the generic terms for property, such as *mulk* or *milkiyya*, which largely refer to the legal discourse, had little meaning to them. They saw the meaning of property as intrinsically tied up with how they had gained access to it. Their access to and control over property differed considerably according to whether they had acquired it through inheritance (*mīrāth*), the dower (*mahr*) or paid employment (*ujra*). Accordingly, this study is in three parts which follow these concepts.

Part I sets out the life stories of four women from very different backgrounds. Placing these stories within the wider context of historical developments is a way to personalise history. At the same time, these stories also form the context for the subsequent discussions of women's access to property through either inheritance or the dower. Part II centres on the *mahr*, the dower, for many women the main way to gain access to property. Here, the four women through whose lives the history of Jabal Nablus was introduced elaborate on their own dower payments or those of their daughters or granddaughters, with related cases drawn in for contrast and further development of the argument. Women's access to wage labour, another device through which they acquire property, is discussed in part III. Here, twelve labour stories are presented to give insight into the labour–property nexus.

*Part I*

# Politics, economy and kinship

This section concentrates on the transfer of property from one generation to the next. Considering general socio-economic trends in the Jabal Nablus region, chapter 2 is introductory in several senses. It introduces four women, Imm Sālim, Imm Shākir, Imm Hilmī and Imm Muhammad by presenting their topical life stories and in this way acquaints us with the women whose inheritance and dower practices will be considered in later chapters.[1] Their stories personalise the historical transformation of Palestine, while the accompanying texts on the history of the specific localities where they live – the village of Al-Balad, the city of Nablus and the Balata refugee camp – contextualise their stories.[2] Chapter 2 introduces the major shifts in property relations. Since most property is male owned and controlled, women's direct access to property is only touched upon; terms such as landowner, peasant and so on refer here to men, unless stated otherwise. In fact, the material presented indicates the importance of men, both husband and kin, to the general socio-economic security of women. This is all the more so as none of the four women considered here is formally employed. (Women's access to property through paid labour will be addressed in part III.)

In chapter 3, on women and inheritance, I briefly return to the life stories of these four women as a starting point from which to discuss the gendered nature of inheritance patterns. It is true that the dower can also be seen as a mechanism for transferring property from one generation to the next, while some property is inherited laterally rather than lineally. Still, inheritance is crucial for the generational transfer of resources amongst property-owners. Major issues to be discussed are whether inheritance rights and practices are gender specific and how various

---

[1] To protect the privacy of the women whose stories I present, all names in this study are fictitious. A married woman with sons is referred to as 'Imm' (mother of) followed by the name of her eldest son. To the name of elderly single women the term 'Sitt' (a polite form of addressing adult women) is prefixed.

[2] While the city of Nablus and the Balata refugee camp are real names, Al-Balad is a fictitious name, as in such a small village (in the early 1980s less than 2,000 inhabitants) individual cases could easily be traced.

15

categories of women are able to gain access to property through inheritance. These questions, however, quickly dissolve under further scrutiny and bring us back to some of the debates presented in chapter 1. Most important in the field of inheritance are the multiple meanings of inheriting property to the women concerned. Women in different positions employ divergent strategies and inheriting property is not unequivocally an effect of power.

# 2     The lives of four women: introducing property and politics

After a sketch of the international context, this chapter introduces the main property-related developments in the Jabal Nablus region through the life stories of four women from diverse backgrounds and locations. Certainly, the historical transformation of Palestine has affected the lives of all of them. Yet their experiences also show considerable variation. The gap between rural and urban life in Jabal Nablus has been wide, the experiences of the wealthy had little in common with those of the poor, and the life courses of the women who came as refugees to Nablus show particular discontinuities.

## 2.1     Palestine: the international context

In Ottoman times, the Jabal Nablus region was the most continuously and densely populated region of Palestine, covering the central portion of the interior hills which run in a north–south direction. While Jabal means mountain, the term Jabal Nablus referred to the whole rural hinterland under the control of the city of Nablus, reaching from the coastal plains on the West to the Jordan Valley in the East. Whereas Jabal Nablus had once been a relatively autonomous region of the Ottoman Empire, in the nineteenth century the Ottoman rulers succeeded in strengthening their control over this area.[3]

The population of the Arab provinces, including Palestine, expected the defeat of the Ottoman empire in the First World War to lead to independence. But things turned out very differently. In true colonial style, Great Britain and France divided the region between themselves with the mandate over Palestine granted to Great Britain. The promise to the Zionist movement, included in the British mandate, to establish a national home for the Jewish people in Palestine was to have far-reaching consequences for the local population. The Zionist aim to build a separate Jewish community with its own institutions, ideally employing Jewish

---

[3] See Doumani (1995 forthcoming) for a comprehensive study of developments in Jabal Nablus in Ottoman times.

labour on Jewish land and buying Jewish produce, could not but entail the dispossession and exclusion of the non-Jewish population. Areas with little or no Jewish settlement, such as Jabal Nablus, were also affected. As British policy supported Jewish rather than Arab development the economic centre of Palestine shifted more and more from the interior hills to the coastal areas (Asad 1976: 4–7; Graham-Brown 1982: 90).

Popular protest did not turn into organised resistance until the mid-1930s, when Jewish immigration increased strongly with the rise of Nazism in Germany. In the spring of 1936 the Arab leaders called a general strike, and an armed revolt broke out which the British army was unable to suppress until 1939. After the Second World War Britain had to admit that it could no longer control the situation and returned its mandate to the United Nations. The 1947 partition plan they came up with was unacceptable to the Palestinians, since the Jews, who by then formed 30 per cent of the population and owned less than 6 per cent of the land, were to be given 54 per cent of it, including most of the irrigated land. But worse was to come. The Jewish armed forces had already driven hundreds of thousands of Palestinians from their homes, when, on 15 May 1948, the state of Israel was proclaimed. As a result of the ensuing war, the new Jewish state came to occupy over 77 per cent of historical Palestine. About three-quarters of the one million Palestinians who had been living there were forced to flee to neighbouring countries. In Palestinian history, this is known as the *nakba*, the disaster.[4]

That part of Palestine that was incorporated by Jordan became known as the West Bank. The new borders separated the interior hills from the coastal areas, disrupted migration and trade patterns and barred land-owners from their property. The large number of refugees fleeing to the West Bank resulted in a sudden increase of the population there from 450,000 inhabitants in 1947 to 850,000 a year later, some of whom were to continue eastward (Van Arkadie 1977: 22). When it became clear that Israel would not allow these refugees to return to their homes in the near future, the UNRWA (United Nations Relief and Works Agency) was established in 1950 to 'assimilate' them into the neighbouring countries and to take care of some of their basic needs. The same year Jordan officially annexed the West Bank and its inhabitants became Jordanian citizens. Expressions of nationalist resistance were suppressed and the centre of power shifted from Jerusalem to Amman. As most foreign aid and public expenditure were directed to the East Bank, higher wages and more investment opportunities there attracted both labour and capital

---

[4] For extensive data on the demographic transformation of Palestine see Abu-Lughod (1971), and for the process of expulsion Morris (1987).

from the West Bank.[5] Beginning in the early 1950s the rapid expansion of
oil production in the Gulf States further encouraged labour migration, in
particular to Kuwait. In 1961 the number of 'Jordanians abroad' from the
Nablus district reached over 30,000 (8.3 per cent of its total population);
more than 70 per cent went to Kuwait and 22 per cent to other Arab
countries (First Census 1963: 315).[6]

When in 1967 the Israeli army defeated those of Egypt, Syria and
Jordan the whole of mandatory Palestine came under Israeli rule. During
the first three months after the war over one-fifth of the West Bank
population fled to the other side of the Jordan river (Mansour 1988: 82).
Except for East Jerusalem, Israel has avoided the formal annexation of the
West Bank, which would have brought up the issue of citizenship of the
Palestinian population, but has opted for rule by force (military occupation).[7] This allowed for the continuation of some measure of Jordanian
influence over the West Bank. Jordanian government departments on the
West Bank continued to function, but were placed under the supervision
of the Israeli military administration, while existing legislature has been
adapted by over one thousand military orders. The major exception to
such Israeli interference has been the shariᶜa court system and personal
status law which have remained under Jordanian control.[8]

Major effects of the Israeli occupation for the Palestinian population
have been the dispossession of resources and economic dependency.
Immediately after occupation, military orders were issued to limit
Palestinian control over land and water resources. By the mid-1980s, over
half of West Bank land was under Israeli control, either for military use or
for establishing settlements, and strict limits were imposed on water use.[9]
Economically, the West Bank rapidly turned into a large captive market
and a pool of cheap labour for Israeli producers. Within a few years after

[5] As a result there was little industrial development on the West Bank; the main sources of
income were agriculture, tourism, the UNRWA and migration. In 1965 industry
contributed about 7 per cent to the West Bank GNP, while remittances from abroad were
almost 12 per cent (Van Arkadie 1977: 24).

[6] In Jabal Nablus, migration was a more recent phenomenon than in the central parts of the
West Bank with a longer tradition of migration to the West, in particular to the United
States and Latin America.

[7] Denying the Palestinians citizenship rights would have meant the institutionalisation of
an apartheid-like system, while granting them these rights would have resulted in a very
substantial non-Jewish minority in the Jewish state.

[8] When in 1988 Jordan formally withdrew its claim to the West Bank, and cut all legal and
administrative links with the area, this was again with the exception of the Ministry of
Awqaf (religious endowments) and the shariᶜa courts. For the legal situation of the
population of the West Bank under Israeli occupation, see Bisharat (1989) and Welchman
(1990).

[9] For a general overview, see Graham-Brown (1984a) and Benvenisti (1986).

the occupation, about 90 per cent of the West Bank imports came from or via Israel and the ensuing enormous deficit on the trade balance of the West Bank was largely compensated for by income from abroad. About one-third of the Palestinians from the West Bank were employed in Israel, or over half if the 'unofficial workers' (those not registered at the labour exchanges) are also included. In the Nablus region, however, with greater distances to Israeli work sites and more local employment available, the number of those working in Israel remained relatively low. In 1980, for example, only 13.8 per cent of registered workers in Israel came from the Nablus region (Graham-Brown 1984a: 211). During the mid- and late 1970s, migration eastward gained momentum as a result of the oil-induced economic boom in Jordan and the Gulf States. From the early 1980s on, however, migration dropped significantly due to the recession in the Gulf and increased Israeli and Jordanian restrictions on Palestinian entry and departure. Still, according to Israeli sources, in 1984 transfers from workers in Israel or abroad formed over one-quarter of the West Bank GNP. And this is certainly an underestimate, as the Israeli Central Bureau of Statistics does not include the remittances of the many migrants who are not considered residents (Mansour 1988: 81–2).[10] Whereas previously outmigration had meant that there was little population increase, the stagnation of migration abroad resulted in a rapid growth of the West Bank population to over one million in the late 1980s.[11]

Politically, with the Arab regimes discredited by the defeat in 1967, the Palestinians realised that they had to take action themselves and by the early 1970s support for the political and guerilla groups that made up the PLO was widespread. Initially the main method of resistance for the Palestinians in the occupied territories – who did not have any political rights, not even freedom of expression – was to stay put and to refrain from legitimising the occupation. By the mid-1970s, the likelihood of the occupation continuing for years to come brought about the development of local grass-root movements, such as voluntary work committees, student organisations, trade unions, and women's committees (Hilter- mann 1991a). After the Israeli army invaded Lebanon in 1982 and the subsequent departure of the PLO from Beirut, these local organisations became increasingly influential in Palestinian politics. The 1987 uprising showed that a new leadership had emerged from inside, coupling the

---

[10] The Israeli authorities consider as non-residents those absent when the 1967 Israeli census of population was held following the June War. As family reunification is difficult to arrange, they can enter the West Bank only with a visitor's permit.

[11] Israeli statistics exclude the Arab population of East Jerusalem. The number of one million includes this population (see CBS 1989: 700).

political demands of the right to national self-determination with attempts at building a less dependent and more self-reliant economy, through, for instance, the boycott of Israeli goods and the encouragement of local (home) production (Kuttab 1989; Nassar and Heacock 1991: 312).

## 2.2 Imm Sālim from the village of Al-Balad, eastern Jabal Nablus

During my research in the village of Al-Balad in the early 1980s I often stayed with Imm Sālim, at the time a widow in her early sixties. With great patience she answered my questions about the changes she had seen during her lifetime, and introduced me to topics I would remain interested in for years to come.

Together with her youngest daughter, Imm Sālim was living in one large room built on top of the old house in which her eldest son and his large family were staying. It was a well-kept, small apartment, with a large wooden cupboard with two mirrors in which they stored their clothing and other belongings, and a large number of mattresses, quilts and pillows for guests, neatly tucked away behind a decorative sheet. A large metal bed – which Imm Sālim rarely used as she preferred to sleep on the ground – stood at one side of the room, there was a small wooden table with some books, an oil lamp and a water jug on it, and along the walls were placed a dozen or so straight wooden chairs, once without doubt the pride of the guest room, but by this time a bit old-fashioned. The only window in the room gave a beautiful view over the village lands and olive trees. A small kitchen had been added onto the room, glassed in on three sides, with a wooden cupboard for provisions, a butane gas burner for cooking and a kerosine heater for cold winter days. Imm Sālim was particularly proud of this kitchen as it indicated that she was not dependent on anyone to prepare her food. At the side was a large open space where we often sat gleaning lentils or grain.

In the last years of Ottoman rule, Imm Sālim's father, a peasant smallholder, had been drafted into the Turkish army; he was one of the few conscripts to return to the village. Imm Sālim, his first child, was born shortly after the British had come to Palestine. Imm Sālim could hardly remember her mother, who died a few years later in childbirth; together with her younger brother and her sister, she was raised by her paternal grandmother. Yet she still vividly recalled the stories of the older women about the war and the days of poverty when the women had to walk all the way to Nablus to sell the wood they had carried on their heads, in order to be able to buy some bread and feed their children.

When Imm Sālim was about eleven she was married. 'It was an

exchange [*badal*] marriage', she explained to me. 'My father had grown restless and wanted to remarry, but he did not have enough money to pay the dower for a new wife and could only marry by giving me in exchange as bride to the new wife's brother.' She did not receive any gold, but her husband's family registered three *dunum* of land (one *dunum* is 0.1 hectare or about 0.25 acres) in her name. As she was still very young, she remained for some time in her father's house before moving in with her husband. 'My father's wife had already given birth when I went to live with him', Imm Sālim said, 'and it did not take long before I was pregnant myself, I only washed [menstruated] twice.'

The house she moved into was very much like her father's, one of the old one-room dwellings, with a low entrance, very small and high windows, and space for the animals. Although her husband's father was already deceased, he and his only brother still held their property together. In this small family, with sufficient land, a large flock of goats and sheep and some cows, the women had a heavy workload. 'We – I and my husband's brother's wife – had to walk for miles to get to the springs to fetch water, and had to go into the mountains to gather firewood', Imm Sālim recalled. 'We weeded, harvested by hand, collected the field crops, and also planted vegetables in the Ghor [the Jordan Valley], but first we had to walk three hours to get there.' In early spring the family often stayed in tents or caves in the rocky hilly lands to the east of the village where there was a lot of grazing land. 'When it stormed, the tent would collapse on our heads, and we had to care for the children, for the animals, for everything. It was very, very hard work. And when the animals were giving milk we had to quickly turn the milk into yogurt [*laban*] and butter. Goats were very important in those days.'

With agriculture dependent on rainfall, life became particularly hard during prolonged droughts, such as in the early 1930s. It was in these days that 'people went into debt just to be able to buy some food to eat', as Imm Sālim phrased it. During such times of hardship, urban traders managed to get hold of much land in the village, or, in Imm Sālim's words, 'the people became indebted just to be able to feed their children, and then the traders took their land for money'. Also the late 1930s, the period of the Arab revolt, were a difficult time in the village. Imm Sālim still vividly recalled how the British imposed strict curfews on the village, made extensive searches and executed 'the two best men of the village'.

Imm Sālim's husband and his brother decided to move out of the old house and to divide the land and the goats between them, when in the mid-1940s the economic situation improved. They both built a new house a little down from the centre of the village, near to each other, but separate. By then Imm Sālim herself had also started to acquire some

property. While she had not received gold at marriage, her husband later
later had given her some gold coins which she had sown on a ribbon and
wore as a necklace (*qilāda*). And from the money her relatives had
presented her at special occassions, such as the religious feasts, she had
bought some animals of her own.

In the mid-1950s Imm Sālim, by then in her early thirties, entered a
new phase in her life; she became a mother-in-law. This was a great relief
as she was in dire need of more female labour in the household. After five
sons had followed two daughers, who were still too small to be able to help
her substantially with all the housework, the work on the land and the
processing of agricultural produce and milk. Her eldest son was about
twenty when she married him to her brother's daughter, 'to have someone
of my own kin around', as she explained; soon thereafter his two younger
brothers were also married, one of them in an exchange marriage to keep
costs down. Although her daughters-in-law were heavily involved in
agriculture, in Imm Sālim's eyes, they had a more comfortable life than
the women from her own generation; 'they were living with us, but each of
them had a room of her own', she said to underline this.

The rapid expansion of the family (later she had another son and one
more daughter) was, however, to cause problems, which were only to
become more serious as time progressed. 'How could six sons and their
households live off the land their father had worked to provide for one
family?' Imm Sālim formulated it herself. As already in the early 1950s
the first young men from the village had gone to Kuwait to find work, the
solution was migration. 'We knew some people from villages to the south
who had gone west, to America', Imm Sālim said, 'but this was much
easier, in those days you did not need anything, no permits or passports,
you just went across the desert.' Her sons soon participated in this process
of male migration, while their wives and children remained in the village.
The material benefits of migration Imm Sālim summarised as follows:
'They sent money to their father who took care that houses were built for
them while they were working abroad. Building a house is the most
important thing.'

The political disaster that struck the West Bank in 1967 was also a
personal tragedy for Imm Sālim. Upon hearing that Israel had invaded
the West Bank, one of her sons, at the time working in Kuwait, set out for
home at once. When together with two other men from the village he
attempted to cross the Jordan River, Israeli soldiers shot and killed all
three of them. His picture still occupies a prominent place in Imm Sālim's
room. Also in other ways the occupation was to affected her life substantially. Whereas by the mid-1960s her husband had already sold many
goats, because with so many men migrating it was difficult to find

someone to tend them, a few years after the occupation Israeli policy forced them to give up goat herding alltogether. A large part of the rocky hills to the east of the village was declared a closed military zone, and a large fertile plain near the Jordan Valley was confiscated for an Israeli settlement. Like many other village families, they lost almost half their agricultural land, and the village as a whole lost most of the land that was communally used for grazing.

In the mid-1970s Imm Sālim was confronted with the sudden death of her husband. By then most of her sons were adult men with families of their own. It did not take long before the land was divided, 'so every one knew what was his'. Each one received about 15 *dunum* of dry-farming land with some olive trees. As at that time three of her sons were in Kuwait and the youngest in Saudi Arabia, their eldest brother took care of their land, using tractors for ploughing and later even rented a combine for harvesting the grain. When I asked Imm Sālim whether her daughters also took their share, she laughed, and said, 'why should they, their brothers have always been good to them'.

Imm Sālim herself was financially well taken care of by her sons and never considered claiming any land as inheritance from her husband. After her husband's death she had stopped working the family land and some years later sold her cow. 'I no longer had anyone to help me', she explained. 'By then I had long married the two eldest daughters and the youngest one was attending school and no longer wanted to care for a cow. First I sold the cow and bought a few goats. Then, a few years later I sold these too, because that had become too much work as well.' Yet, she did control the land which had been part of her dower. 'When the land was divided, they gave me the land that was registered for me as my marriage gift', Imm Sālim said. A few years later she handed over one *dunum* of it to her youngest son to build a house on. 'He had land, but far away from the road and the brother he liked to live close too', Imm Sālim pointed out. 'He actually offered to exchange it (for land he had inherited), but I told him "you can keep the land, I do not need it."' On the other two *dunum* she continued to grow grain, one year barley, and the other year durra. Her eldest son took care of the ploughing and sowing and her brother was in charge of the harvesting, receiving in return the straw for his cow. The few olive trees Imm Sālim herself owned yielded three canisters of olive oil (each containing 17 kilos) in good years; two of these she and her daughter used for home consumption and the third one she sold.

Imm Sālim's youngest daughter, the one who was still living with her, studied at the local university in Nablus. Her older brothers, already in their forties, did not particularly like the idea of their sister travelling every day to Nablus to continue her education. But Imm Sālim supported her. 'I gave her money for clothing and transport to Nablus', she underlined, 'so she did not have to ask them, and they could not say anything about it. I still have some money and gold for myself, which I can spend any way I want. My sons take care of everything we need. They can afford to do so.'

By village standards the family had become well-off. Her elder sons had built houses nearby, while the younger ones built villa-like houses in the plain, on agricultural land, next to the road to Nablus. Imm Sālim was proud of their achievements, but she found it difficult to have them away for such a long time. Actually, one of them had left Kuwait in the mid-1970s and gone to work in Israel, 'so he could come home at least a few times every week', Imm Sālim said, 'but the problem is, when you work in Israel you can eat and drink, but you cannot build, so he returned to Kuwait. And this had become difficult too, as by then there were all sorts of regulations.'

When I talked with Imm Sālim shortly before the intifada she emphasised how much easier her life had become, as she no longer had to care for the goats, and had little work on the land, with water in a cistern near the house, a gas stove to cook on, and kerosine for heating. She pointed out how lucky she was, a mother of many sons, who were reasonably well-to-do and kept their ties with their mother and the village. But at the same time life was difficult. There was no freedom. If previously you could go wherever you wanted to, now it might be dangerous even to go into the mountains near the village; at least four children from Al-Balad had been killed by explosives the Israeli army had left behind. With the use of new hybrid seeds, artificial fertilizer and so on, food had lost its taste and prices were rising every day. And there was always fear. If a man returned late, his mother and his wife were afraid that he would be in prison or even dead. If your son was abroad and you fell ill, 'he would need one hundred permits before he could come and visit you, that is if they would allow him to return at all.'[12]

### Villages: from peasantry to rural migrant workers

In the early mandatory period, about three-quarters of the population of Jabal Nablus, a mountainous area with fertile valleys and dry-farming dependent on irregular rain fall, lived in the rural areas, mostly in small villages like Al-Balad. In Al-Balad, as elsewhere in that region, winter crops, in particular wheat and barley, were rotated with summer crops

---

[12] Even before the intifada, young men (between 16 and 26) who left the West Bank had to stay abroad for six months before they were allowed to return; after the intifada, this was extended to one year and in individual cases longer periods are demanded.

such as lentils and sesame and at the base of the village olive trees were planted. From the beginning of the century peasants from Al-Balad also went to cultivate land in the Jordan Valley, a few hours walk to the east, which was irrigated by natural springs and where later they built mud brick houses, the hamlet of Nazlat al-Balad.

In those days the main source of livelihood in this area was agriculture. Although in the hill areas some produce was also marketed, peasant smallholders still mainly directed production towards subsistence. Social differentiation in the rural areas was, however, on the increase. Already around the mid nineteenth-century the Ottoman empire had started to introduce new land tenure laws. Whereas previously the contact between the state and the peasantry had been indirect, through tax farmers as middle men, the 1858 Ottoman Land Code (OLC) intended to register land rights in the name of the cultivators in order to increase productivity and tax income (Issawi 1982: 146). Yet the result of the OLC was that the cultivators more often than not lost their rights, as the peasants did not know the procedures and were distrustful of state officials, fearing taxation and the draft. Land commonly became registered in the name of the rural shaykhs and the urban notables (Schölch 1982: 22). A similar process took place in Al-Balad. There, differentiation also increased within the dominant lineage, the *dār al-shaykh*, part of a larger landowning clan in the region. Some became large landowners by registering land in their own name, while others lost access to land.

In the mandatory period it became increasingly difficult to distinguish between large landowners and traders, as the wealthy tribal families settled in Nablus and also operated as large traders, while urban traders succeeded in increasing their landholdings in the village by taking land from indebted peasants (Graham-Brown 1982: 141). Whereas large landowners became increasingly prosperous, the Palestinian peasantry became impoverished. In the Jabal Nablus region, peasants generally did not lose their land due to Jewish settlement, but British policy, in particular the taxation system, and the droughts and failure of the harvests in the early 1930s created a very precarious situation and increased their dependence on money lenders. Forced to sell their land because of indebtedness, many of these peasants still kept access to it as share-croppers. Most commonly, the production factors of land, labour, seeds, and plough animals each gave the right to a quarter of the produce, while in irrigated agriculture water was counted separately and the produce was divided into five parts. Thus, tenants who could supply only labour received a quarter to a fifth of the harvest. In Al-Balad, few share-croppers were landless labourers cropping on larger estates; most were smallholders possessing insufficient land of their own, while raising live stock was also an important source of livelihood.

Whereas in the early 1920s peasants without access to land had few possibilities other than working as agricultural labourers, ten years later the first public works had been started, such as road building and construction works in the harbours, and demand for cheap Arab labour in the citrus groves had also increased. At first, few labourers came from the more remote areas, such as Jabal Nablus, to the coastal plains, but their number increased with the stagnation in agriculture and in local manufacturing in Nablus. With seasonal employment outside agriculture available, share-croppers were more often also able to contribute other production factors besides labour and received a larger part of the produce (Graham-Brown 1982: 122). In the middle of the 1930s, however, economic recession set in, resistance to Arab labour in Jewish enterprises increased and during the Arab revolt work outside agriculture further diminished (Graham-Brown 1982: 144). Only in the early 1940s when the war effort led to control on imports and rapidly rising food prices peasants succeeded in paying off their debts. Employment opportunities with the British administration, such as in building and servicing army camps, also increased rapidly. Still, in the hill areas, such as Jabal Nablus, labour outside agriculture remained largely supplementary to income from agriculture (Tamari 1981). In Al-Balad only a few men went to work outside the village for longer periods of time.

Beginning in the Jordanian period, this started to change. In the Jabal Nablus region, population growth and partible inheritance had already resulted in peasants having insufficient land for their livelihood. Cut off from the coastal areas, with high unemployment on the West Bank itself and a booming economy in the Gulf area, those looking for work headed eastward. Around the mid-1950s migration to Kuwait was already firmly underway in Al-Balad with a smaller number of men searching for work on the East Bank, some of them enlisting in the Jordanian army.[13]

Different developments took place in irrigated agriculture in the Jordan Valley (only about 5 per cent of agriculture on the West Bank is irrigated).[14] There, state support for large landowners and the abundant supply of cheap labour in the refugee camps induced cash crop production, such as fruit and vegetables. In irrigated areas such as Nazlat al-

[13] Data from the first Jordanian census, held in 1961, show to what extent men had been leaving Al-Balad to work elsewhere. The number of men per 100 women was 76 for those between 15 and 30 years, 72 for those between 30 and 45 years, and 114 for those of 45 years and older (First Census 1963: 48–9, 58–9, 68–9).

[14] For a detailed case study of a village in the Jordan Valley, see Tamari and Giacaman (1980).

Balad, both larger landowners and smallholders started to develop citrus groves, the latter usually selling the produce beforehand for a set price to a commission agent, who arranged picking, packing and transport, work often done by the refugees. Smallholders also increasingly turned to growing vegetables, with some of those with insufficient land entering into share-cropping arrangements. While previously many households in Al-Balad had access to land both in the village itself and in Nazlat al-Balad, these developments led to a greater specialisation in the type of land worked. Households with many migrating members commonly exchanged their land in Nazlat al-Balad for land in Al-Balad. They did not have enough labour to develop irrigated agriculture and preferred to have dry-farming land nearby. In households which had become involved in irrigated agriculture, migration was much less common.[15]

Since the beginning of the Israeli occupation, dry-farming has become more and more supplementary to wage labour. While most of the population still lives in the rural areas, very few households are exclusively dependent on income from agriculture. In Al-Balad in 1981, dry-farming agriculture was the main occupation for only 13 per cent of the men and most of them were elderly; the majority of those employed outside agriculture were also working outside the West Bank, either in the Gulf States or in Israel.[16] Only in irrigated areas has agriculture remained the main source of employment. But while the Jordanian administration provided some support for (larger) landowners, Israeli state policies have threatened its viability. In the Jordan Valley, where most irrigated agriculture is located, Palestinian land has been confiscated and the access of Palestinian farmers to water is restricted, while Jewish colonists receive state subsidies to develop capital intensive agriculture (Pollock 1988: 248).

These transformations in the socio-economic structure of villages tie in with changes in the gender division of labour. Also previously when production was still mainly directed towards subsistence, there was a certain division of labour with ploughing and threshing mainly done by men, and women active in weeding, processing grains and in particular milk (into yogurt, butter, and later also cheese). Yet many tasks such as

---

[15] Data from the first Jordanian census, held in 1961, show that in Nazlat al-Balad migration was more limited; usually it was not the 'heads of households', but younger sons who would go and work elsewhere. There the number of men per hundred women was 86 for those between 15 and 30 years, 106 for those between 30 and 45 years, and 110 for those of 45 years and older (First Census 1963: 48–9; 58–9; 68–9).

[16] In 1981 37 per cent of the male labour force working outside agriculture was employed on the West Bank and 63 per cent abroad: 28 per cent in the Gulf States, 27 per cent in Israel and 8 per cent in Jordan (based on data on more than half the total male labour force of Al-Balad). Not included here are the men who have migrated together with their wives and children, many of whom have settled in Jordan.

planting and harvesting were done by men and women together, and it was evident that both were extensively involved in agriculture. Men generally would spend more time on this work, but women were also valued for their labour in both direct care for household members and agriculture. Imm Sālim expressed this when she emphasised that she had married her elder sons because she needed the labour of her daughters-in-law. Only in the *dār al-shaykh* households did women refrain from working the land.

When younger men increasingly turned to non-agrarian work, the relations between the generations and the gender division of labour changed. With inherited property less important as a source of livelihood and employment opportunities available elsewhere, these men became less dependent on their fathers, and extended families started to break up earlier. Imm Sālim's husband had continued to live with his brother and to keep land in common property even after their father died, but Imm Sālim's youngest son, who worked in Saudi Arabia, built a house before he had married. At the same time, in agriculture itself a process of feminisation of labour has come about. This does not mean that younger women have taken over male tasks or have become more involved in agriculture than their mothers and grandmothers. On the contrary, due to partible inheritance, land confiscations and closures many smallholders have less land and commonly spend considerably less time on agricultural production than previous generations. But agriculture has become feminised in the sense that women's input has increased in comparison to that of men, as it is by and large male tasks (in particular the time consuming ploughing and threshing), which have become mechanised. Not all women are, however, similarly affected. In particular, women in better-off migrant households increasingly refrain from working the land in an attempt to bid for higher social status, while in irrigated agriculture both men and women have remained involved in working the land. Still, on the whole, the greater centrality of male wage labour and cash income for the livelihood of households, and the marginalisation of agriculture, largely directed towards subsistence and defined as women's work, has resulted in women's labour being less valued.

## 2.3    Imm Shākir and Imm Hilmī from Nablus city

### Imm Shākir: wealth in Nablus

When I asked a Palestinian colleague, herself from a prominent Nablus family, whether she would be willing to introduce me to an elderly upper-class Nablus woman, she arranged an appointment with Imm Shākir. It was in the summer of 1989 that we went together to visit her in a villa which looked nice enough from the outside, yet it was the interior which really expressed her very high standard of living, with its marble floors, abundant use of luxurious wood and leather sofas. At the time, only Imm Shākir and her husband were living there, while there were separate quarters for her live-in servant. After some small talk, my colleague left so I could speak with Imm Shākir in private.

Imm Shākir, born in 1927, was the eldest of three girls and five boys in a well-off Nablus family. Her father owned land, but was 'not really a large landowner', she said, explaining that her family's wealth was based on commerce rather than on large land-ownership. Her father was also engaged in wholesale trading, but most of his income was derived from the agency he held for a British tyre company, and he was also involved in the sale of cars. Imm Shākir spent her early childhood in the old family mansion, a very large house near the centre of town, where her father's brothers and his unmarried sisters were also living. It was when the British army sequestered it in 1942 that they decided to establish separate households and had houses built for themselves. By then Imm Shākir, having finished primary school in Nablus, was boarding at the (American Quakers) Friends' School in Ramallah. As she explained, in those days there was no secondary education for girls in Nablus and the Friend's School, with an English language programme, was well-known for its high educational standards.

Shortly after graduation, when she was nineteen years old, Imm Shākir was married. She called it 'a family marriage'; her father and her husband's father were close friends and she herself had not spoken with the prospective groom before the marriage contract was signed. 'My own family may have agreed to us sitting together before marriage', Imm Shākir said, 'but his family was more conservative.' With some amusement she recalled how uncomfortable her husband initially had felt about the less strict gender segregation in her family. She would have preferred to postpone marriage for a little while, but had agreed to the marriage as her family considered him a very good match. His family was wealthier than her own; they were large landowners, and also owned a sesame mill, a soap factory and a bus company. Her husband later set up a company in building materials and then moved into the import of cars. After his father died, everything was divided between him and his two brothers with only the soap factory, started by their great-grandfather, remaining common property.

During the engagement period and at the wedding, Imm Shākir received a lot of gold, both from her own kin and especially from her husband. When I asked her whether she ever sold gold to buy more fashionable jewellery, she aptly pointed out that she never needed to do so because 'whenever there was a new model on the market my husband would buy it for me'. The dower itself her husband, or rather his father, paid in cash to her father, who in turn gave the full amount to his daughter. 'My father deposited all of it in a bank account for me', Imm Shākir emphasised. 'From his own money he gave me gold and provided the furniture for the house.' In answer to my question what she did with the money, she said: 'a year later my father returned the money to my husband and allowed him to administer it for me, "as she is for you and you are for her", he said.' His decision seemed both prompted by some religious unease about having money in the bank and taking interest from it and by the fact that his daughter's marriage seemed well established and she already had a son. Most of the money was invested in shares in a company in Amman, which gave Imm Shākir at least a few hundred JD (Jordanian Dinars) yearly income. Yet, as she said, 'of course, I do not need it at all, my husband brings me everything I need. But if I want to do something myself, if I want to give something away to a poor neighbour, without telling her of course, then I will do that from my own money.' As Imm Shākir stated emphatically, the shares were registered in her own name.

After living with her in-laws during the first six months of marriage, 'naturally in separate quarters', the new couple moved into one of the apartments her husband's father owned in the same building. Within ten years Imm Shākir had five children, four sons and one daughter; that was enough. In the early 1960s they moved into the new villa her husband had built, where they are still living. As was common for a woman of her background, soon after marriage a refugee woman from Haifa ('from a good family', as Imm Shākir stressed), came to live with her to help with the housework and the children. Imm Shākir herself never worked outside the house. 'If a woman has studied and marries late', she said, 'then it is good if she works. But when you have children, caring for them is the most important thing.' Yet reflecting on her own life, she added immediately, 'But ten years ago I thought, I wish I had a job, not for material reasons, but to pass the time.' In fact, starting in the early 1950s she became active on the board of several charitable institutions. 'When I was pregnant and I did not feel well', Imm Shākir recalled, 'my mother-in-law advised me to become active, to have something to do; she herself had founded one of these institutions in the mandatory period.' The president of one of these organisations, the wife of the mayor of Nablus, asked Imm Shākir to take care of the bookkeeping. This she continued to do until the late 1960s, when, as she said 'it all became very complicated and it had to be done by a registered accountant'.

When I talked to Imm Shākir her mother was still alive, but her father had died in the early 1960s. Discussing inheritance practices, Imm Shākir stressed that for the first ten or fifteen years nobody claimed their inheritance rights. 'My brothers were still studying abroad, the money was needed for the upkeep of the household, their education and then their marriages', she said. Once every one had become settled – only one brother is living in Nablus, the other three have long ago established themselves in Amman and one of the smaller Gulf States – Imm Shākir and her two married sisters started to take a share of the rent of four apartments and some stores in an apartment building her father had owned.

Imm Shākir's children are all well educated. After the 1967 war one of them actually went to Amman to complete his high school education in order not to be affected by the school strike on the West Bank in the aftermath of the war. Her four sons studied either engineering or medicine abroad, in the United States and in the Arab world, and are living in Amman and in Cairo; two of them set up an engineering company in Amman and own two concrete factories there. Her only daughter graduated from the American University of Cairo, and after working for a short time in Nablus married in Amman, where her husband holds a high position in a well-known bank. 'A number of men came to us to ask her hand, but she herself has chosen', Imm Shākir stressed. For three of her sons, Imm Shākir made the first selection of brides she deemed suitable. The one who studied in the United States also agreed to this, heeding his mother's warnings that a foreign woman would always want to return to her own country. A firm believer in 'like-marrying-like', Imm Shākir explained her motivations as follows: 'It is important that he marries a girl from a good family background, with good morals and of the same social level, one with a university education, so that they can understand each other in life. Everywhere there are great families and those that are not. Sometimes even between cousins it does not work out, how could it be if they are from different backgrounds?' The only son who has chosen his wife himself married a distant paternal relative, who studied at the same university.

When I spoke with Imm Shākir it was one and a half years after the start of the intifada, yet she did not refer to it much except for the inconveniences it caused her husband's business activities and the problems of mobility everyone had to face. Neither did she express the unease Imm Sālim felt about having her children abroad. In part, this is due to class-informed ways of propriety, with restraint and self-control highly valued amongst the elite. Yet her sphere of action was also very different. She was still involved in some charitable activities and had been travelling a lot, accompanying her husband on his working trips to Europe and on vacations to the Far East. Even if travelling had become more difficult during the intifada, she still was able to go abroad regularly to visit her children and relatives.

### Imm Hilmī: poverty in Nablus

I met Imm Hilmī through her neighbours, a refugee family whose house was built around the same courtyard in the old city of Nablus. When I last talked to her, in the summer of 1988, she was living together with her twenty-two year old single daughter in one large room with untiled rough concrete walls and a small kitchen attached to it. A large Nablus family of nine occupied two rooms in the same courtyard. An elderly refugee widow, estranged from her only son, rented Imm Hilmī's very old, second room. Imm Hilmī was in ill health, having serious problems in walking, and her eyesight was also bad, even though she wore thick glasses. During our talks she sprinkled her sentences with religious expressions.

Imm Hilmī, born in the late 1920s, was the second of five children. 'There was much poverty', she emphasised, recalling her youth. 'My father died when I was about five, six years old. Neither he nor my mother had a brother, who could take care of us, so we were totally dependent upon her, there was nobody to help us.' Her mother turned to all kinds of informal work, 'breaking almonds for the traders in the market, making sweets to sell to the people and that kind of thing'. Although life was difficult, Imm Hilmī was sent to school, but because of her bad eyesight, this only lasted for one year. Thereafter she stayed at home, helping her mother.

When Imm Hilmī was about twenty years old she was married, 'because of poverty', she said. Her husband, a quarry worker in his mid-thirties, she had not seen before, as, in her words, 'in the past people used to be very strict'. As dower, she received a little gold and a small chest in which they put her clothing. Because her husband was an orphan, they were married in the house of his mother's sister. When within a few days it became apparent that he did not have the basics to furnish a house, her mother ended up lending him some money to do so. And things did not turn for the better. When Imm Hilmī was pregnant for the first time, there was an explosion in the quarry where her husband was working. Hit by the flying debris, he suffered a concussion and lost his teeth. He never fully recovered, or, as Imm Hilmī put it, 'one day he worked and ten days not', adding 'but what can you do when you are married and pregnant? We had children and our life was poverty and worries.'

In the early 1950s Imm Hilmī accompanied her husband to Jordan where he went to look for work in the stone quarries. They stayed there for some years, until on a cold winter day he used benzine to light a fire and was badly burned. Destitute, the family – by then Imm Hilmī had two small sons – returned to Nablus. 'We moved into one of the ruined houses that had been destroyed by the earthquake', Imm Hilmī said. 'I sold my bracelets to fix it up, we did so bit by bit.' Her husband, no longer able to work in the quarries, started to collect old bags and from the material that was still good he made new ones, going around the houses with a donkey to sell them. Around the mid-1970s he died as the result of an accident, the aftermath of which Imm Hilmī still vividly recalled. 'I and my daughter went with him to the hospital', she said. Expressing the lack of compassion of the better-off, she continued: 'Maybe his mind became afraid, and he said, "take care of the donkey". The doctors laughed at him and I started to cry. After he died, the wealthy people in the neighbour-hood sent us some rice and sugar, because the younger children were still small. That was maybe enough for one week but not for two.' By that time, three of her sons had already left the house. They had quit school at a young age to go and work in Jordan, like their father, as quarry workers.

Soon after her husband died, Imm Hilmī married off her eldest daughter. 'She was thirteen years old then, but I said that she was fourteen. She was not lucky. Her husband suddenly died, leaving her with four small children, three boys and one girl.' Imm Hilmī did not want her to stay with her in-laws, because 'she was still a young girl and her brothers-in-law were also living there.' Instead, Imm Hilmī convinced her widowed daughter to leave her children and arranged another marriage for her. Unfortunately, this marriage did not work out. When she already had three daughters from her new husband and was again pregnant, he took another wife and repudiated her. Together with her children she moved in with her mother, 'without any money', Imm Hilmī stressed, 'because at the time we did not know that he had to pay her maintenance.' Mediators came and went, and in the end her husband took her back. 'Because of the children she has to bear it with patience', Imm Hilmī reflected.

In answer to my question whether she herself had worked, Imm Hilmī said 'not really', but then continued to tell me about how she used to rip rags apart, how an aunt had taught her to adorn head scarfs with small beads, to crochet scull caps and to take these around the houses. This she had to give up when her eyesight deteriorated further. The last years she sometimes cleaned sheep heads. 'Not all people who buy heads know how to clean them', she explained. 'I learned it from a neighbour. She brings them from the butcher and if she has many and is busy she gives me some to clean.' Her youngest daughter did the same work.

Imm Hilmī much regretted that she had neither a brother nor a son in Nablus. One of her sons was living in the northern part of the West Bank, the others had settled in Jordan. Imm Hilmī regularly visited them for considerable stretches of time, but was always happy to return home. 'They all have large families and are living in small houses, their children are small and make a lot of noise, and they have a hard time finding work,' she sighed. When I asked her whether they supported her financially, she said 'They do not give me anything, they would like me to give them something! And believe me, if I had something I would give it to them.' Imm Hilmī further emphasised that she herself had fixed up the room where she was now living. 'The land is my husband's but I was the one who had water and electricity installed. There was a little money from my husband's work, and I had saved from my own work and from the work of this girl. But if a good man comes to ask her hand, I will marry her.'

One year later her daughter was married to one of the sons of the large Nablus family living at the same courtyard. I did not talk to Imm Hilmī again, as she died shortly afterwards. After three months of marriage, her daughter's husband was arrested when a rifle was found in his house during a nightly army raid. His brothers had previously fallen victim to the army's aggression; one brother had a leg broken, and two others had been shot.

### Social differentiation in the urban context

Strategically located in a valley between two high mountains and with an abundance of spring water, the city of Nablus was an important administrative and trade centre in Ottoman times. The increased influence in the area of the Ottoman rulers from the 1850s on had strengthened the urban elite. With the new land laws, many urban traders succeeded in becoming large estate owners and the Ottoman state sought the support of the learned urban notables, the religious establishment, in setting up a central administration (Smith 1984: 19). In those days Nablus was also a centre of artisanal production, and particularly well-known for its olive oil soap; between 1860 and 1882 the number of soap factories, often named after the family owning them, increased from fifteen to thirty (Schölch 1982: 49–50). Cotton, wool and silk cloth were produced in a large number of weaving mills and many gold and silver smiths worked in Nablus.

By the turn of the century Nablus was the second largest city in Palestine with over 20,000 inhabitants (Migdal 1980: 16). The town's centre was the great mosque, surrounded by shops, religious schools, baths, workshops and so on. Sections of the market were designated for specific craftsmen, such as jewellers, metal workers, and quilt makers.

These commercial areas were part of what is nowadays called the old city, where at that time the large majority of the inhabitants, both rich and poor, were living. The mansions of the prominent families, large, fortress-like buildings, were near those of the poor, whom they employed in their shops or workshops, in the warehouses nearby, and also in their houses. The common people lived in the old, often square, one-room lime-stone houses with a domed roof, arranged around an open or enclosed courtyard. More modern housing could be recognised by the red-tiled roofs.

From 1880 on, when trade with Europe was becoming increasingly important, the economic centre of Palestine started to shift to the coastal areas, and the Jabal Nablus region became more and more peripheral to the Palestinian economy; Jerusalem and especially the coastal cities grew much more rapidly.[17] During the mandatory period, increased imports further undermined the position of the artisans and soap producers and from the early 1930s on economic stagnation in the Nablus region led to more decline. Only in the 1940s did the situation of the artisanal sector improve, but higher incomes in the city were more often than not offset by a high rate of inflation (Graham-Brown 1982: 153). The position of the learned families also deteriorated. Their members were still appointed to high government posts but they had become dependent on the British, as *waqf* income (from religious endowments) now had to be paid to the state, administrators were paid by the state, and the state had to approve appointments (Smith 1984: 62). Traders and large landowners, on the other hand, often managed to strengthen their position. In Nablus a small number of families rented out the stores in the market area and virtually controlled the trade in food, agricultural produce and imported consumption goods (Graham-Brown 1982: 138). With increased trade opportunities, the number of commission agents and agents for foreign companies, such as the father of Imm Shākir, grew rapidly. And some of the younger sons of estate owners, often educated abroad, started to invest their capital in cash crops, in particular citrus.

The lay-out of the city started to change after a large earthquake had struck central Palestine in 1927, destroying hundreds of houses in Nablus. Many of those who could afford it started to build houses, set apart and often surrounded by gardens and trees, along the east–west axis on the lower slopes of the mountains. Imm Shākir, for instance, never lived in the old city. This slow and gradual expansion of the city gained

---

[17] According to a British survey the population of Nablus increased in absolute numbers from 16,000 in 1922 to 17,189 in 1931, that is by 7.8 per cent (Mills 1933). In the same period the population of Jerusalem increased by 37 per cent and that of Haifa by 87 per cent (Taqqu 1977: 57). Comparing the population increase of Nablus with that of the coastal cities, Graham-Brown (1982: 110) gives even more divergent percentages.

tremendous momentum after 1948 when the population of Nablus almost tripled as a result of the sudden influx of refugees; between 1948 and 1950, some 40,000 refugees came to Nablus city, a considerable number of whom were to continue further eastward (El-Khatib 1985: 57). If some of these refugees were wealthy, the large majority came without any resources and were destitute. Even more disadvantaged than the Nablus urban poor who had their ties of patronage with the Nablus elite, many of them ended up at the bottom of the urban hierarchy. Soon refugee camps were set up at the edges of the city, but refugees living in Nablus itself, often in the old city, like Imm Hilmī's neighbours, remained a sizeable minority.[18]

The rapid economic expansion in the Gulf States in the 1950s gave a strong impetus to the local Nablus economy. It created a market and encouraged migration, not only to the Gulf States but also to the East Bank. Both the better-off and educated, such as Imm Shākir's brothers, and the poor and unskilled, like Imm Hilmī's husband and later her sons, went to work there. Having no agricultural land to take care of, urban migrants were more inclined to have their families accompany them than their rural counterparts. Still, as migration was commonly seen as temporarily and maintaining a presence in one's place of origin was highly valued, revenues were often invested in private housing and, as a result, building activity in Nablus, increased considerably. By the early 1960s the urban population was recorded as slightly over 45,000 and the city had extended to its limits, reaching the neighbouring villages to the east and west; in 1963 Balata, Askar, Rafidia and Jneid were actually incorporated within the city limits (El-Khatib 1985: 84).

With the Israeli occupation trade relations with the Arab world were disrupted, those abroad were commonly not able to return to their hometown as the Israeli authorities did not consider them residents, and the West Bank became economically dependent on Israel. While the population of the city of Nablus gradually increased, by the mid-1980s reaching about 85,000, Jabal Nablus still remains little urbanised with only about one-third of the population of the district living in the city. It is true that there are more local employment opportunities in the city than in the rural areas with many employed in the numerous small workshops, in the building trade, or self-employed as peddlers and small traders. Many of Imm Hilmī's neighbours, for example, are involved in these often irregular and informal jobs. But lacking industrial development and with a skeleton administration, Nablus has not attracted a large number of

---

[18] The Jordanian census does not provide data on the refugee population. According to Israeli census data shortly after occupation about 15 per cent of the Nablus city population was of refugee origin (CBS 1967: 90).

rural dwellers. Migration abroad is often seen as a better option, and those unable or unwilling to migrate may well prefer to go and work in Israel than remain dependent on the Nablus elite.[19]

Through time, the relation between the old city and the newly built areas has changed. The old city is still both a residential and a market area, with grocers and wholesalers, furniture and clothing stores, soap factories and metal workshops, as well as mosques, doctors clinics, and so on. Densely populated, with narrow, winding alleyways, where access by car is difficult and loads are carried by animals or porters with small handcarts, the old city has, however, increasingly become a run down area. Certainly, a few of the prominent families are still living there, in large and hard to maintain houses, surrounded by walls to ensure privacy, or hold property as a *dīwān*, a meeting place for the men at special occasions, such as funerals. Most of the prominent and middle-class families have, however, left the old city, and even the aspiring poor have often succeeded in finding housing on the mountain slopes, leaving the old city area to those with no other options.

With the intifada the old city, as the centre of Palestinian resistance against the Israeli occupation, has become even less attractive because of the very severe Israeli repression. Also before the intifada the army had already blocked off part of the entrances to the old city with concrete filled oil drums, and curfews were most often imposed on this area of town. It is true that with the intifada, curfews are also regularly imposed on Nablus as a whole: in 1988 Nablus city was under curfew for fifty-eight days; in 1989 for sixty days (JMCC 1991: 112). But in the old city the effects are more severe, as living conditions there are very cramped, amenities limited and people often do not have sufficient food stocks due to poverty. A disproportionate number of the victims of direct military violence, such as Imm Hilmī's neighbour's sons, come from the old city and the poorer adjacent neighbourhoods.

The life stories of Imm Shākir and Imm Hilmī both point to the importance of male kin and husbands for women's socio-economic security and illustrate the great social differentiation in the city, previously largely based on property ownership and political position, with access to professional posts through higher education and social networks becoming increasingly important. Imm Shākir, starting from the relatively secure position as daughter of a well-off trader, landed in a marriage with one of the wealthier men of Nablus, and became the mother of professionally successful sons. Imm Hilmī, on the other hand, attributed

---

[19] The novels of the Palestinian writer Sahar Khalifa (1976; 1980; 1990), born and raised in Nablus, vividly depict the antagonistic feelings of the poor and the refugees towards the Nablus elite.

her poverty to her father's premature death and the absence of father's and mother's brothers. Due to poverty, she married an orphaned man, who was hardly able to provide for the household, and her sons left school at an early age to start working. If Imm Hilmī's relation with her sons indicates that the presence of impoverished male kin is no guarantee for support, a woman's situation is often even more difficult if she has no kin.

In the city, a married son would often set up his own household at an earlier stage than his counterpart in the rural areas. In the case of the wealthy, economic ties grounded in property still remained important, but a professional career may give a son some independence and living separately (and well) has become an indication of high status. Amongst the poor it could be a survival strategy to remain living together, but often a father may not be able or willing to maintain a son and his wife, or they themselves may want to leave in search of better opportunities. The major difference with rural smallholders was, however, that in agrarian households women's work was much valued, and daughters were often seen as an important productive support to the household. In the city, on the other hand, women were more often seen as an economic burden on the household. Poor, urban women in particular may have a very difficult time fending for themselves. Imm Shākir with her high school diploma could have found herself a well-paid job if she had wanted to, but she did not need to do so. Poor women, however, had little chance to complete their education. Imm Hilmī, illiterate as her mother had been, had no option other than, again following in her mother's footsteps, to turn to home work to earn something. How the relation between class, education and employment has developed is further discussed in part III.

## 2.4     Imm Muhammad from Jaffa, living in Balata camp

In the early 1950s, Imm Muhammad's family had been living in the same courtyard as Imm Hilmī. Actually, one of her relatives was still living there and it was his wife who took me to Imm Muhammad in the Balata refugee camp at the edge of Nablus city, where she had moved to after marriage. In 1988 and 1989 I often stayed with Imm Muhammad. She was living together with her much older, slightly confused husband, three unmarried daughters and her youngest son in a recently fixed up small house, consisting of three rooms around a central hall, a very small kitchen and a bathroom. On the flat roof, where we could sit in the shadow of the watertanks, her youngest son kept rabbits, chickens and doves in a shed. They had started to add another floor to the house for him to set up his own household after marriage. The walls were already high enough so that we could sit there during the curfews without being spotted by the army. The small windows in the front of the house they had closed off with concrete blocks after soldiers had shot and killed a woman near their house early in 1988 and had broken all the glass.

Imm Muhammad, in her mid-fifties, started her life story by returning to her roots. 'Originally we are from Jaffa', she said. 'Both my father and my mother were from Jaffa and I was born there.' Stressing the impact of the 1948 disaster (*nakba*) on her life, she continued, 'Now we are refugees without property or land; even the land our house is built on we do not own. We have managed, but like it was in Jaffa, no.' Recalling life in Jaffa, she told me about the house they had there, with a kitchen and even a bathtub. Her father had owned a small citrus grove, selling the crop to middlemen, who took further charge of it. Her mother, who was able to read and write and dressed in city clothing, wearing a half long coat and a face veil, did not need to work on the land. But her life had been difficult. Most of the children she had given birth to had died very young; only Imm Muhammad, her elder sister, and a younger brother and sister survived. Further comparing the situation in Jaffa with her life in Balata, Imm Muhammad summarised the differences as: 'There we were living like city people. Here in Balata I dress like the peasant women, because most of the people here are from the rural areas.'

At the time of the *nakba* Imm Muhammad was about twelve years old. 'The Jews came, nobody dared to leave the house', she said, recalling those traumatic experiences. 'We were afraid, because those who went outside were shot. Corpses were everywhere. As soon as possible, when there was a lull in the fighting, we left.' They ended up in Salt (on the East Bank), where in Imm Muhammad's words, 'we were living under the trees'. There she also had to face a major personal tragedy. 'My mother died there after giving birth', she said. 'It was snowing and we were not used to snow. I took care of the baby, but she only lived for three months, she had diarrhoea continuously and also died. It was very, very difficult, the people there were bedouin, they spoke differently from us and washed their clothes in cold water. We left, because we did not know how to live there, and came to Nablus.'

While they were still on the East Bank a marriage was arranged for Imm Muhammad. Her father's female paternal cousin (*bint ʿamm*) had also died and when her father went to offer his condolences her son asked Imm Muhammad in marriage. Her father agreed to the marriage, to the dismay of Imm Muhammad, who emphasised that she had not really wanted him, as he was much older than herself. Back in Nablus, like many other refugees the family first rented a house in the city. 'It had a roof of corrugated iron and we lived there with many', said Imm Muhammad.

'When the people in Nablus no longer wanted us', as she put it, 'the camps were set up. First there were only tents, that is where I gave birth to my elder children.' Pointing to the smallest, very low room in her house, she added, 'Some years later they built one small room for every household, you can see it, it is so low that you had to bend down to enter it. Everything else was in the open.'

Imm Muhammad had nine children, six girls and three boys, one of whom died in an accident. Initially the household was fully dependent on the UNWRA rations and the little money her husband made selling vegetables and fruit from a handcart. Imm Muhammad herself never worked for wages. 'That was not possible with the children', she explained, 'but we did have some goats, we held them where we later built the kitchen.' As was common in many camp households, her children started working when they were still at school. In the vacations her daughters would work on the land in the Jordan Valley picking vegetables and carrying the boxes, work one of her female neighbours arranged for them.

After the Israeli occupation the family went through a particularly hard time. There was very little work at first, and Imm Muhammad's husband had broken a leg, so he could not do anything at all. Then her father died, while her only brother, who was disabled, was in prison. Discussing inheritance, Imm Muhammad underlined that the little money her father had managed to save was spent on the marriage she arranged for her brother when he was released from prison. At that time they also divided her mother's gold, a necklace with sixteen small coins. Eight of these were given to her brother, with Imm Muhammad and her sister taking four each, as Islamic law prescribes; Imm Muhammad later gave these to her daughters. Soon after her second son died in an accident. 'I was very, very upset for a long time and the younger children suffered because of that. One of my daughters left school early to stay home with me.'

Imm Muhammad was particularly proud of her eldest daughter. Part of the dower gold Imm Muhammad had received at marriage she had sold when this girl wanted to go to teacher training college. 'It is thanks to her that we managed to improve our situation', she told me several times, 'she succeeded in becoming a teacher.' Her eldest son was financially less successful. Trained as a carpenter and employed in a workshop in Nablus it took him ten years to save enough money to be able to marry. As renting a house in Nablus turned out to be too expensive, he bought a house in the camp that needed a roof and a lot of other work. When in the mid-1970s, already in debt and badly in need of money, he and his sister managed to get permission to work in Saudi Arabia it was a great relief. Whereas he had a relatively low-paying job as a clerk, his sister worked there as a teacher in a village government school and also gave private lessons. 'My son paid for his own family', Imm Muhammad pointed out, 'but it was with her money that we were able to improve the house, and she also paid off part of his debts.'

When I talked to her in 1988 Imm Muhammad still had three daughters and her youngest son at home. The eldest daughter, the teacher, has been unemployed ever since returning from Saudi Arabia. Her brother had refused to stay there any longer as life was very difficult and his wife, living by herself in the camp with five small children, did not accept it any more. While his sister would have preferred to continue working in Saudi Arabia she had to come back with him because as a single woman she could only work there if accompanied by a *mahram* (a male within the forbidden degrees of marriage). Upon returning, her brother worked for a short time in Nablus, but when there was only work for half the week he started working in Israel, not as a carpenter but as a common labourer. Imm Muhammad's second daughter worked in a small cheese factory near the camp for a while, but was laid off with the intifada, while her youngest daughter should have been in school, but was at home because the schools were all closed. Her youngest son, trained by the UNRWA as a builder, had just spent three months in administrative detention, and worked irregularly.[20] Imm Muhammad hoped that the following year, he would go to work in Saudi Arabia together with his eldest sister, but was afraid he may not be allowed to leave the West Bank because he had spent time in jail. They were also thinking about arranging a marriage for him, but had to face the problem once more, that there was not enough money. Imm Muhammad was planning to give him one of the bracelets she still had, and also one of his sisters would give him one. But first he had to build a second floor onto the house, so the new couple could live separately.

When I visited Imm Muhammad again in 1989 the situation had further deteriorated. Her youngest son had been shot, one of her daughters had to undergo an operation because soldiers had hit her in the abdomen which had resulted in blood coagulation, and her eight-year old epileptic grandson had also been shot. A diabetic herself, the continuous stress had also affected her own health. Although health care is officially provided free by the UNRWA, in practice having someone in the hospital

---

[20] Administrative detention refers to imprisonment without charge or trial. Although Palestinians had been placed under administrative detention before the intifada, after the intifada had gained momentum their numbers greatly increased. Of the 18,000 Palestinians whom the Israeli authorities acknowledge to have arrested during the first year of the intifada, 3–4,000 were placed under administrative detention (Al-Haq 1988: 147).

is expensive. No one had regular work, except her eldest son who was still employed in Israel. But he had to maintain a wife and five children as well, and his earnings also dropped considerably, because as a result of strikes and curfews, he worked fewer days.

### Refugees: sudden dispossession

The large majority of the refugees who came to Nablus in 1947/48 were from the rural areas and found themselves suddenly without any sources of livelihood. Certainly, the wealthier urbanites also lost their houses and estates. But in the later mandatory period, they had also started to invest their profits in interest-bearing bank deposits, in shares, government bonds and other financial paper, which they were able to transfer (Smith 1984: 117). And they may have had other advantages, such as family or business contacts in Nablus city, a British-style education, or work experience as officials for the British administration, which made it easier for them to find work in the Gulf States, often for British and American companies. The rural population, on the other hand, did not have these resources; the peasant and bedouin women had only been able to take their gold with them.

When these refugees reached Nablus, some found shelter in schools or mosques, others moved into the ruined houses in the old city, the caves in the mountains, or slept in the open in the olive groves. When it became evident that Israel would not allow the refugees to return, three camps were set up near Nablus in 1950 to coordinate the relief efforts. As Imm Muhammad pointed out, at first, the refugees were only supplied with tents and rations. Then after some years the UNRWA built one room huts for them. In the largest camp, Balata, about 15,000 refugees were settled, mainly peasants from numerous villages in the Jaffa, Ramleh and Lydda districts of central Palestine and bedouin from different clans in that region. Imm Muhammad's family was one of the few from a semi-urban background.[21]

Having lost their land and flocks the refugees had little choice but to work as agricultural labourers for the large estate owners, as day labourers in the market area, as sellers of vegetables, fruit and so on, or to become totally dependent on UNRWA relief and rations. Only those with some money were able to rent agricultural land for cash, as had been common

---

[21] The UNRWA and Jordanian officials, in consultation with the major of Nablus, chose the site as some refugees had already settled there in the course of the 1948 war. The fertile, cultivated land belonged to the inhabitants of the village of Balata and was located near the village itself. Yet, the villagers were not consulted. At first they did not receive any compensation at all; later they were paid a rent far below the market value (Ammons 1978: 100).

practice in the coastal areas. Because of the availability of cheap labour, industry was attracted to Balata camp; in 1953, one of the leading Nablus families set up a vegetable oil factory, which was to be followed by metalworks, ceramics, glass, sweets and woodwork (Ammons 1978: 120). During and shortly after the 1967 war roughly one-third of the population of Balata camp fled a second time, reducing the camp's population considerably. Lacking resources and with unemployment rampant in the first years after the Israeli occupation, a large number of those who stayed went to work in Israel in order to escape dependence on the 'charity' of the UNRWA and the Nablus elite.

It was the very same refugee families, often originally from villages considerably more urbanised than those of the Nablus region, who did everything they could to give their children an education. Yet, with little employment opportunities on the West Bank for those with higher education, such as Imm Muhammad's eldest daughter, graduation was often followed by migration. For those who stayed (by 1988 the camp still had about 14,000 inhabitants), it was often revenues from abroad which improved their standard of living. While most houses still have the one UNRWA room they started out with, almost all households have upgraded their dwellings at their own expense by adding rooms to it, building an indoor kitchen and sometimes a second floor for a marrying son. Yet the situation in the camps is still visually different from the neighbouring villages and urban quarters. Not only are houses in the camps exclusively built of cement and cinder blocks, and not of stone, but the camps have also become exceedingly cramped, with the expanded houses coming very close together and the alleyways extremely narrow. Still, facilities in the camps may well be better than in the more remote villages. It is true that the supply of running water and electricity may be irregular, and that the educational and medical services the UNRWA provides are still wanting. Yet, in many smaller villages such as Al-Balad, with no piped water, only private electricity generators, and dependent on Israeli-run education and medical care, the situation in terms of public services is worse.

With the intifada, houses in the camps have become of particular importance for daily life, because of the numerous and extensive curfews: in 1988 Balata camp was under complete curfew for 123 days, in 1989 for 99 days (JMCC 1991: 112). Like the old city of Nablus also before the intifada the camps had been centres of resistance against the occupation. After the beginning of the intifada in Gaza on 8–9 December 1987, it was in Balata camp that the first demonstrations on the West Bank took place, and on 11 December the army killed two women and two children in the camp; during the first year of the intifada ten people from the Balata camp were shot dead by the army (Yahya 1991: 98). And, as the events in Imm Muhammad's household show, the camps have continued to be hit hard by military repression.

In many ways the situation of women in the camps is similar to that of Nablusi women in the old city, having to cope with poverty, insecurity, army violence, arbitrary arrests, and dependence on men, who may hardly be in a position to provide much support. Yet there are also major differences in their life stories. If the Nablusi poor have often experienced some gradual improvement in their socio-economic situation, refugee women lived through the *nakba*, sudden dispossession and downward social mobility. Only more recently has their situation improved to some extent. How this ties in with the greater emphasis on education and female employment in the camps is to be elaborated on in part III.

## 2.5 Property: from production to consumption?

The material presented here indicates a major, albeit ambiguous, historical shift in the meaning of property from productive resource to consumer good. For many households, wage labour, often outside the West Bank, rather than productive property has become the main source of livelihood. In the 1980s, most of Imm Sālim's sons were working in the Gulf States or had previously done so. By then only few households in Al-Balad were still fully dependent on dry-farming agriculture, a situation which contrasted sharply with that of the mandatory period. Imm Shākir's sons were professionally trained and held high-ranking positions abroad. Admittedly, two of them, both engineers, were factory owners, yet in contrast to their grandfather's generation, secular education had been of great importance to their career, and even amongst the elite property had lost some of its centrality. While Imm Hilmī's family also previously had not owned property, the greater opportunities abroad meant less dependence on the local elite than previous generations had experienced. It was Imm Muhammad who had seen the most rapid, complete and negative transformation 'from property to wage labour'. While her father had been a moderately successful smallholder producing for the market, her son was working as a common labourer in Israel.

Remittances and savings were first and foremost spent on housing. One reason for this pattern was that there were few opportunities for productive investment; local producers have a very hard time competing with the well-protected and subsidised Israeli products, which flood the West Bank market. Also, there is virtually no banking system on the West Bank. After 1967 the Israeli authorities closed all Arab banks, while Israeli banks only have very limited functions and are generally distrusted. The instability of the Israeli currency, with its many devaluations and strong inflation from 1974 on, stimulated the West Bank population to keep their savings in Jordanian dinars (JD) (both currencies are legal tender on the West Bank). However, Jordanian banks have virtually no branches on the West Bank and more recent events, such as the devaluation of the JD in early 1989, when it lost about 40 per cent of its value, have also made this currency less attractive. As hoarding large amounts of cash or gold is considered risky, investing in real estate, in particular one's own home, makes sense.

At least as important as these material considerations is the cultural centrality of home-ownership in a society which greatly values autonomy in the sense of households not having to depend on others. To the prominent families in the city houses symbolised their social position. Prominence, after all, was not defined simply by wealth, but rather by 'deep-rootedness', by having a family tree going back for centuries, of which the old family mansions, the *dīwān* and the soap factories could be seen as the physical embodiment. And while rent acts are strongly supportive of tenants, also to many poorer but aspiring urbanites owning one's own home is a major goal in life. In the villages, where rented housing was, and still is, not very common, an increasingly large part of income is spent on housing, with extended family households splitting up earlier, and standards for suitable housing becoming higher and higher. Migrants often build in the village, as these houses signify their ties to their place of origin; in the eyes of his fellow villagers all the money a migrant earns abroad means nothing if he does not build in the village. Refugee families in the camps, on the other hand, driven from their homes, had to start from scratch, and while many of them have spent considerable sums to improve the minimal housing originally provided by the UNRWA, they find themselves in an ambiguous position. Even if they buy and sell houses in the camps as if these were their property, in fact they are only selling occupancy rights, as the land these houses have been built on has been leased by the UNRWA. That the Israeli occupational forces are well aware of the cultural centrality of home ownership is evident. To prevent Palestinian residential expansion they have demolished many houses allegedly because of lack of proper permits, while they also use the demolition and sealing of houses to punish the families of Palestinians suspected of 'security offences' (Al-Haq 1988: 152).

Still, the shift from property as productive resource to a means of consumption is far from total. Both in a symbolic and material sense agricultural land is still valuable. It is true that landownership in itself no longer conveys social status, but it has remained central in the identity and sense of belonging of the rural population, crucial for their dignity and self-respect as expressed by the saying 'the one who has no land has no honour.' Also to those working abroad land ownership is still a symbolic tie to the village. Few migrants sold their land in order to be able to migrate; it was rather their income from migration labour which made it possible for them to hold on to their land. Neither has its material importance totally disappeared, as both the situation of migrants to the Gulf States, often without residence rights, and commuters to Israel, many of whom officially are not allowed to spend the night there, is precarious. Land is still seen as a form of security, a provision for old age, and a source of supplementary income for wage labourers.[22] At the same time one specific type of 'property' has become increasingly important. Many families, first the better-off urbanites and the refugees, but gradually also the villagers and the urban poor, have spent a large part of their income on their children's education. Even if education is a very different type of asset than land or other forms of productive property, it can be seen as a form of personalised property.

Turning to gender relations, a preliminary conclusion from the life stories presented here is that men (both kin and husbands) are of central importance for the socio-economic security of non-employed women. Yet, the life stories also reveal that women have some direct access to property through inheritance and the dower. The following chapters will focus on this property, the changes in its meaning and how these tie in with the ambiguous shift from property as a productive resource to a means of consumption.

---

[22] Tamari (1981) argues that one reason why villagers working in Israel are often employed in the building trade is that this type of work can be easily combined with peasant farming.

# 3    Women and inheritance

One way for women to gain access to property is through inheritance. According to the prevalent laws of succession in the region a woman is entitled to inherit both from her kin and her husband. Many women I spoke with, in the city as well as in the rural areas, were aware of their inheritance rights. But at the same time they underlined that if urban women might take their share in the estate, rural women by and large refrained from doing so. Such an urban–rural dichotomy is also prevalent in the literature on the subject. A summary of how the literature has dealt with this issue is presented first. This is followed by a brief description of the ways in which women's succession rights have been defined in the legal system. The main body of this chapter concentrates on the question of under which circumstances various categories of women inherit and what this means to them.

## 3.1    Historians and anthropologists: an urban–rural dichotomy?

In the literature on inheritance practices the urban–rural divide tends to coincide with disciplinary boundaries, historians largely focusing on the cities and anthropologists mainly paying attention to the rural areas. Detailed case studies by historians indicate that Muslim women in Ottoman cities did, indeed, inherit. Gerber (1980: 232, 240) argues that in seventeenth-century Bursa the law of inheritance was fully effective concerning women and in many cases they inherited. According to Jennings (1975: 98, 111) in the same period a large number of women in Kayseri made inheritance claims which were supported by the court. And Marcus (1985: 120) indicates that in eighteenth-century Aleppo, women were active as dealers in residential housing, with inheritance one of the means by which this had come into their possession. The anthropological literature on rural areas, on the other hand, emphasises the great divide between Islamic law and inheritance practices with women often not receiving their share in the estate. Granqvist's research indicates that in

the 1920s in Artas, a village near Bethlehem, women rarely inherited
(1935: 256). Rosenfeld (1960: 66) also argues that women in the villages of
the lower Galilee generally did not take their inheritance share. According to Antoun (1972: 140), in the 1960s women in a village on the East
Bank often refrained from claiming their rights in the estate. Equally,
Ammons (1978: 169) points out that in the early 1970s in the village of
Balata, near Nablus, women did not inherit.

Still, this does not imply that urban women generally took their
inheritance share while women in the rural areas consistently did not do
so. The emphasis historians give to women inheriting seems, at least in
part, to stem from their unease about pre-conceived notions of the
particularly 'depressed' (Gerber 1980: 231) or 'despised' (Jennings 1975:
53) position of women in 'Islamic societies', and may be seen as a result of
their attempts to set the record straight. In fact, they acknowledge that not
all town women inherited (Gerber 1980: 233) and provide circumstantial
evidence that women's inheritance practices may well have depended on
the nature of the property involved. Jennings (1975: 101) indicates that
women more often sold buildings than land, while both Gerber (1980:
233) and Marcus (1983: 144) argue that women were more prominent in
the trade in residential housing than in either commercial or agricultural
property. Although women did not necessarily acquire this property
through inheritance, it is likely that they did so at least in part. As such,
their inheritance shares in productive property were probably more
limited than their shares in housing.

While anthropologists usually stress that rural women do not receive
their inheritance share, they have also pointed to situations in which they
did inherit. In studies of rural inheritance practices, both Peters (1978)
and Mundy (1988) provide examples of villages (in Southern Lebanon
and Highland Yemen respectively) in which women as a rule took their
share. Both argue that whether or not women inherit is tied in with the
structures of production, in particular with the nature of the property
holding unit. Women seem to stand a better chance to inherit land if it is
individually owned rather than held in one way or another by a collecti-
vity. In addition, Pastner (1980: 152) states that if women are sometimes
less apt to receive their share in land, they may then be compensated for
by movable property.

The urban–rural duality is further undermined if it is acknowledged
that neither urban nor rural women can be seen as a homogeneous
category. Various authors point to the importance of taking factors such
as class, the absence or presence of competing heirs, and the stage in the
life cycle into account. In some villages women in smallholder households
took their share, while women in wealthy families where rank is founded

on property ownership, were often either excluded from inheritance or, as (potential) heirs, strictly limited in their marriage options (Peters 1978: 337). Even in villages where women generally refrained from taking their share, daughters without brothers may inherit (Granqvist 1931: 76ff.; Rosenfeld 1960: 67). Widows in polygynous households with competing wives or the latter's children present, were particularly prone to claim their share, as reported for Arabs in Israel (Layish 1973: 31) and the Hatay in Southern Turkey (Aswad 1967). In a Highland Yemeni village, women only take a share in their father's estate when they are in mid-life and have adult sons, doing so in order to transfer the land to them (Mundy 1979: 169).

So, the simple question whether women receive the share they are legally entitled to, raises a host of issues. Although the urban–rural dichotomy is common in the literature, authors also point to the importance of taking a closer look both at the nature of the property concerned and the women involved. Which women inherit and what type of property do they receive? When do they obtain their share and how do they gain access to it? Neither is the meaning of inheritance to women immediately transparent. Under what circumstances do they refrain from claiming their rights, in which cases are they forced to give these up and what induces them to demand their share? In what follows, I will look into the most common cases of women inheriting, daughters and wives, focusing first on women's succession rights as defined in the legal system and then on social practice.

## 3.2    The legal discourse: property and person

Even if the law is not always applied, it does provide a point of reference in debates on women and inheritance. In the Jabal Nablus region, as in other areas once part of the Ottoman empire, succession is regulated through two different legal systems, with the nature of the property involved determining which system is applied. Property held in full ownership (*mulk*), such as urban real estate, buildings, vineyards, orchards and movables, is inherited in accordance with the Islamic law of succession. Most agricultural land (but not the plantations) is not *mulk* but *mīrī*, land to which individuals could acquire rights of usufruct and possession, but with ultimate ownership vested in the state. This right of possession is also inheritable, but a secular law of succession is applied.

The Islamic law of inheritance is prescriptive and strongly partible; it restricts the right of testation and stipulates allotments to a large number of heirs, divided into two categories.[1] First in line are the Quranic heirs (*ahl al-farā'id*), who are entitled to a fixed percentage of the estate, varying from one-half to one-sixth. This category mainly consists of close kin, such as the father, mother, daughter and sister of the deceased, and the widow or widower. The remainder, which may well be the major part, is divided amongst the male agnatic heirs (the *ʿasaba*), with the nearer agnate excluding the farther. Certain categories of women, such as the daughter and the sister, turn from *farā'id* into *ʿasaba* heirs if there are male heirs of the same category; in that case they receive one-half of the share of their male counterparts.

While in Islamic law women have inheritance rights, these then are generally more limited than those of men. Looking into the shares of widows and daughters, male preference is clear. A widow is entitled to a fixed share of one-eighth of her late husband's estate if he had children (not necessarily by her) and one-quarter if not. If there are more widows they have to divide this share. A widower in a similar situation would take twice as much: one-quarter and one-half of his wife's estate respectively. Daughters receive a fixed share if the deceased has no sons: one daughter is entitled to half the estate, two or more sharing two-thirds of it. Thus, if a man dies without leaving sons, a considerable part of the estate goes to his male agnates. If, on the other hand, there are sons, these are the first heirs and daughters turn into *ʿasaba* heirs, entrusted with one-half the share of a son. Comparing the rights of female heirs, there is a strong preference for kin. Not only is the share of a widow smaller than that of a daughter, but also a mother and under certain circumstances a sister may inherit more.[2]

In Islamic thought, a man's greater inheritance rights are justified by linking them to his maintenance obligations (*nafaqa*). A husband is always responsible for the maintenance of his wife, independent of her own means, while she has no such obligations towards him. A father is to provide for his single, divorced and widowed daughters if they have no means of their own, and for his sons until adulthood. If he is too poor to maintain them and their mother has adequate financial means, she is obliged to support them, yet this is considered a loan to her husband, which he is to repay. A widow holds custody rights (*hadāna*) over her minor children, but their father's closest agnate is their natural guardian

---

[1] The right of testation is limited to one-third of the estate and cannot be made in favour of a legal heir, unless all other legal heirs agree. Yet, it is possible to circumvent the law by bestowing property as a gift (*hiba*) or dedicating it as an endowment (*waqf*).

[2] If the deceased had only one sister, she is entitled to one-half (if there were no children) or a quarter (if there were children). A mother receives respectively one-sixth and one-third of the estate.

and owes them maintenance, while she herself is to be maintained by her own relatives if she has no means of her own.[3] Sons are always responsible for maintaining their impoverished parents, daughters only if they can afford it. Maintenance to impoverished and disabled kin is to be provided by those who inherit from them and have sufficient means to do so, with their contribution depending on the percentage of their inheritance share.[4]

If *mulk* property is inherited according to Islamic law, a very different law of succession is applied to *mīrī* land: the Ottoman *intiqāl* (succession) system. While early forms of *intiqāl* severely restricted the number of heirs, only recognising the rights of sons, later legal reforms extended the number of heirs; by 1868 daughters were also able to inherit. Codified in 1913 as the Ottoman Law of Succession, its main principles are gender neutrality and the distribution of the estate on the basis of generations. The major heirs are the children of the deceased, and if there are none, then the parents, the surviving spouse receiving one-quarter of the estate if the deceased had children and one-half if there were none (Schölch 1982: 21; Mundy 1988: 12).

In the last seventy years, only limited changes have been made in the laws of succession (see Welchman 1988: 879). The shari'a courts are still responsible for drawing up a list of heirs and calculating the percentage of the estate each heir is entitled to, also for *intiqāl* inheritance. The law itself remains silent about when the estate is to be divided and it is common practice for the estate to remain officially undivided for a considerable length of time, with heirs only asking the shari'a court to register their shares if they want to formally donate or sell their share.

In short, women's inheritance rights are regulated according to two different systems. In regard to real estate and movables, Islamic law is in force. In that case, women's rights are generally more limited than those of men, and while spouses and close matri-kin (such as mothers) hold rights, there is a distinct preference for agnates. *Intiqāl* law, on the other hand, applied to virtually all agricultural land (except that planted with trees), expresses gender neutrality, allocates a greater share of the estate to spouses and does not recognise the special position of agnates. Yet comparing these two systems out of context is problematic, as Islamic

---

[3] According to Hanafī law, the mother's custody ended when a son is seven and a daughter nine; these age limits were raised in the 1951 Jordanian Law of Family Rights (JLFR; art. 123ff.) to nine and eleven years and in the 1976 Jordanian Law of Personal Status (JLPS; art. 154ff.) to the onset of puberty. Thereafter the children are returned to their natural guardian. If the mother is denied the right of custody (because of not devoting herself to her children, in particular if remarrying), it passes to the maternal grandmother, her other female agnates and then to the paternal grandmother.

[4] See JLPS (1976) art. 172 and 173.

inheritance law ought to be seen within the framework of the total shariʿa system. In Islamic legal thought, women's lesser inheritance rights are seen as compensated for by women's rights to maintenance, and women are defined as protected dependents.

## 3.3 Daughters: kinship rather than property

Three of the four women whose life stories I constructed in the previous chapter, had fathers who owned at least some property. Imm Sālim's father from Al-Balad, a smallholder with some land and goats, had only recently died. To her, a great-grandmother whose adult sons provided her with everything she needed, it was inconceivable to take from the land her brothers had cultivated for decennia. Imm Muhammad's father from Jaffa had lost most of his property in 1948, yet at the time of his death in the late 1960s he owned a dilapidated house in the old city, had a little cash and a number of goats. Imm Muhammad and her two sisters gave the money and goats to their only brother so that he could marry, and it was self-evident that he was also the one who would live in their father's small house. Imm Shākir, whose father belonged to the Nablus elite, refrained from claiming her inheritance for a considerable period of time, and then only took a share in the income from it.

That none of these three women took her full inheritance share is no coincidence. It is true that both Islamic and intiqāl law entitle women to a share in their father's estate. Yet amongst small property owners the most striking commonality in women's life stories is that few daughters with brothers would ever take their share and even amongst the wealthy they often did not receive what they were entitled to.

### Giving to brothers: problems of dependence and pleasures of identification

Historical data indicate the prevalence of male ownership of land in the rural areas. In nineteenth-century Palestine, a form of land ownership between individual and communal ownership, the mushāʿ system, was common in the grain-growing plains and the valleys in the hilly areas.[5] In regions with sufficient land and limited labour these village lands were divided into a number of categories and the rights of cultivation were allocated and periodically redivided according to the number of men or

[5] In those days the main issue was not individual ownership, but access to land and the rights of usufruct including part of the yields. Villages were collectively held responsible for the payment of taxes, and cultivating cereals often in combination with raising goats demanded a rotation scheme and some coordination.

plough animals in the household. When the population increased at the end of the nineteenth century and in particular during the mandatory period, the land was redivided on a smaller and smaller scale, a permanent division between the different lineages became increasingly common, and only within these units land was redivided (Simpson 1930: 31).[6] When *mushāʿ* land was divided definitively it was usually registered in the name of men (Granott 1952: 226; Cohen 1965: 6; Owen 1981: 256).

Some authors such as Peters (1978) and Mundy (1988) link women's exclusion from inheriting land to such more collective forms of landownership. In a similar vein, Layish (1975: 307) argues that in Israel changes in the system of land tenure 'especially, the transition from *mushāʿ* (joint ownership) to individual ownership' greatly encouraged Muslim women to take their inheritance share.[7] In West Bank villages like Al-Balad, where as far back as people remember the *mushāʿ* system did not prevail, there is, however, no positive link between 'individual ownership' and female inheritance, and women usually refrained from claiming a share in their father's estate.

Women themselves point out that it not so much the nature of land tenure but rather that of kin relations which is at stake. When in the 1920s Granqvist asked in Artas, a village near Betlehem, why a woman does not take her share of the inheritance, the answer was 'but then she would have no more rights to her father's house' (1935: 256). Women in Al-Balad in the 1980s by and large expressed very similar sentiments; by leaving her share to her brothers, a daughter reaffirms and strengthens her ties with her closest male kinsmen. And such ties are of great importance to women, as they both identify with their father's house and lineage and are dependent on it. With women remaining lifelong members of their own patrilineage, also after marriage they continue to share in its status and feel a special closeness to their natal household. Leaving her share in the father's estate to her brothers, a woman at once enhances their status and by implication her own and accentuates their obligations towards her. Just as a woman could return to her father's house if she intended to leave her husband or if he had repudiated her, after his death she would then be able to turn to one of her brothers, who would be responsible for housing her and providing for her. The relation between giving up a claim to land and maintaining kinship ties is also embodied in the gifts a man is obliged

---

[6]   In 1923 in the whole of Palestine 56 per cent of the village land was *mushāʿ*; 37 per cent in the north and 80 per cent in the south (Granott 1952: 237); the British mandatory authorities attempted to abolish the *mushāʿ* system, but were not very successful. In some villages in the Jabal Nablus region, such as Talluza, *mushāʿ* was common until the 1950s (Ammons 1978: 69).

[7]   'Changes in the system of land tenure' in Israel also have meant large-scale confiscations of Palestinian land.

to present to his sisters on a number of occasions, such as at the end of Ramadan (also Rosenfeld 1960).

That renouncing her inheritance rights is central to the brother–sister relation is evident from what happens if a woman demands her share. Then her kinship ties with her brothers are usually disrupted at once and she is no longer able to invoke their help and support. As the position of a woman in her husband's house often depends on the support she can count on from her own kin, this would simultaneously undermine her position *vis-à-vis* her husband and in-laws (also Granqvist 1935: 144). Neither is this easily compensated for by her newly gained access to land. Although the gender division of labour in agriculture is not very marked, some tasks are gender specific; ploughing in particular is considered men's work. Men can always ask women – their wives, daughters or sisters – to work on the (male) 'household lands', but when a woman needs male labour for cultivating her land, she has no such automatic claims to men's labour. In particular, when a woman is no longer able to ask her brothers or other relatives to help her, she becomes increasingly dependent on her husband.

If women then 'take land from their brothers' they do so under very specific circumstances. In some cases a husband presses his wife to claim her share, rather than she acting on her own initiative. In fact, she may well do so in spite of her own wishes. Imm Sālim related to me the tale of one of the very few women in Al-Balad who had claimed her share in her father's estate. 'This woman', she said, 'was forced by her husband to do so. He had got into a fight with one of her brothers and that is why he wanted her to take the land. Pressured by him, she did so and it destroyed her life. Her brothers had always been good to her, and they continued to present many gifts at the feasts to her sister, who had not claimed her share. But in her case, after her brothers had given her the value of the land in cash, they cut off their kin relation with her. This affected her so much that she fell ill and never fully recovered. Her husband did not really take care of her; he spent her money, and in the end left her to herself.' Under particular circumstances, however, it is socially condoned if a daughter claims her share. If her brothers do not treat her well, neglect her and do not provide for her, a daughter claiming her land is not condemned. Still, it remains a risky thing to do. The only woman from Al-Balad of whom I heard that she was considering to claim her share was in her late forties and already had adult sons. She intended to take her share in her mother's estate (consisting of four olive trees), as her brother had not supported his sisters nor taken care of his aged mother.

Inheritance practices in the city of Nablus are remarkably similar to those in the rural areas. If the literature tends to emphasise that urban women inherit, daughters of small property owners in Nablus usually did not claim their rights in their father's estate. With the family house and workshops seen as indications of their deep-rooted presence in the city, this property was not only economically central but also had a strong symbolic meaning. In artisanal households, skills, tools and workshops were usually transmitted from father to son, and the house, often the only other type of property, was destined for the sons, their (future) wives and children. For small metal workers, sweet makers, carpenters, shoemakers and so on, it was inconceivable to split it up. It is true that previously in the city more cash was available than in the rural areas, but this usually was not sufficient to formally 'buy out' a sister.

An urban daughter often opted for the very same strategy her rural counterpart followed, that is strengthening her brothers' position by leaving her share with them rather than taking it herself. And she did so for the very same reasons, as also in the city women identify with and are dependent on their father's house and lineage. In fact, with the gender division of labour more evident, women's economic dependence in the city was underlined even more strongly. By refraining from claiming their inheritance rights they did their brothers a favour and enhanced the status of their own family, while at the same time indicating that they were sufficiently well-off in their husband's house not to need to claim their inheritance.

Although there are strong historical continuities and to many women the relation with their brothers is still of great importance, over time the conjugal relation has become more accentuated. Writing about the 1920s Granqvist (1935: 156) acknowledged that marriage was important for a woman, as unmarried women were an easy target for gossip, but emphasised that it was a brother who would protect and help her in time of need. After all, 'the husband is only a garment which a woman puts on or throws off again, or she herself can be "thrown off" by her husband, but the brother is the one, who is always there' (Granqvist 1935: 253). Women in Al-Balad in the 1980s, on the other hand, tended to put a greater emphasis on the central role of husbands as providers. In response to my questions as to why women did not take their inheritance share, Imm Sālim's granddaughters and many others pointed out that their brothers needed the land 'because they have to take care of their wives and children; women themselves can do without, as their husbands will provide for them'. Yet even if they consider husbands as the main provider, they still recognise the importance of having a brother in times of hardship.

This shift from brother to husband as source of economic security for women ties in with changes in the social and economic structure of the village. Whereas previously most households were smallholders with both men and women producing for subsistence, at present most consumption goods are bought on the market, the large majority of the younger men work outside agriculture, and women's subsistence work in agricultural production has become economically less important and socially devalued. Inherited property has become less central as a source of livelihood and lineages have lost many of their political and economic functions. The result is not only a stronger emphasis on men as providers but also a shift in responsibility from fathers and brothers to husbands. Yet, this shift is far from complete and women do not go so far as to take the risk of disrupting their kin relations by claiming their share in their father's estate. Even in the city, where the emphasis on conjugality has a longer history, women often still prefer to underline their kin relations by refraining from claiming their inheritance share.

### No brothers: controversies about inheritance

While anthropologists emphasise that rural women generally do not inherit, some point to the exceptional position of daughters without brothers who do take their share (Granqvist 1931: 76ff.; Rosenfeld 1960: 67). In the Jabal Nablus region, the position of such daughters in relation to their father's estate is also very different from that of women with brothers. If it is frowned upon if women 'take their brother's share', it is not socially disapproved of if daughters without brothers claim their inheritance rights. But in practice these daughters were regularly disinherited. Their problematic situation is evident in the inheritance story of Imm ʿAbdulrahīm, a poor widow, employed as a cleaner in a Nablus hospital, related to me.

Imm ʿAbdulrahīm's father was from N., a village to the west of Nablus, but she herself was born in the Majdal, in the coastal region, where in the 1930s her father had started to work in the orange groves. Only a few years old when he died, she did not recall him. Her mother then remarried a man from the Majdal and the two small daughters were taken in by their father's brother. When Imm ʿAbdulrahīm was about twelve, she herself was married to a relative of her mother's second husband.

A few years later, during the fighting of 1948, the young couple had to flee the Majdal and came to N., where her late father had owned some land. Her father's brother had, however, taken this. 'He did not want to give us any', Imm ʿAbdulrahīm stressed. 'We had nothing. He only let us live in the old house.' Still very young and with a refugee husband, she felt herself in no position to challenge her paternal uncle. Recalling those days, Imm ʿAbdulrahīm emphasised how difficult the situation had been. 'My husband went everywhere to find work. For a short time we lived in the Jordan Valley working as sharecroppers, then he worked for two years in Kuwait while I remained in N., and after that we lived for a while with our three children on the East Bank where he worked as a stonecutter.' When her husband was no longer able to do that work and they returned to N., Imm ʿAbdulrahīm and her sister finally attempted to get their share of their father's land. 'This was twenty years after he had died', she said. 'At first, my father's brother refused adamantly. Through the mediation of others we tried to convince him and in the end, after lots of problems, the two of us together received one-quarter of our father's land, although we were entitled to more.' This land Imm ʿAbdulrahīm then used as security to borrow money so her husband would once more be able to go and work in Kuwait. Unfortunately all was lost. Her husband did not find work and died soon after he returned in the mid-1960s. She had to sell the land and was left a widow, twenty-five years old with a son of twelve, two younger daughters, and an infant son.

Cases such as this one are fairly common. If 'daughters without brothers' receive a share in their father's estate, it is often considerably less than what they are legally entitled to. Imm ʿAbdulrahīm, for instance, not only had to wait many years before she received the land, but even then did not obtain the full amount, as she and her sister together were entitled to two-thirds of this olive-tree planted land rather than to one-quarter of it.

A daughter without brothers usually has good reasons to try to claim her land. She knows that her father's brothers will generally be less concerned about her well-being and less dependable in providing for her than brothers would have been. So, even if her husband is to profit most from the inheritance, it could still be a sensible strategy for a brotherless woman to take her share. The problematic situation of such a daughter is also socially recognised, as she is not condemned for claiming her share. On the contrary, a man attempting to disinherit his late brother's daughter is often censured. Still, it may be very difficult for her to gain *de facto* control over the property. If she is already married her father's brother, usually many years her senior, will try to ignore her claims and whether she receives anything may well depend on her husband's standing in the community. If she is still single her father's brother is not only her contending heir, but also her legal marriage guardian. To forestall further problems about the estate he may try to marry her to his own son, as in that way no land will be lost to strangers. As Granqvist noted in Artas, a daughter without brothers could inherit, but she had to marry within the lineage 'in order to prevent a stranger taking possession of the property and inheritance of the family' and a disproportionate number of brotherless girls had married their paternal cousin (*ibn ʿamm*)

(1931: 76, 78). Elsewhere on the West Bank this type of cousin marriage is also one of the most common forms of forced marriages, both for women and for men. A man might have to marry a woman many years his senior only to hold on to the land. This in turn may induce him later to take a second wife.

Even if brotherless women are not always successful in their attempts, compared to women with brothers they tend to take their inheritance share relatively often. Turning to historical changes in inheritance practices, this implies that demographic developments have to be taken into account. As younger women at present probably stand less of a chance of finding themselves in the position of 'brotherless daughter' they are also less likely to become potential heirs than the generations of the 1920s and 1930s.

## 3.4    Widows: children rather than property

Two of the four women whose life stories I constructed in chapter 2 were widowed. Imm Sālim from Al-Balad renounced her share in favour of her sons when the land needed to be officially divided so they could get a permit to build on it. In the case of Imm Hilmī from the old city of Nablus the estate, her husband's house, was not divided. Whether an elderly woman renounces her share or not usually does not make much difference in practice; both Imm Sālim and Imm Hilmī continued to live in their late husband's house.

Widows in general are often more concerned about being able to keep their children than about taking a share in the husband's estate. As mentioned previously, according to Islamic law a widow has custody rights over her minor children, but their father's closest agnate is their natural guardian and owes them maintenance, while she herself is to be maintained by her own relatives. In practice, this means that if a widow is not unequivocally supported by her in-laws, she usually has to give up her children. For her own relatives are often only willing to support her if she returns to them, and are not prepared to maintain her children. They may want her to remarry so she will be provided for, her reputation (and in consequence, their own) will be better protected and, previously in the rural areas, perhaps also to claim part of her dower (Granqvist 1935: 311; see chapter 5). Unless she marries her husband's brother, a remarrying woman has to give up her children. So, for a widow the crucial question is whether she will be able to remain in her husband's house or has to return to her father's house. The outcome depends on the interplay of numerous factors, such as her age and reproductive history (sex and age of her children), her access to resources (house or land) and her relations with her own family and in-laws.

### Rural widows: between kin and affines

When women in Al-Balad explained to me the situation a rural woman would find herself in after her husband had died, they often presented two extremes as generalised examples. In the case of a mature widow with sons there were strong incentives for her to remain in her husband's house and to refrain from remarriage. She would then be able to raise her children while her husband's estate would often not be divided for a long time, except if he had (children by) another wife. Also, if she renounced her share for the sake of her sons, she may well have a relatively independent position through *de facto* control of her sons' land, often with more autonomy than in her husband's life time.[8] And when her sons were grown up, they would not only be legally obliged to provide for her, but the claim of a mother on her sons was also emotionally and morally very strong. Under such circumstances it was unusual for her own kin to ask her to return, and if they did so, it was unlikely that she would respond to them. The case of a young, childless widow, on the other hand, was very different. A widow chooses to stay in her husband's house for the benefit of the children; without children, she has no reason to remain with her in-laws. Even so, if her in-laws had taken a liking to her, they might prefer her to stay with them, as they had already paid a dower for her, donated gifts to her, and she might even want to claim her inheritance share. The only solution then was for her to marry one of her husband's brothers.

If under such circumstances the outcome is almost predictable – a mature widow staying with her sons, a young childless widow returning home, unless a brother-in-law marries her – many cases are not so clear-cut. When, for instance, Imm Sālim's son and two cousins were killed in 1967 attempting to cross the Jordan River, three women in Al-Balad were widowed at once. What were their options?

There was little doubt that Imm Sālim's daughter-in-law, at the time twenty-seven years old, with a nine year old son and three younger daughters, would stay with her children. It is true that during her husband's lifetime her relation with Imm Sālim had occasionally been tense, yet, as she pointed out, there were strong family ties between them; she and her husband were from the same lineage and her brother had also married one of Imm Sālim's daughters. And she herself had worked hard to get things her way. Through lending out some of her own money for the

---

[8] See the numerous examples in Granqvist (1935: 319–25).

use of land and cultivating it herself, she had helped her husband to save in order to build a separate house next to his father's house. When she was widowed, no one suggested she ought to leave her husband's house. Her father-in-law had sufficient land, and her son would inherit his father's share. In the meantime, she continued cultivating the land and her in-laws provided for the household. To further decrease her dependence on them, she started working as a seamstress, while she was also supported by one of her brothers in Kuwait, who was well-off, sent her many gifts, and in the late 1970s also got her son a job in Kuwait.

The second widow was a little older, about thirty. She also had four children, an eleven year old daughter and three sons under seven, but her situation was more ambiguous. She was not only from another lineage and another part of the village than her husband, but her relation with her in-laws was strained, as she and her husband had been turned out of her husband's father's house, when space was needed for his brothers who also wanted to marry. As his father had little land, her husband used the money he earned in Kuwait to lend it in exchange for the use of agricultural land (which she had cultivated), and to buy a few *dunum* of land to start building a house. She herself had only a few goats. After her husband died her in-laws hardly provided for her. Still indignant she told me how her brother-in-law had even suggested she return to her father's house, but she had refused to leave her children and, as she said, her own brothers had been good to her; they had not forced her to return home. With some bitterness she pointed out that although her in-laws were better off than her own relatives, who worked as share-croppers, her brothers cared more for her and the children, bringing them vegetables from the market where they worked, and other gifts.

The third widow was only nineteen when she lost her husband, was from another lineage, had two small daughters, two and four years old, and was pregnant. For a short time she had lived together with her husband in Kuwait, then she had sold her gold to help him build separate rooms at his father's house. When she was widowed her father did not want her to stay with her in-laws, as she was very young and they were strangers (non-kin). Then a marriage was arranged with her husband's brother, who was a year younger than she. As she said, 'he married me for the sake of his brother's children'. By the late 1970s, she had three sons by him.

The above cases show that the position of Imm Sālim's daughter-in-law was the most secure. She belonged to the same lineage and there were multiple ties of kinship, her husband had built a separate house and she had a son. The second widow's position was weaker as she was from a different lineage and her relation to her in-laws was strained, yet as a widow with sons, (the beginnings of) her own house, and the support of her own relatives, she was able to manage. The third widow, however, was simply too young to stay with her children. Her father feared gossip about the reputation of his daughter, a young, widowed woman, living in the same household with her husband's brothers, young men. So her husband's brother married her, the only person a woman may marry without losing her children.

The last case points to the highly problematic position of a younger widow with only daughters, a situation fraught with tensions and with an unpredictable outcome. If the widow herself often would prefer to stay with and care for her daughters, her future is insecure, as her daughters are to marry and will usually not be able to provide for her. Her late husband's brothers are not obliged to maintain her and might well cheat her and her daughters out of their rights to the estate. Her own relatives may urge her to return home, but have no obligations towards her daughters and may pressure her into remarrying. Emotionally this is an extremely taxing situation both for her and for her daughters. That women without sons fear such a future is evident from the cases in which a woman encourages her husband to marry another wife in order to have sons, because once a man has sons, his brother is no longer able to take his property and her daughters have (half-)brothers to protect them. In Al-Balad, for instance, a woman in her early forties told me about the problem that she only had one blind daughter, and then continued to describe in great detail and with pride how she had convinced her husband to take a second wife and how she had selected one of her own relatives, a woman in her late twenties. Everything had worked out well, her husband now had three small sons and she took care of them as a second mother in order that later they would treat her daughter, their half-sister, well (see also Granqvist 1935: 211–12).

## Urban widows: the burden of providing

In the city too, widows would often attempt to stay with their children and not remarry. Yet, due to the nature of the property involved and the gender division of labour, an urban widow's economic situation would deteriorate considerably and she might well be worse off than her rural 'propertied' counterpart. After all, in the villages, at least until quite recently, women's work in agriculture had been essential, a widow could do a large part of the work herself, and for specific male tasks she could invoke the help of male relatives or in-laws. In practice this may well have meant that she was amongst the last ones to be helped, yet men's position as providers gained currency in the rural areas only with large-scale labour migration. In the urban cash economy, on the other hand, women were largely excluded from earning a living; an urban widow was often not able to take over even part of her husband's work, be it artisanal or in trading. The loss of a husband could then indeed mean the loss of a provider and might make her dependent on charity and gifts. Such problems drove Nuzha, who was twenty-six and had four sons when she was widowed in 1983, to remarry.

Telling me about her plight, Nuzha strongly emphasised the injustice that had befallen her. Married at fourteen, she had got along quite well with her husband, whom she described as a quiet man, fifteen years her senior. His father had already died, and he had inherited a shop, where he sold clothing and needlework. 'In the beginning our financial situation was difficult', she pointed out. 'I helped him by knitting and crocheting things he could sell in the store. Later I also worked as a hairdresser at home and bought lots of things for the house. Gradually our situation improved.' She did not, however, get along well with his mother, with whom they were living with. As Nuzha phrased it, 'She was very domineering, all the time she told him what to do, and he did it.'

Then her husband suddenly died. According to Nuzha, problems developed almost immediately. 'It was incredible, already after three days his family told me that I had no rights, because I was still young. They said that I would remarry and then the estate would go to my new husband. Imagine, I had four sons, the eldest was twelve, I wanted to take care of them, not to remarry!' To underline her commitment to her children, she added, 'And I had renounced my inheritance rights for the sake of the children.' Refusing to leave the children, Nuzha stayed with them in their rooms. But her in-laws did not give her anything. Nuzha recalled how one of them sat in her husband's shop, but as she said, they did not give her any of the proceeds nor did they replace anything. After having spent the money she had saved from her work as a hairdresser, she felt she had no choice but to raise the problem and his family and her father came together. Unfortunately, this did not work out. When someone told her father that he could easily afford to pay for her, which in Nuzha's eyes was true since he was a reasonably successful trader, he became very angry. In Nuzha's words, 'He said he was prepared to provide for me, but that he was under no obligation to take care of the children, and told me to come home and leave the children behind.' Nuzha tried everything she could to avoid this. Through an old friend of her husband she had heard that the men in the market were willing to help her with the store if she wanted to run it. When she suggested this to her father, he flatly refused the idea. 'He was afraid people would blame him for not taking care of his daughter', Nuzha explained. When gossip spread that she was talking to men, she had to give up the idea.

Nuzha had no other option but to move in with her father. Only her youngest son accompanied her, the others were divided amongst her husband's brothers. But her father was yet to cause her further trouble, as Nuzha, still resentful, pointed out. 'He did not allow my sons to stay overnight at his house, so their paternal uncles became angry and forbade them to come at all.' She started to despair. 'Only after I threatened to kill myself did my father relent and let them stay with me,' she said. But that also did not work out. 'We were living there with five in one room. And he did not make them feel at home at all. When they were eating he would watch how much they ate, when they wanted to watch television he did not allow them, because it was "not from their work" . . . ' At that time other problems also developed. Nuzha had previously given her father 1,000 JD from her work to invest in his business. 'Never did I see anything from it', she underlined, 'and he got annoyed when I asked about it. Really, a woman becomes a beggar if she has to depend on her relatives.' Still, for a long time, whenever a man came to ask her in marriage, she refused, because she wanted to stay with her children. In the end, however, she considered the offer of a man, who had left his wife and children four years earlier, and said he would accept her sons. 'By then I really wanted to leave my father's house', she explained. 'I was no more than a servant for my family and I wanted some freedom.' But her father did not agree to the marriage. 'He was afraid that people would say that I had married because he did not take care of me', Nuzha pointed out, 'so, he placed many obstacles, but we married none the less.' When I last spoke to Nuzha she was living with her husband, together with her youngest son in a virtually unfurnished house. Her father had refused to give her the dower her husband had paid and the latter was not willing to spend any more.

Even if Nuzha's case, a mother of four sons more or less forced to remarry, is rather exceptional, it highlights the problems an urban widow may find herself confronted with. In the urban context, women, and also children, are often seen as an economic burden. As Nuzha's case indicates, she is separated from her children because her in-laws refuse to maintain her, while her own father does not want to spend money on her children. Both parties limit themselves to what they are legally obliged to provide. In the rural areas, a widow may lose her children too, but in the days that agriculture was still the major source of livelihood, this happened for very different reasons. There, the importance of women's labour was still recognised and children were seen more as an asset than as a burden. If a rural widow had to give up her children, it was because her kin wanted her to return home, while her in-laws did not want to lose the children.

The social position of a widow, of her father and of her late husband also influences whether and under which conditions she is able to stay with her children. If such a widow has resources of her own, if she has wealthy relatives who support her, or a well-off late husband whose estate her sons inherit, she has at least the financial means to raise her children. The life story of Imm Hilmī presented in the previous chapter, on the other hand, illustrates the problems women from poor households have to face. When her mother was widowed with five small children, neither she nor her late husband had a brother to provide for her and the children, so she turned to all kinds of work to be able to feed them. Imm Hilmī herself became a widow when she was already an elderly woman with mature sons. Yet, her sons were not able to support her financially, so she had to do odd jobs, and she married off her eldest daughter at thirteen. After ten years of marriage, this girl's husband suddenly died. As she was living with her husband's family, together with her brothers-in-law, her mother would only allow her to stay there if one of them would marry her. When this did not materialise, Imm Hilmī asked her daughter to return home and married her again. The children, three boys and one girl, remained in their paternal grandfather's house, but his relatives were not able to take care of them and they were placed in an orphanage. A woman from a poor background was often confronted with the problem that neither her brothers-in-law nor her own brothers were able to provide for her and her children. She would then either have to remarry and lose her children or have to fend for herself.

Turning to processes of historical change, the narrowing of age differentials between groom and bride has resulted in younger women being widowed less often.[9] Yet, the position of those women who find themselves widowed may well have worsened. For a widow with sons the main question is not so much whether she receives her legal allotment, but rather how she can deal with the property concerned. In the mandatory period, this was easier for rural than for urban women, as in the villages the gender division of labour was less strict and more consumption goods were home produced. Gradually, however, it has become virtually impossible to depend on dry-farming agriculture for a living and the rural population also has become more dependent on non-agrarian wage labour. As a result, the position of rural widows has weakened considerably as also to them losing a husband has come to mean losing a provider.

[9] In Al-Balad, for instance, in the period 1928–47 the age differential between groom and bride was more than ten years in 40 per cent of marriages (n = 20), for the period 1947–67 this was 32 per cent (n = 25), and for the period 1967–81 17 per cent (n = 30).

## 3.5     Those with a better chance to be given

Under specific conditions women stand a better chance to receive property, that is, if they are from a wealthy family, if they are single and elderly, or if they inherit from their mothers. Also, when property is donated *pre mortem* they sometimes receive more than would have been the case otherwise.

### 'Wealthy women': receiving gifts rather than claiming rights

Daughters of small property owners often argued that they did not claim their share in their father's estate as there was little to divide and their brothers needed it to be able to provide for their households. This then raises the question as to what happens in the case of women from a wealthy background. Does wealth make it easier for women to receive their share?

To some extent this is, indeed, the case. It is true that among the wealthy, the large traders, high office holders, owners of flour mills or soap factories, renting out shops and houses, productive property was also usually transmitted patrilineally and remained under male family control. But if enough cash was available in such households, women were more often 'bought out' or were allowed to share in the income from the property. In such households giving daughters, even those who are married, a share in their father's estate was seen as enhancing the status of the family as a whole. Even then, however, women commonly received less than what they were legally entitled to and often only did so after a considerable lapse of time. As the life story of Imm Shākir indicates, after her father's death the household's strategy was to keep productive property together and invest in the education of her younger brothers. Only when they were financially secure did their (married) sisters start to receive their inheritance. The latter did not, however, gain control over the property itself but began to share in the income from it, and even then not fully to the extent they were entitled to according to Islamic law. Imm Shākir did not mind much, one way or the other. Married to one of the wealthier men of Nablus, with her sons well-established as professionals, she felt no need for pressing the issue.

Women from wealthy families who are interested in their financial situation, have to face the problem that it is not deemed proper for a woman to inquire after her father's estate, as the case of Khawla, a successful professional woman in her early forties, indicates. When her father died in the mid-1950s, Khawla was only fourteen. He had been a wholesale trader in cloth, and together with his brothers and sisters owned large estates in the villages to the east. With her mother staying in the family home, the property remained undivided for a considerable period of time; it was not until the early 1980s that it was officially split up. By then Khawla had been married to a well-known businessman for over fifteen years, had two teenage daughters, one of whom had a health problem, and had herself taken up professional employment.

When her father's estate was divided, three of her brothers and two sisters were still alive. In line with common practice, her brothers made all the arrangements for the division of the estate. Pushed by her concern for the future of her daughters who, as she stressed, would not have a brother to protect them, Khawla wanted to know what was going on, but found it difficult to ask. 'The majority, also the educated people, consider it a shame for a woman to inquire after her inheritance share. They say she is negligent of her brother [bitqāsir akhūhā]. So my sisters remained silent, they were too shy to ask. But I was strong, and because I fought they also received their share.' And indeed, her brothers were not very pleased about their sister's inquisitiveness. As Khawla put it: 'I have inherited by fighting, not in court, but by telling them "I will not sign anything unless you show me everything". After all, they did not work hard for it, my father did and he left it for all of us.' She still thinks that they took a little more than their share, but, as she said, 'that does not matter, they are my brothers'.

Khawla acquired various property rights. She started telling me about the agricultural land of which her father had been a co-owner. 'The land in the east is not subdivided, my father's generation did not divide it, so it is for his children and for the children of his brothers and sisters.' With some nostalgia she recalled how previously the peasants used to bring so many sacks of sesame and wheat and also canisters of olive oil, adding, 'but now the share of the peasants is larger, and then my father and uncles had contact with them, now nobody cares, every one has his own business. The income is kept in a treasury, and one family member is responsible for it, the one who is always in Nablus. We keep it for family occasions, for funerals and celebrations. Instead of collecting from all of us, this income covers everything.'

Her father had also owned a large house, which the Israeli authorities had sequestered as a school. Khawla's share was one-eighth. 'If we sell it the land will be worth more than 100,000 JD', she said. 'But the rent is very low, it is paid in Israeli Shekel (IS) and with the devaluation of the IS, my share has decreased from the equivalent of about 90 JD per year to that of 40 JD.' Yet, as Khawla emphasised, 'we do not care for the rent but for the land.' Other real estate her father had owned in Nablus was roughly worth another 100,000 JD. Part of this was sold, and on the remainder of it some of the other heirs had built houses. Khawla did not do that. 'With my brothers, my sister and my husband all so close together it would become very complicated', she explained. 'I bought a piece of land far away from them. At the time, in 1981, it cost only 5,500 JD; now it is worth three times as much.' The rest of the inheritance Khawla put into building this house. 'I have sold about 15,000 JD worth of bank shares and up till now the house has cost me about 35,000 JD.' She still had shares worth about 8,000 JD in a bank and a factory in Amman which brought in about 180 JD annually. Her main impetus to build a house had been to secure her eldest daughter's future. 'So she will have a good house in the future. I want to make sure that she is safe.'

Khawla had not considered putting her inheritance share in the name of either her husband or her relatives. Reacting to my question whether she had not considered letting her husband administer it, she said: 'No, I do not do that. I give him part of my income, but the rest we keep separate. Men always like to be in control of the spending. They also like to have a woman write the property in their name, or at least to be appointed as her representative [wakīl]. But then it will mingle and it will be taken for granted that it is his money and when you want anything it is as if you have to ask. And particularly without sons, you have to be careful.' Neither did she consider putting it in the care of a relative. 'You will loose either money or relationship; that is what will happen in the long run', she stressed.

Presenting her inheritance story, Khawla emphasised that her brothers had been good to her, allowing her to study abroad at a time when few women did so, but she still had a difficult time convincing them that she wanted to be involved in the division of their father's estate. The problem was that by doing so she acted against the unwritten rule that a woman ought to be satisfied with what comes her way and should not actively seek her inheritance share. So, if daughters in wealthy families are often given part of their share in the estate, they should not bring up the issue themselves. Khawla did so because she was both able to and felt a pressing need. As a professional woman in her forties, with her own income, she was not too dependent on her brothers and would not need to return to them. Still, the main factor which pushed her to act was to secure her daughters' future.

Not all prominent families display the same inheritance practices. Although during the British mandatory period there were no longer sharp lines of distinction between the learned families and the large estate owners, it was amongst families with a learned tradition that women were more likely to receive the share to which they were entitled. Even though, as Khawla said, amongst educated families women did not automatically obtain their rights, the daughters of learned families, their fathers often high religious functionaries, stood a better chance of inheriting. With the large estate owners from a rural background, on the other hand, a different pattern emerged. If urban, upper-class ideology disapproved of disinheriting daughters totally, these families were confronted with the problem that their major resource was agricultural land. If a married daughter would take her share in the inheritance, perhaps pressed by her husband, considerable tracts of land might be lost to strangers. A common solution then was to only allow a daughter to marry her paternal cousin (*ibn ʿamm*), so the land would remain in the same lineage; if it was not possible to arrange such a marriage, such a daughter would have to remain single (see Canaan 1931: 178). Peters (1978: 337) describes a similar pattern of strict marriage arrangements for daughters of large landowners in a village in South Lebanon. There, however, daughters inherited as a rule. In the Jabal Nablus region, on the other hand, it was the sheer possibility that a daughter might claim her share that had these effects.

Even if at present in some upper-class families landed estates are still an important source of wealth, these restrictions on women's marriage arrangements have gradually disappeared. Inherited property is no longer as pivotal as it had been previously, education has become more important and such strict marriage rules are now considered old-fashioned. But in the rural areas, these traditions on occasion still influence marriage strategies. In Al-Balad and other villages to the east of Nablus, it is still common for *dār al-shaykh* women to only marry within the lineage, even if many of these families have become impoverished and may own less land than the average peasant.

### Single elderly daughters: rights to housing and maintenance

Quite a number of older houses in Nablus are inhabited by women only; sometimes a woman lives there by herself, more often a mother with her daughter or two sisters are staying together. If most of those who could afford it have left the old city, some of the large houses where the prominent families used to live are still inhabited by the elderly unmarried daughters. One of these houses, for example, is the home of three single sisters, the daughters of a high religious functionary, who were pensioned after long careers in education and administration. When their father died in the mid-1960s, their brothers had already moved out and were living and working in Amman, and the three sisters, together with their mother, remained living in the old house.

Single women from less prominent families also regularly became the main occupants of their father's (or occasionally mother's) house. But in such cases the situation was not always as clear-cut, as the case of Sitt Salwā, a woman in her late sixties, whose father had only owned a small workshop and a house in the old city, indicates.

Sitt Salwā was the eldest daughter in a household of two girls and four boys. Leaving school when she was in the fifth grade – because of the Arab revolt and the general strike in 1936 – she became apprenticed for some years to an experienced seamstress, and then went to work as an independent seamstress herself. In the early 1950s, when she was in her mid-twenties, she also started to take care of the infant son of one of her brothers. Her responsibilities further grew when her mother fell ill. By then all her brothers had married and had moved out of the house. As Sitt Salwā put it, 'My sisters-in-law left my mother to herself.'

Sitt Salwā's position as a seamstress deteriorated when after the Israeli occupation in 1967 the independent sewing trade collapsed, but it was a personal tragedy – the death of her foster son in the civil war in Jordan 1970 – which affected her so much that she quit sewing altogether. When a few years later her mother passed away (her father had died some years earlier), she intended to stay by herself in the family home. Yet her brothers were not very happy with the situation, fearing people's censure that they were not willing to care for their sister. Indeed, for some time she went to live in her eldest brother's household, but, as she pointed out, 'his wife could not bear it'. Sitt Salwā felt that she was not treated well and had little privacy. After a quarrel she returned to the family home in the old city, which she much preferred. Although for some time her brothers remained angry with her and refused to pay her maintenance, in the end everyone accepted the situation and the relation with her brothers was mended. She never considered claiming her inheritance share, but received her mother's two gold bracelets.

This episode had given her a realistic perspective on what to expect from brothers. 'For a single woman everything is seen as excessive,' she stressed. 'Her brother brings three or four large bags of rice to his own house, but to her he does not even bring ten kilos, and then he says "what do you want with all of this, it will last you for over a year". I would have to count every single grain if it was to last me that long! When I met my brother while I was carrying some hand brooms, he said, "what are you doing with those, are they for sale? Didn't I give you a broom?" I said, "Is one broom enough, don't you sweep with it?" '

The above indicates that in the case of elderly single women the inheritance issue is structurally different from that of a married woman. In the case of a single woman without means of her own, her brothers are legally obliged to provide for her. If tensions arise, these tend to be expressed in terms of maintenance obligations rather than in terms of inheritance rights. Even if a single woman were to receive a share in her father's estate, her brothers are her first heirs. It is quite common, therefore, for elderly single women to hold strong usufruct rights to the family home. When it became increasingly common for married sons to move into a house of their own, the most convenient solution for everyone was for an elderly unmarried daughter to remain in her father's house. Although emotional ties between a sister and her brother can be very close, and in the early years of his marriage a sister may have more say in her brother's household than his wife, this tends to change through time, when her sister-in-law has (grown) children. Many times I heard older women warn girls reluctant to marry that they would end up living in their brother's house as a servant for his wife. This was of particular importance in the urban setting where many women are not employed (the relation between remaining single and professional employment is addressed in chapter 9) and a single woman is more likely to be seen as an economic burden to her brother's household than in the rural areas, where she may support herself through raising goats and so on. It is particularly under such circumstances that a single elderly woman often prefers to remain in the family home. More recently, with the great socio-economic changes in the villages, a similar process is starting to take place there. Thus, while an elderly single woman usually does not demand her share in the estate, the rights she holds to the use of the family home tend to be socially recognised and are of central importance to her.

### Inheriting from mothers or women's ties to gold

In the Jabal Nablus region, women generally have a better chance to receive gold than to inherit their share in landed property. A single village woman, in her mid-twenties and employed as a teacher in Nablus, pointed out to me that she would renounce her rights in her father's estate (of agricultural land) for the sake of her brothers, because 'you never know when you will need them', but that she would take her mother's gold. Actually, she was expecting her mother to sell some of it in the near future and give her the money, so she would be able to buy herself a small, second-hand car and go home more regularly. Indeed, it generally seemed more difficult to disinherit women from gold than from any other type of property. As the case of Imm Muhammad showed, her father's property was given to her brother, but her mother's gold was divided according to the shari$^c$a rules. Admittedly, she herself planned to give one of her bracelets to her son, who badly needed money to be able to marry, yet she had already given some coins to her daughters.

It is, however, not so much the nature of the property that is at stake, but rather the relation between testator and heir. Gold is, after all, mostly inherited from mothers. Because of the strong emotional bonds between a mother and her daughter it is rather common for a woman to support her daughter through donating some of her gold to her. Women from very different backgrounds did so. An elderly woman, from a well-off Nablus family, married into a prominent large landowning rural family, gave each of her six daughters one of her gold bracelets when they were married. It was intended as a memorable gift, the economic value of little importance. At the other end of the spectrum, Imm Ahmad, from a poor Nablus family also gave her gold to her daughter when she was married, but in this case financial reasons were paramount, as the groom, an orphan, was not able to pay it himself. It is true that in poorer households women's gold could be the main form of property and as such it could not always be spared for daughters. A mother may instead give her gold to her son if he wanted to get married, so he was saved the expense of buying gold for his wife. Yet it was also common, both in Nablus and in the rural areas, for a mother to give her gold to a daughter she felt particularly responsible for and close to, for example a daughter who had postponed her own marriage to take care of her mother when she was getting on in age. And if she did not do so in her lifetime, such as in the case of Sitt Salwā, this close mother–daughter tie gives women a particular claim on their mother's estate, which often consists of gold.

### Pre mortem *gifts: old traditions and new developments*

*Pre mortem* gifts are often associated with attempts at disinheriting women. In the Jabal Nablus region, however, women also acquired property in this way. It was suggested above that some daughters had already received their mother's gold during her life time. Yet this is true not only of mothers; a father may also give his daughters part of his property before he passed away. In some cases he would do so following the rules of the shariᶜa, in order that his children would know what was theirs and could work with it. Sitt Sukayna, a single, elderly woman, recently retired from a prominent position with the UNRWA and still active in charitable associations, told me how her father decided to split up the property before his decease.

The wealth of Sitt Sukayna's family, which, she said, 'used to rule in Ottoman times', was based on large landed estates in the villages in the north. Her father, who owned thousands of *dunum* of dry-farming land, part of which he had developed into orange plantations, held a high administrative post both in British and Jordanian times, but retired when he was transferred to the East Bank. Reflecting on how he divided his property, Sitt Sukayna, who herself had a long career in teaching and administration, said: 'During his lifetime when he was getting on in age, he decided to divide the land according to the rules of religion to make it easier for us. He told every one of us – four brothers and three sisters – what was theirs.' The house, some of the plantations and part of the dry-farming land he left to one brother and the three sisters together. The other brothers each had their own estates, but they also put one in charge of the land.

Sitt Sukayna, who was living together with her mother and another single sister in the house they inherited, did not show great interest in the land. 'I am not involved', she said. 'I do not have time for it; our brother takes care of it. He is living in the village and it is easier for him to work with the peasants. At the end of the year we all receive our share.' She estimated hers at roughly 2,000 JD, adding 'it does not give very much these days. During the Jordanian times it was very good, but now you have to spend much, for fertiliser, for water, for labour.' As nobody disagreed after their father died, they kept it the way he had divided it.

In other cases a father gave away part of his property in order to deviate from the inheritance rules. It is true that daughters could be disinherited this way. A father may, for example, give most of his property to a favourite son. Yet it was also not uncommon for a father to purposely donate part of his property to his daughters. For a man without sons this could be an expedient way to guarantee that his daughter received her share and his brothers would not cheat her out of it. This was a consideration for the father of Imm Hishām, an elderly widow from a well-known learned family.

Imm Hishām's father had only two daughters. He had married Imm Hishām's mother while studying in Turkey in Ottoman times and taken her back with him to Nablus, where he was appointed as qādī (religious judge). Not able to get used to life in Nablus his wife returned to Istanbul leaving, or forced to leave, her infant daughter in the care of her ex-husband's mother. Imm Hishām's father remarried, and his second wife also only gave him a daughter. Turning to the subject of inheritance Imm Hishām explained that, when he was getting on in years, some friends advised her father to donate the house he had built to his daughters. They argued that his brothers' material situation was good and if the estate was to be divided according to the shari'a every heir would only receive a small share. Imm Hishām underlined that at first her father had hesitated as he did not want to deviate from the shari'a. When he realised that it was allowed, however, he agreed, and gave the house to his wife and daughters. After her stepmother died a few years ago Imm Hishām and her half-sister – who both had been married and were living in their (late) husbands' houses – sold their father's house and put the money into a bank account, 'to lose almost half of it with the devaluation,' as Imm Hishām put it.

Another reason for a father to donate property to his daughters was to guarantee a *single* daughter that she would remain well provided for. This happened, for example, to two elderly sisters, the younger daughters in a middle-class, urban family, one of whom, Sitt Miryam, explained their father's considerations to me. 'Shortly after the British came my eldest sister and only brother went to study in Turkey. She was one of the first women from Nablus to study abroad.' With pride she added that on returning to Nablus her sister had become appointed as school director at a very young age and had an impressive career. Turning to her own life story she said: 'But I and my younger sister did not like the idea of leaving for a long time to study, so we were trained as seamstresses. We earned money ourselves, but our father always insisted that he provide for us. He did not want us to spend any money. After his death, when our brother was already married and had his own family, our eldest sister took over his responsibilities and took care of us. She built a new house for herself and for us, next to the house our brother had build after he married, and she also built a mosque.' About her father she said that he had given his children the opportunity to learn but had little money to leave to them. He had, however, bought a piece of land in Amman. 'That land he gave to the two of us, because we had not finished our education. We sold the land in 1956 for 500 JD and bought shares in an oil company. Living without men, that would give us income.'

More recently not only daughters but also wives occasionally receive property as *pre mortem* gifts. With the rapid growth of migration and the weaker ties between the older and the younger generation, a man may fear that after his death his sons would not care well for their mother. To strengthen her position, he may register the house in the name of his wife during his life time so his sons would not be able to sell it. After the Israeli occupation there was an additional reason for *pre mortem* gifts of land and real estate. If the legal heir was a non-resident, his or her share could be considered absentee property (*amlāk ghā'ibīn*) with the (Israeli) state claiming it. In order to avoid this property was sometimes given away *pre mortem*. If only a daughter had remained on the West Bank, she would then be the one in whose name the property was registered.

## 3.6    Inheriting property: what does it mean?

As mentioned previously, much of the literature on women and inheritance in the Middle East refers to the rural–urban dichotomy. The property rights of women in the city are seen as better protected because of the greater influence of scriptural Islam and the different nature of the property involved, real estate and movables versus agricultural land. It is true that location (urban or rural) and the nature of property involved have some impact on women's access to inherited property. Yet it seems that the kinship position of women, social stratification and marital status are more important. The presence or absence of specific contending heirs is central to whether women claim their inheritance share or not. It is the daughters without brothers and, to a lesser extent, the widows without sons or with (children by) competing wives, who show most interest in inheriting. The daughters in wealthy households are the ones who stand the best chance to being given a share in the estate, or at least part of the income from it. Single, elderly women most often hold usufruct rights in their father's house.

But what is the meaning of inheriting property for the women involved? Historians, who by virtue of their sources often have more information about the property than about the women concerned and their motives, commonly consider property ownership as the embodiment of power. Anthropologists, on the other hand, have argued that refraining from claiming property rights does not necessarily imply giving up all rights to it. The material presented here points to the multiple meanings of inheriting property. In the Jabal Nablus region, women inherit under very diverse circumstances and with widely divergent implications, and acquiring inherited property does not necessarily tie in with gendered power. Some women may receive (part of) their share automatically because they are from an urban, wealthy family background and men can raise their own status by giving to their sisters. Yet the latter are not supposed to inquire about their rights, but ought to accept what they are given. In such cases, women's access to property is first and foremost an expression of their class position. Incidentally, it is this specific category to whom people refer when they argue that urban women indeed inherit. Others inherit because their husbands put great pressure on them to claim their share. Rather than an indication of power, under such circumstances inheriting property points to a highly problematic situation. These women are not only likely to lose kin support, but, as a result, also find themselves in a weaker position in regard to their husband and his kin. Then there are women, in particular daughters without brothers, who claim their share because they find themselves in a highly vulnerable situation. Such as girl does not only stand a good chance that, after her father's death, his brother will take possession of the land but she may also be forced to marry her paternal cousin (*ibn ʿamm*), whether he is suitable or not, to preempt the possibility that the land goes to strangers. In a similar vein, daughters in large landowning families, as potential heirs, previously had severely limited marriage options, having to choose between marrying their paternal cousin or remaining single.

While inheriting property is not always an indication of gendered power, neither is refraining from taking one's share necessarily an expression of total subordination. Daughters may renounce their rights to the estate as they both identify emotionally with their brothers, sharing in their prosperity, and in order to underline their brothers' obligations towards them. And when a widow leaves her share to her sons, rather than a sign of powerlessness, this tends to strengthen her position.

*Part II*

# The dower

If women often refrain from claiming their share in the estate, this does not imply that they have no direct access to property at all. For many women, marriage presentations, the *mahr* or dower, were and are the most important means by which to acquire property.[1] In part II, I will discuss the historical shifts which have taken place in women's access to such 'dower property'. Changes in the value and the nature of the property involved will be addressed and related to the variations in the meaning of the dower to different categories of women.[2]

In chapter 4 I summarily discuss the dower as part of the process of arranging marriages in three discursive fields: anthropological theory, Islamic law, and locally held conceptions. After these introductory notes, chapter 5 concentrates on the prompt dower, the gifts the bride receives when she marries, while the deferred dower, that part of the dower women obtain when they are repudiated or widowed, is the central topic of chapter 6. Both chapters set out with a description of historical changes in the dower as registered in the marriage contracts. To discuss possible incongruencies between the written texts and payment practices, this is followed by the words of the women themselves as they speak through court cases and, in particular, through marriage and divorce stories. The summaries of court cases indicate under which circumstances women were able and willing to turn to court to gain the rights they were not automatically granted. Oral history may throw light on those issues which

---

[1]  In this text I will use the terms *mahr* and dower indiscriminately. In the legal literature on the area the most common English translation of the Arabic *mahr* is 'dower' (Layish 1975: 40; Anderson 1951b: 186). It can both refer to the gifts the bride is to receive at marriage (prompt dower) and what she obtains at divorce or widowhood (deferred dower) and is sufficiently general to invite providing concrete detail on who gives and who receives. Other terms used in the literature on Palestine, such as brideprice/bridewealth (Granqvist 1931: 111; Kressel 1977; Rosenfeld 1980) or dowry are misleading, as the former is associated with payments (or gifts) for, rather than to, the bride and the latter with gifts from the parents to their daughter. The problems with considering the *mahr* as an 'indirect dowry' (Goody 1973: 2) will be discussed in section 4.1.

[2]  Part of this discussion on women's access to dower property has been published as Moors (1994). I am grateful to the publishers, E. J. Brill, for permission to reprint this material.

women did not raise in court, either because they were not conscious of their legal rights or because they considered it more expedient not to do so. I will end with taking a second look at some anthropological theories and their heuristic value for understanding the relation between women, their dower and access to property.

# 4    The dower: marriage, gender and social stratification

When I was in Al-Balad in 1981 one of Imm Sālim's granddaughters, Hanān was married. The first time I talked to her the marriage contract had already been signed and with pride she showed me the gifts she had received at the engagement party from Misᶜad, her *fiancé*.[3] Hanān was pleased with the marriage. Misᶜad was no stranger to her, on the contrary, she had known him all her life. He was not only from the same lineage, but his mother also was her father's sister, while his late father had been her mother's brother. He was only a few years older – she was eighteen at the time, he twenty-two – and had for some years been working in oil production in Kuwait, a job he had found through another brother of his mother who held a good position there for the past twenty-five years.

Misᶜad's mother had been the driving force behind the marriage. A widow with only one son (and three younger daughters) she was very attached to him and counted on his support in the future. Therefore, she had carefully selected her future daughter-in-law. Looking for a girl both her son and she herself would get along with, Hanān seemed suitable. Tall and with a light complexion she fit the local standards of beauty, Imm Misᶜad also knew her as compliant and, of course, she was her brother's daughter. The only person who seemed a bit hesitant about the marriage was Hanān's mother, who recalled the times when her relation with Imm Misᶜad, her husband's sister, had been tense. Being the younger of the two and of a less forceful nature, she had usually lost out to her. She was worried that her daughter might have a difficult time with her mother-in-law.

As the families involved were so close, there was no need for the usual first step in arranging a marriage, the informal visits of the mother or sisters of the prospective groom to check out the girl and find out about the demands of her family. Neither was there much discussion about the dower. The bride's father, one of the poorer members of the family, was

---

[3] While bride and groom are legally married once the marriage contract is signed, the bride only moves in with the groom after the marriage celebrations have taken place, which can vary from a few days to several years after the signing of the contract.

neither willing nor able to pressure his widowed sister for a high dower, so they agreed on a token prompt dower of 1 JD and 1,000 JD deferred. Soon after Mis⁽ad, accompanied by male kin and trusted friends, had formally asked for the hand of the bride from her father, the marriage contract was drawn up at the shari⁽a court. This was an all male event, the bride having authorised her father to act as her representative; still, as she told me, a court official had asked her whether she agreed to the marriage.

The signing of the contract was followed, as Hanān explained, by the engagement (*khutba*) or 'display' (*shūfa*), a party for the bride and her female friends, with the bride and groom officially seated together for the first time. For this occasion Mis⁽ad had given Hanān clothing, a pretty pinkish party dress and the first presents of gold, a necklace, a set of earrings and a watch. These were to be considered gifts, and were not part of the dower. Soon thereafter Mis⁽ad again left for Kuwait. During the engagement period the groom usually comes to visit the bride and brings her small presents, clothing, or sweets. Mis⁽ad, being abroad, now and then sent his *fiancé* some money.

The wedding was held about eight months later. With some help from his mother and his mother's brother in Kuwait, Mis⁽ad had managed to save enough to buy the gold, for although only a token prompt dower was registered, all had agreed that the bride would receive gold similar to what other brides were being given at the time. The main festivities started the night before the wedding. The last night Hanān was to spend at her father's house, the 'henna night', many of her female friends and relatives came to sing and dance for her, while she wore some of the gowns the groom had already sent over to her. The evening ended when henna was applied to her hands and feet.

The next day the wedding was held. It was a day of hectic activity. Imm Mis⁽ad spent most of the time overseeing the cooking of a lavish lunch, consisting of thirteen *mansaf* (large platters of rice, bread, yogurt and lamb), which would be eaten by the men and the women separately. In the morning the groom himself went in procession, followed by the men and then the women of the neighbourhood, to take his bath in the house of one of his paternal cousins. At the same time the bride with some close female kin went to a beauty salon in Nablus to have her hair done. Upon returning she was dressed at her father's house in a white wedding gown and some make-up was applied. Her friends came to sing for her there, until the sad moment that she had to leave her father's house.

By then many women had started to gather at Imm Mis⁽ad's house, the older ones to help with the cooking, the younger ones preparing the room with festive lightning and decorations, clapping their hands and singing, while the room became more and more packed with women and children, waiting for the coming of the bride. Escorted by her father and other close male relatives Hanān walked in procession to her husband's house, where she became the centre of attention, seated on a chair on top of a table so everyone could admire her. A cassette recorder played music, women started to sing and some of them danced, most of all the close female relatives of the groom, who celebrated the arrival of a daughter-in-law, while her mother showed more restraint as she was losing a daughter. About an hour later the groom entered the room. He was seated in a chair beside her and, a little later, after more singing and dancing, he put the dower gold on her, a coin bracelet costing 340 JD, two 'snakes' (hayāya) bracelets of 400 JD, a necklace and some rings, all in all over 850 JD in gold. Some pictures were taken of this ceremony which were to be followed by many more of various relatives together with the bride and groom. Others came forward, not only women but also some closely related men, to present gifts (nuqūt) to the bride and groom separately, usually money, the amount of which was registered as they would return these gifts at a suitable occasion. Only the presents from her closest kin, like her father and brothers, does a woman not need to reciprocate.

Hanān only lived for some months with her mother-in-law. Then, as she had hoped, her husband took her with him to live in Zerqa, in Jordan, where they rented an apartment in the same building where a brother of her father (and his mother) was living. Had she remained on the West Bank, her husband would only have been able to visit her once every six months as he was under twenty-six. Working in Kuwait, he could not house her there, but he would be able to come to Zerqa every month when he had time off. She expected it would take him another three and a half years to build himself a house in the village.

The above case is presented here as an example of the setting in which dower arrangements were made in Al-Balad in the early 1980s. In this introductory chapter various theories about the dower are discussed. First, the work of some authors who have contributed to the debate on marriage transactions and women's property rights is addressed, with particular attention paid to their divergent views on the relation between the dower and social stratification. As registering the dower in the marriage contract is required according to shari'a law, this is followed by a discussion of the law system and the major historical modifications which have taken place. Yet, the legal system is only part of the story; the place of the dower within the wider context of locally held views on marriage and social hierarchy will be the central topic of the last paragraph.

## 4.1 The *mahr* in academia: property, gender and social status

As mentioned in chapter 1, marriage presentations or payments have been extensively debated in anthropology, yet anthropologists have mainly concentrated on the gifts exchanged *for* women. The presentations women themselves receive have largely been neglected. As a consequence, possible changes in women's access to property through marriage payments have remained invisible.

Goody's work (1973; 1976; 1990) is interesting as he considers the *mahr* as a specific kind of dowry and underlines the importance of the *mahr* for women's potential access to property. In *Bridewealth and dowry* (1973) he argues that although these marriage transactions might appear as each other's mirror image, bridewealth being paid by the kin of the groom and dowry by the bride's side, they are, in fact, of a very different order. As bridewealth is paid to the male kin of the bride, it forms a horizontally circulating fund, while dowry, passing vertically (from parents/father to daughter) becomes part of the conjugal fund of the new couple, and can be seen as a kind of *pre-mortem* inheritance. The *mahr* has often been characterised as bridewealth because of the direction of the gifts, from the groom to the bride's side. Yet, Goody classifies the *mahr* as a type of dowry, because it is not part of a circulating fund, but functions as the starting capital for the new couple. He calls it an 'indirect dowry', as the bride receives the gifts from the groom, and not from her father (1973: 2).

Goody's work is, however, problematic in that by labelling the *mahr* as 'indirect dowry' he overlooks possible historical, social and locational specificities. Although conceding in his later work that marriage transactions in Arab societies are not necessarily identical, he rejects the possible occurrence there of marriage payments with some similarity to bridewealth. On the basis of very limited evidence, mainly from North Africa and North Yemen, he dismisses the work of authors who 'dealing with Palestine have asserted that the gifts from the groom's family are said to be used by the bride's family to acquire their own brides' by simply stating that 'in most parts of the Near East that is not the case' (1990: 375). Indeed, according to Islamic law the *mahr* is a sum registered in the marriage contract, to which the bride herself is entitled. Yet Granqvist (1931: 118, 135ff.) has already pointed out that in practice in rural Palestine the bride's father, receiving the *mahr* from the groom's side, might not give the full sum to his daughter, but keep part of it himself (for similar variants elsewhere see Pastner 1980: 153ff.). Also Kressel (1977: 444) and Rosenfeld (1980: 197), who both did research on marriage payments among Palestinians in Israel, indicate that the bride does not always receive the full amount and discuss variations and changes in the shares the bride and her father take.

If the full *mahr* does indeed go to the new couple, another problem arises, the ambiguity about who receives and controls the gifts, the bride or her husband. Goody states that 'the bulk goes to the bride herself and thus forms part of a joint (or sometimes separate) conjugal fund [...]' (Goody 1973: 2). Yet Islamic law does not recognise marriage in community of goods. While this does not necessarily imply that women are in full control of their property, neither is it self-evident that property is held in common. In a similar vein, Schlegel and Eloul (1988: 302) suggest that the indirect dowry can be a way for nuclear families to establish property rights in a polygynous or extended family household in anticipation of eventual fission. Their focus on the relations between the generations and disregard of gender, also makes it problematic to trace changes in women's access to property through the *mahr*.

Turning to the relation between marriage presentations and socio-economic differentiation, Goody links the occurrence of either bride-wealth or dowry to the nature of property relations and, following Boserup (1970), to women's participation in agriculture. He states that in (sub-Saharan) Africa, where there is little economic differentiation, women generally do not inherit and bridewealth is seen as a compensation for the loss of the labour and childbearing capacities of a woman. In the more hierarchical societies of (pre-industrial) Europe and Asia ('Eura-sia'), property is transferred to both sons and daughters, with daughters often receiving (part of) their inheritance share as a dowry. Women's agricultural labour is restricted and women are basically seen as mothers to heirs of property. Marriages need to be carefully balanced and settlement of property on both sons and daughters is to guarantee an equal match (often through in-marriage) and to uphold the prestige of the family. Goody's emphasis on like-marrying-like implies that the (indir-ect) dowry tends to reproduce property inequalities among women.

Schlegel and Eloul (1988: 304) take a somewhat different position. They argue that in poor villages the 'bridewealth aspect' of the *mahr* tends to be emphasised, as the labour value of women is more important than status considerations, while among the urban middle and upper classes the dowry side is accentuated. This implies that the *mahr* actually underlines property inequalities among women. Tucker (1988: 177), on the other hand, in her historical study on marriage and the family in eighteenth and early nineteenth century Nablus argues the reverse. In her view, the *mahr* was a more significant sum in lower-class marriages, providing the wife with significant property, while among upper class women the *mahr* was a relatively less important transfer of wealth and, as such, less central for women's property ownership. These issues will be taken up again in chapters 5 and 6. But first I will turn to the place of the *mahr* in Islamic law.

## 4.2    Islamic law and marriage contracts: the paradox of property and person

In mandatory Palestine, jurisdiction in matters of personal status of the Muslim population was held by the shari'a courts. These applied the latest Ottoman modification of classical Islamic law, the Ottoman Law of Family Rights (OLFR) of 1917. This law was largely based on Hanafi doctrine, one of the four major Sunni schools of law, but also made use of the opinions of the other law schools to facilitate the introduction of certain reforms. In 1951 Jordan enacted the Jordanian Law of Family Rights (JLFR) to replace the 1917 OLFR, and in 1976 the Jordanian Law of Personal Status (JLPS) was issued, which repealed the 1951 JLFR.[4] The major impetus behind the legal reforms implemented in these laws was to update the law to 'the needs of a changing society' (Welchman 1988: 886).

According to the 1917 OLFR, marriages were to be registered with the shari'a court and a representative of the court was to fill out the marriage registration forms (Anderson 1951a: 118). During the period of the British mandate most marriages were already recorded in court, usually the one located nearest to the bride's place of residence. As written documents have become increasingly important in everyday life, from the mid-1950s on virtually the entire population registered their marriages at the courts (Doumani 1985: 8).

Beginning in the 1920s marriage contracts were recorded on printed forms and kept in separate registers. Such forms included space to record the name, age, place of residence, religion and profession of bride and groom, the names of agents or guardians, of witnesses, and of the court registrar. The marital status of the bride was defined as virgin (*bikr*) or non-virgin (*thayyib*), the amount and nature of the dower were taken down, including whether payment of part of it was deferred to dissolution through repudiation or widowhood, and specific marriage stipulations could be included.[5] In the early 1950s the Jordanians introduced a new registration form which solicited, in addition to the above, information about the place of birth and the nationality of groom and bride, and the

---

[4] As mentioned in chapter 2, also after the Israeli occupation Jordanian personal status law is applied to the Palestinian population of the West Bank.

[5] Until the early 1930s information on the profession, age and place of residence of the fathers of groom and bride was also recorded; thereafter this practice was discontinued.

marital status of the groom. Also a separate category of 'addenda' (*tawābiʿ*) to the prompt and deferred dower was created.

The various laws mentioned have introduced some reforms in the arrangement of marriages. According to Hanafī law, women whose marriages had been arranged during their minority (that is pre-pubescent girls) by their fathers or grandfathers could not sever these marriages after reaching puberty. The 1917 OLFR put this practice to an end, by prohibiting the marriage of boys under twelve and girls under nine. In addition, boys between the ages of twelve and eigtheen and girls between the ages of nine and seventeen (considered the minimum and maximum ages for the onset of puberty) could be married only with the permission of the court (Anderson 1951a: 116).[6] In the 1951 JLFR, the minimum age for such a marriage was raised to fifteen for both boys and girls, and a new article (art. 6) was introduced, stating explicitly that if the age differential between bride and groom was more than twenty years, then the judge was to ensure that the youngest partner was not forced into the marriage and that the marriage was not contrary to her interests.[7]

While minor girls had no say in their marriages according to Hanafī law, women in their legal majority could both refuse marriages arranged for them and arrange for their own marriages. The 1917 OLFR states that a mature woman (of at least seventeen) could ask the court permission to marry if her marriage guardian had insuffient reasons for refusal; in the 1976 JLPS this age limit was lowered to fifteen if the girl's marriage guardian was not her father or grandfather (art. 6a/b), and if she had previously been married she no longer needed the approval of her guardian at all (art. 13). The main valid reason for a marriage guardian to refuse was that the groom was not at least equal (*kufūʾ*) to the bride, for according to the law equality of the groom and bride is a condition for a valid marriage (Anderson 1951a: 119).[8]

Turning from arranging marriages to its effects, the marriage contract requires that a man pay the bride a *mahr* and provide her with maintenance (*nafaqa*), irrespective of her own financial means. With regard to the dower the only legal innovation is that the 1917 OLFR explicitly forbade the bride's parents or relatives to accept money or goods in return for giving their daughter in marriage. The dower is considered the bride's

---

[6] The judge could do so on the ground of sufficient maturity and, in the case of the bride, with the condition that her marriage guardian would consent.

[7] The 1976 JLPS limits this regulation to girls under eighteen (art. 6c).

[8] In Hanafī law equality was measured in terms of religion, freedom, lineage, profession (of the bride's father), piety, property (referring to the ability to pay at the time of marriage the prompt dower and maintenance) and wealth; although the 1951 JLFR only explicitly mentioned property, according to Anderson (1952: 194) the other criteria also still applied.

property and she cannot be compelled to use it to purchase her *jihāz* (gold, clothing and household goods that she brings into the marriage) (Anderson 1951b: 188; 1976 JLPS art. 61–2). Neither can her husband legally exert control over it. Marriage does not result in community of property between husband and wife; each partner independently controls any property owned before marriage or acquired thereafter. Married women are free to use their property as they please; they do not need their husbands' permission to dispose of it (such as by donation or sale).

In respect of maintenance, this previously referred to food, clothing and a separate dwelling (*maskan sharʿī* or *bayt sharʿī*). The 1951 JLFR further extended a man's financial obligations towards his wife and children as he was also to pay for their medical care and his adult son's education (Anderson 1952: 200), and the 1976 JLPS explicitly obliged him to pay for his wife's funeral (art. 82). At the same time, the way in which maintenance was calculated changed. According to the 1951 JLFR maintenance no longer was determined with reference to the financial standing of both husband and wife (as formulated in the 1917 OLFR), but rather with exclusive reference to the husband's financial means (Anderson 1951b: 189, 193; 1952: 199).

Whereas a woman has no financial obligations with regard to her husband, he has a qualified right to limit his wife's freedom of movement, a right that may have financial implications. After a husband has paid the dower, his wife is obliged to live in his house. If she leaves the dwelling against his will without a valid reason (such as ill-treatment or not being provided with a suitable dwelling) she legally may be declared 'rebellious' (*nāshiza*). Her husband then no longer is obliged to pay her maintenance and may have her forcibly returned to the marital home. Because the 1951 JLFR explicitly states that women are allowed to leave the conjugal home in case of maltreatment without losing their rights to maintenance, it has become more difficult for a man to suspend maintaining his wife by claiming that she was rebellious. Legal sanctions against a rebellious wife were further limited by the formulations of the 1976 JLPS which no longer allowed for her forcible return to her husband's house (Welchman 1988: 875).

While the general principles of the law still stand, expressing a paradox between person (men's qualified control over women) and property (women's rights to maintenance and the dower and their freedom to act with property in general), some changes have taken place in the legal system. In respect of marriage, the reforms implemented first by the Ottoman and later by the Jordanian state, express two major trends. To start with, the legal position of women has improved. They gained a greater freedom to act *vis-à-vis* their male kin (with regard to arranging marriages) and later also in relation to their husband (freedom of movement). Secondly, while Hanafī law already recognised not only the importance of patri-kin but also of the conjugal tie (such as by requiring separate housing, *maskan sharʿī*), the reforms have placed a greater emphasis on the conjugal relation (in particular by calculating maintenance only according to the financial means of the husband).[9]

Contextualising the dower within the legal system, it is evident that the dower is gendered property *par excellence*, and part and parcel of a marriage system which highlights gender differences. The relation with social hierarchy, on the other hand, is less clear-cut. It is true that equality between groom and bride is a condition for a valid marriage, but there are no limits set to the dower and the parties involved are free to agree about the sum registered. It remains to be seen whether like-marrying-like also translates into dower differentials and the reproduction of property inequalities amongst women.

## 4.3    Local perspectives: marriage as relation in process

As Hanān's case indicates, selecting a partner and contracting a marriage are still seen as a family affair. As elsewhere in the region, in Jabal Nablus marriage is the only way to organise social reproduction. The marriage contract does not only define the legal rights and obligations of husband and wife, and legitimises the children of the union, but it also creates relations of affinity and alliance between the two families of husband and wife.

In discussing marriage preferences, women themselves often refer to the advantages of like-marrying-like. When Imm Shākir said, 'sometimes even between cousins it does not work out, how could it be if they are from different backgrounds?', she underlined the importance of this principle. To Hanān's family it was self-evident that if a suitable relative were available she would marry him. Indeed, the idea that one should marry someone of similar background is a widely held sentiment. Yet 'sameness' is a highly complex notion with various meanings in different contexts.

In local terms, 'sameness' is associated with 'closeness' (*qarāba*), a relative rather than an absolute concept and a term which also means 'kinship'. In the mandatory period, in particular in the rural areas, one aspect of kinship was especially important, the cultural preference for an *ibn ʿamm* marriage, extending from the most preferred first paternal cousin to all members of the lineage or the clan (also Granquist 1931: 66–

---

[9] Antoun (1990: 57) also questions the widespread assumption that Islamic law only emphasises patrilineal kinship rather than conjugality.

69). Elderly women in Al-Balad, such as Imm Sālim often highlighted how problematic it had been previously to refuse a first paternal cousin. In this case, closeness implied sameness in terms of 'sharing blood'. Yet it could also refer to 'sharing space' such as, for example, living in the same village, with co-villagers preferred over suitors from elsewhere. In the urban context amongst the better-off sameness referred not only to 'sharing class' but also to 'sharing culture' as is illustrated by the reluctance of old prominent and propertied Nablus families to marry their daughters to men without similar, long-established roots in the city. In concrete cases, these meanings of 'closeness' could contradict each other; kin could live far away, deep-rooted Nablusi families may be impoverished and so on.

In some respects closeness could have a different meaning for men and women. If women shared the cultural preference for an *ibn ʿamm* marriage, feeling closer to members of their own lineage than to strangers, they simultaneously held their own preferences which could contradict this. To strengthen her ties with her own kin, a mother, such as Imm Misʿad, may attempt to have her sons or daughters married to her brothers' children. In cases where married sons remain for a long time in their father's household, a bride herself may prefer a marriage with her mother's sister's son (*ibn khāla*), as then her mother-in-law would be her mother's sister, a relationship generally seen as emotionally close.

If 'sameness' is important, a marriage to a 'stranger' (*gharīb*) could also have its advantages. A girl's kin may be interested in forging an alliance with those seen as higher in the social hierarchy in one way or another, such as peasants marrying their daughters to better-off urbanites, women from poorer learned families marrying wealthy traders and so on. Individual women themselves often expressed contradictory feelings about these marriages. Excited and with great expectations about the rise in social status such a marriage would entail, they also recognised that marrying up would imply less protection from their own family and as such a greater dependence on their husbands and in-laws. As a woman from Balata camp explained to me 'if you marry a wealthy man, you will be no more than a piece of furniture in his house and he can repudiate you or take a second wife whenever he wants to'.

Even if there is not one standard for evaluating hierarchy (wealth, education, politics, religion, location and so on may play a role), some historical trends can be indicated. With kinship losing some of its central importance and younger men having access to wage labour, these men have more say in their own marriages. It has also become easier for girls to refuse an unwanted suitor, and sometimes even to express their own preferences. Although some of the landowning clans in the region still refuse to allow their daughters to marry non-clan members, this has become considerably less common than previously, and it has generally become easier also to avoid an *ibn ʿamm* marriage. Imm Sālim had no problem in turning down her youngest daughter's first paternal cousin; she did not like his family much and did not deem him suitable as his educational level was much lower than her daughter's. Even if some of the prominent Nablus families are hesitant to marry their daughters to outsiders, such marriages regularly take place nowadays. Increased social mobility, in particular through migration and education, has started to undermine both existing hierarchies within Nablus and those between Nablus, the camps and the villages. It has become more common for educated men from the villages and the camps to marry urban girls.

In 'evaluating' brides, individual characteristics have also become more important. It is true that family background still counts, and previously a woman's age, appearance and virginity (not having been married previously) were also important. Yet, the latter criteria have become more emphasised with the decline of the importance of women's agricultural labour in the villages, seclusion less strictly adhered to and younger men having more say about their marriages. Furthermore, new elements, such as education, or even holding a (professional) job, have become important in selecting a bride. While girls generally like the decreased control of the older generation, some of them, in particular those in the rural areas with little education are more ambivalent about these developments. Commenting on a man who had demanded to see the girl he wanted to marry before writing the contract, a woman in her early thirties from Al-Balad exclaimed, 'Is she a cow that he needs to see her?'

With the intifada, as previously in times of great political fervour, politics have also become an important consideration. When one of the women activists in Balata camp was asked in marriage she immediately asked her brother in prison to gather information about her suitor's politics. Even in less engaged times both men and women (or their families) with a particular ideological conviction would opt for a partner with a similar outlook. After the intifada had gained momentum politically non-committed households would also at least take care to check out whether the prospective groom was not involved in collaboration.[10]

Closeness plays a role not only in the process of arranging a marriage but also with regard to the dower. When there is already a special relation

---

[10] During the occupation, the Israeli authorities set up a network of collaborators and informers. Whereas already prior to the intifada there were some efforts to boycot them, the uprising has enabled activists in a number of cases to settle their scores with them. Measures taken against collaborators have varied from interrogation to expulsion from the community and execution (see, for instance, Yahya 1991).

between the families of the groom and the bride, the bride's father may more often choose not to press for a high dower. Granqvist (1931: 122ff.), for example, indicated that in Artas the dower asked from a stranger was higher than that from a co-villager, with the amount demanded from a paternal cousin lowest. Although there were no such clear-cut rules in Al-Balad, closeness there also influenced dower discussions, as Hanān's case indicated.

For the girl involved, closeness could have a specific meaning. If a relation had already developed between the girl and the suitor, in the sense that they had met and talked together and she agreed with the marriage, she herself may actually attempt to lower the dower in order to have the marriage come through. Admittedly, drawing up the marriage contract officially is done by the older male relatives of bride and groom with a representative of the shari'a court; women are often not present when the contract is written up and a bride, if she has authorised a male relative as her representative, does not even need to attend the signing of the contract. Yet female relatives have an informal influence and some brides themselves have a say in how the dower is recorded. In particular, if a woman is not very young, is educated and if her marriage guardian is her brother rather than her father, he will commonly take her opinion into account.

Age also ties in with closeness and may have particular implications for the dower. For a younger girl, one aspect of closeness implies marrying a man not much her senior. A small age differential between bride and groom is generally seen as conducive for love to develop, as such a man is perceived to be less domineering. When her youngest son and his wife came to visit Imm Sālim, she pointed out to me (to their great embarrassment) how much they loved each other, as they both had been very young when married and 'from the same generation' (he had been almost sixteen, she fourteen). To a mature woman, on the other hand, marriage more often means looking after one's interests rather than great expectations of romantic love. Having to decide between either marrying a less attractive husband (perhaps an older villager, a widower with children at home, or a man who is already married) or remaining single, she may choose the first option, but then want guarantees, such as suitable housing or possibly a high dower. Under such circumstances a high dower could 'compensate' for a relatively unattractive groom. In extremis, a father may politely refuse an undesirable groom by demanding an extraordinarily high dower. Occasionally, however, this backfires if the groom, contrary to expectations, agrees and manages to pay. When Nuzha's father, for instance, wanted to prevent her second marriage, he demanded, as she said, 'a ridiculously high dower for a widow', yet her husband signed the contract.

In short, the marriage and dower system allows considerable room for manoeuvre for the parties involved and in itself expresses various, sometimes contradictory, tendencies. Through the dower, women gain access to property, yet at the same time it is part of a legal system which defines women as protected dependents. It can simultaneously be a power resource for women and the expression of their gender subordination. It underlines gender differences, yet it is also a system which recognises the importance of social 'sameness' of men and women as marital partners and differentiates women according to their background. Even if writers on the dower hold different views as to the nature of this differentiation, whether it accentuates social hierarchy or undercuts it to some extent, and local models allow for considerable leeway, social hierarchy is part and parcel of the dower system. In the following chapters, both aspects of the dower will be addressed, the dower as gender-specific device for women to gain access to property and the dower as means to differentiate between women.

# 5    Marriage: the prompt dower

What women receive when they marry is the starting point of this chapter. Here I will return to the four women introduced in chapter 2 and discuss their marriage stories in greater detail, adding some of the stories of their daughters and granddaughters for the sake of historical comparison. In the Jabal Nablus region, the prompt dower is registered in two very different ways, either as 'regular prompt dower', with the registered sum bearing at least some resemblance to what is given, or as 'token dower', when a very small sum is recorded (often 1 JD), creating a complete break between the amount stated in the contracts and the gifts received. These two dower patterns will be discussed successively, with particular attention paid to the divergent meanings registering a token dower can have for different categories of women. Next, the sometimes detailed registration of household goods in the contracts is considered and shifts in the nature of the gifts are discussed. The dower will then be contextualised within the process of socio-economic change by relating the value of the dower to the transfer of property from fathers to sons. Before summarising the historical trends in women's access to property through the dower I will briefly discuss 'intifada marriages'.

## 5.1    The regular prompt dower: contracts and social practice

*The contracts: towards equality between women?*

Starting with the regular prompt dower, which major historical developments do the marriage contracts indicate? Are there important differences between what is registered for women in different locations? My calculations of the average sums registered as prompt dower indicate that these have generally followed economic trends with only limited differences between the city and the rural areas.[1] While in the 1920s and 1930s the

---

[1] This analysis of marriage contracts is based on a 10 per cent sample of urban contracts for every fourth year in the period 1928–1988, including 1987 (n = 652), and of the village

dower both in Nablus and in the countryside remained quite stable, varying from 30 to 50 PP (Palestine Pounds), the protracted economic growth and inflation of the 1940s led to a dramatic increase in the amounts registered. In 1944, for example, the average urban dower had reached 126 PP, a sum approximately three and a half times that of the 1930s.

Whereas the economic decline of the 1930s was not reflected in the registered dower, the shattering impact of the events of 1947/48, resulting in the collapse of the Nablus economy with a large number of virtually destitute refugees settling in or near Nablus, was evident. The average dower dropped considerably, gradually reaching its low point in the early 1950s, with the smallest sums recorded in the refugee camps, where the economic situation was particularly difficult. In 1952, for example, the average dower was 100 JD in the city, 110 JD in the villages and 60 JD in the refugee camps. Only by the late 1950s when migration gained momentum and the economic situation was improving did it rise again. By 1964 the average urban dower reached 210 JD, an increase perhaps also stimulated as many poor refugees had moved from the city to the camps. Still, in the villages and in the camps the average dower had also rapidly increased, to 170 JD and 140 JD respectively.

The influence of the 1967 war on the registered dower was less dramatic than had been the case after 1948. The first years showed stagnation but no decline and soon the dower went up again, with differences between city, village and camps further diminishing. In particular during the later 1970s this increase gained tremendous momentum; between 1976 and 1984 the average urban dower more than tripled from 450 JD to 1,400 JD, while in the villages it went up from 440 JD to 1,170 JD and in the camps from 450 JD to 1,210 JD. While by the late 1970s a period of recession had already set in, which was to continue throughout the 1980s, it was only from the mid-1980s on that the dower in Nablus and the villages started to stagnate and in the camps actually declined. In 1988, the first year of the intifada, the average dower was 1,390 JD in Nablus city and 1,120 JD in the villages, while in the camps it had decreased to 910 JD.

Whereas geographical differences were limited, what about social differentiations within these various locations? During the mandatory period the urban dowers were considerably more divergent than those in the rural areas. In Nablus city the relation between the top and bottom 20 per cent was four and a half to one, while in the rural areas this was less

and camp contracts of every twelfth year in the period 1928–1976 (for the camps beginning in 1952) and then for every fourth year in the period 1976–1988, including 1987 (n = 656). The year 1987 has been covered to gain better insight into the specific impact of the intifada (1988). In addition, as many contracts as could be located for Al-Balad were considered (n = 220).

than two and a half to one; in individual villages the differences were even smaller. In Al-Balad, for example, in the 1920s and 1930s the prompt dower was rarely less than 30 PP or more than 60 PP and in over half the cases it was registered as 50 PP. To some extent the urban differential was more pronounced as in the urban contracts a very low dower was registered for women who had been previously married, while in the villages this was not the case.[2] But when we exclude women who remarry, the urban differential was still almost three to one. Village differentials were probably smaller as the population there was socially more homogeneous; by this period, many wealthy estate owners had already moved to Nablus. Still, the urban differential in no way mirrored the great differences in wealth between urban households. In fact, there was no direct correlation between the occupation of the groom and the dower. It is true that men who held a high-status position registered a high dower, and those with a low-status profession a low dower, but there was a very large intermediate category of men who registered varying amounts. This suggests that the relatively limited dower differentials mentioned above reflect the maximum divergencies between the rich and the poor. So, on paper at least, the prompt dower was much more important for women from poor households than for those of wealthy families.[3] To poor urban women the dower represented a considerable sum of money and for women in the villages the registered dower was also relatively high.

In the Jordanian period the social differences between the registered sums increased, but not uniformly. In Nablus city the relation between the top and bottom 20 per cent of the dowers for women marrying for the first time grew only slightly to a little over three and a half to one, whereas the differences in village dowers increased rapidly to five to one. So, in contrast to the mandatory period, the dowers in the rural areas now became more divergent than in the city. An important reason for the increased differentiation in the rural areas was the rapid growth of migration labour, which initially may have created greater social inequalities in the rural areas. Whereas in 1952 76 per cent of rural men still registered their occupation as farmer, by 1964 this had decreased to 48 per

[2]  In the sample years up to and including 1952 the bride had been previously married in 22 per cent of all marriages contracts; thereafter this was on average the case for only 5 per cent.

[3]  This is also one of the main conclusions of Tucker (1988). In the eighteenth century and the first half of the nineteenth, a middle- and upper-class dower was about twice to three times the dower of a lower-class woman. While in those days marriage contracts were formulated by notaries in such a way as to reflect the class background of the parties involved, in the twentieth century it is no longer possible to directly link the dower and the social background of groom and bride. On the printed marriage forms the profession of the groom is registered, but in such a summarily manner that no direct link can be made with class.

cent. It is likely that the large differences between the villages, as to when migration started, the number of migrants involved and their destination, also contributed to greater dower differentials amongst rural women. In the camps, differences also became more prominent. By the late 1950s the greater differentials there were due mainly to a rapid increase of high dowers, indicating that some men were able and willing to pay a larger sum as dower.

It was by the mid-1960s that differentials in the urban dowers started to decrease; this coincided with the start of a trend to register a token dower in the contracts. This process continued during the Israeli occupation, when it also made itself felt in the camps and villages. The employment situation had 'stabilised' in the rural areas with only 21 per cent of the village grooms registering as farmer in 1976 and no more than 15 per cent in the early 1980s. In the 1970s and 1980s the top and bottom 20 per cent related to each other as less than two and a half to one in all locations.

In short, during the whole period urban dowers differed little from those registered for women in the villages, while the dower in the refugee camps was slightly higher than that of poorer urbanites. The increased social differentiation of the 1950s and 1960s was short-lived and was soon to be followed by greater dower similarities. On paper, then, the dower has become ever more important for poorer women and rural women as a means to gain access to property. What did this mean in practice?

### The villages: from daughter to wife

Imm Sālim's description of her marriage in the early 1930s is a strong example of the great divergences between the registered dower and what a rural bride herself received in the mandatory period. Reflecting on her youth, she explained under which circumstances her marriage had been arranged. 'As my mother had died while I was still a small girl', she said, 'my father wanted to remarry. But in those days many people were poor, and he did not have enough money to pay the dower for a new wife. So instead of paying the dower, he promised to give me in exchange as bride to the brother of his future wife.' Being married as an exchange bride (badīla), her dower was the same as that of her father's new wife. 'For each of us 50 PP was recorded', Imm Sālim recalled, 'of which 10 PP were to be meant for me.' When I asked her whether she had received any gold, she smiled and told me that in those days exchange brides did not receive much. 'People did not have much money at the time. Instead of gold my in-laws registered three dunum of land with olive trees for me, for the future.'

In various ways, the contrasts between the text of the contracts and social practice were great in those days. Imm Sālim was about thirteen years old when she moved in with her husband. At the time, marrying at such a young age was not uncommon. Elderly women in Al-Balad told me time and again that they were married when still very young, often just after reaching menarche (see also Granqvist 1931: 34). Yet I did not find any marriage contracts for Al-Balad in which the age of the bride was recorded as under seventeen. Although according to the 1917 OLFR only the permission of the court was required to give a girl in marriage if she was younger than seventeen (and older than nine), people apparently preferred either to simply record the girl's age as seventeen or to postpone registering the marriage until she had reached that age.[4]

That Imm Sālim did not receive the full sum written in the contract was also standard practice. At that time it was common in rural Palestine for the father of the bride – who, as her marriage guardian, usually received the dower – not to pass the whole sum on to his daughter (Granqvist 1931: 118; 135ff; Rosenfeld 1980: 197). In Al-Balad, for instance, the bride's share often was limited to one-third of the total prompt dower. Women who married in the 1930s regularly mentioned sums of 10 PP or 20 PP. In the 1940s, when the average dower went up to 150 PP, the bride herself frequently received 50 PP.

The summaries of court cases also show that rural women in the Jabal Nablus region did not always receive the prompt dower specified in the marriage contracts.[5] In 1940 for example, C., from a small village to the east of Nablus, turned to the court to raise a complaint against her

---

[4] Oral information shows that during the mandatory period in Al-Balad, 55 per cent of the girls were younger than 16 years old, and 30 per cent were even younger than 14 years upon marrying (n = 20). Over time the marital age went up and the recorded ages (as noted down in the marriage contracts) started to conform more closely with oral information:

*Marital age of girls in Al-Balad in texts of contracts and through oral history in different periods*

| Age | 1920–1948 text | oral | 1949–1967 text | oral | 1968–1987 text | oral |
|---|---|---|---|---|---|---|
| < 18 yrs | 20% | 70% | 35% | 68% | 42% | 47% |
| < 16 yrs | — | 55% | 15% | 44% | 17% | 13% |
| < 14 yrs | — | 30% | — | 24% | — | — |
| n = | 55 | 20 | 40 | 25 | 111 | 30 |

[5] I have analysed summaries of dower cases for the same years as the sample of marriage contracts (see note 1). For the years under investigation, dower cases never exceeded 10 per cent of all court cases. Most dower cases were filed by women demanding their deferred dower.

paternal cousin (*ibn ʿamm*). She stated that he had been her marriage guardian and had received the whole prompt dower of 40 PP, but had only given her 28 PP. In his defence he argued that he had, with her permission, handed 7 PP to her father's brother (not his own father) and had bought her a cow for 5 PP. According to C., however, she was to receive the cow in addition to her dower and had never given her cousin permission to hand over anything to her father's brother. As C. refused to take the oath that the cow had indeed been intended to be added to the dower, her cousin only had to pay her the 7 PP her uncle had received.[6] This case is typical in that women generally only raised a case against their own kin, if not their father, but another relative had been their marriage guardian. For a rural girl it was self-evident that her father would take part of her dower. Because a woman would return to her father's house in case of marital problems, turning against him would weaken rather than strengthen her position *vis-à-vis* her husband and his kin. As uncles and other patri-kin had less obligations towards their female relatives, women were more often willing to raise a case against them in court.

Imm Sālim found herself in a specific situation as she had been married through an exchange marriage. In the 1920s and 1930s, when only limited cash was available, such marriages were rather common in the villages.[7] These exchanges could take on various forms. Usually a woman was offered in exchange for a wife for her brother. But it also occurred, as in the case of Imm Sālim, that a widower would give his daughter in marriage in exchange for a bride for himself, which often resulted in great age differentials between groom and bride. In such marriage contracts, an identical regular dower would be registered for both brides, yet this full amount did not need to be paid as the father's shares (in the case of Imm Sālim, 40 PP) would cancel each other. In exchange marriages brides also frequently received less than the average bride's share, for such marriages often were an indication of poverty.

At her wedding Imm Sālim received neither money nor gold, but a piece of land was registered for her. In those days the norm was already that the dower ought to be paid in cash. The bride's father would take it and use part of it (the bride's share) to buy his daughter gold and household goods, which would remain her property;[8] also he may give his

---

6 Mahkamat Nablus (Nablus court, MN), sijill (register, s.) 8/88, p. 260, no. 127; 30/8/1940.

7 Oral information showed that between 1928 and 1947 in Al-Balad about 30 per cent of the marriages were exchange marriages (n = 20). In the village of Artas near Bethlehem, such marriages were also common; there, 26.5 per cent of all marriages were exchanges (Granqvist 1931: 111).

8 Every woman had her own (locked) chest, and in the later period, a cupboard. Granqvist (1935: 236) mentions the case of a woman who left her husband because he had forcibly opened her chest.

daughter a number of goats as (part of) the bride's share. Yet, at least until the 1940s it could be difficult for rural men to pay the whole prompt dower in cash. Only few men were working for wages, so the dower had to be saved from the sale of agricultural surplus and live-stock. Instead of paying cash the father of the groom might offer to register a piece of land or a number of olive trees in the name of the bride (see also Granqvist 1931: 119). In the case of a marriage between close relatives, an average dower was often registered, but payment was less strictly enforced.

Comparing Imm Sālim's marriage arrangements with those of her three daughters, the experiences of different generations of rural women become visible. Her eldest daughter, Imm Rushdī, who never went to school and was married in 1958 at age thirteen, stressed with some regret in her voice that her marriage had been much more similar to that of her mother than that of her younger sisters. 'My mother first had three sons; I was the eldest daughter', she pointed out. 'After my two eldest brothers were married and the dower for their wives had been paid, little money was available for the third and he also wanted to marry. So, an exchange marriage was a convenient solution and I was married very young because I was an exchange bride.' Her husband was her second paternal cousin, whose father had a little land and live-stock in the village and in the Jordan Valley. His sister, the woman she was exchanged for, was already eighteen. In Imm Rushdī's view her dower did not amount to much, 'I think it was about 80 JD; I received some gold, about eight Turkish gold coins.'

The marriage arrangements of Imm Sālim's second daughter, Imm Nidāl, were quite different. She was married in 1971, eighteen years old, to her paternal cousin. He was a few years older and had started to work in Kuwait at age fifteen after finishing preparatory school. Her prompt dower was 200 JD and a deferred dower of 200 JD was also recorded in the marriage contract. When I asked her whether her father had taken anything from it she adamantly denied this, saying 'the full dower was given to me, my father did not keep anything for himself. He took the dower and brought me a pair of heavy gold 'twisted wire' [mabarīm] bracelets, but no household goods as I was to move with my husband to Kuwait and did not need these.' Imm Nidāl went to live with her husband in Kuwait as he had no residence permit for the West Bank, having been absent in 1967. When some years later he managed to get his papers, they returned to the village. After living a few years with her in-laws, they then moved into the new house her husband had built on his father's land.

Tāhiyya, the youngest daughter, was married in 1984, when she was twenty-five years old. Her mother had told me that her first cousin (ibn ʿamm), a brother of Imm Nidāl's husband, had wanted to marry her, but they had refused. By then they considered themselves economically better-off and Tāhiyya was studying at the time, so they had a different future in mind for her and did not consider her cousin suitable. Tāhiyya continued her education, took a BA in sociology and as one of the best students was offered a job as teaching assistant in Nablus. After working there for one year, she married. Actually, as she told me later, she had considered applying for a scholarship to study abroad, but had not done so as she knew her brothers would not agree. Her marriage was arranged through a friend of one of her brothers. Tāhiyya agreed to the marriage because the suitor was a very religious man, well-educated and holding a good job as a Jordanian government employee in Nablus. In her marriage contract, a token prompt dower of 1 JD and a deferred dower of 5,000 JD were registered. At the engagement her future husband gave her gold jewellery worth about 400 JD. At the wedding she received gold for another 700 JD. Her husband had already rented and furnished an apartment in Nablus. Living with them in a room of her own was her husband's widowed mother, who was very happy with Tāhiyya and expressed the change of times when she exclaimed 'where do you find a bride nowadays who agrees to have her mother-in-law living with her?'

It was in the later Jordanian period that the dower system started to change in Al-Balad. The marriage of Imm Rushdī was still similar to that of her mother; each had married as an exchange bride at a very young age and her husband worked full-time in agriculture. By the time Imm Nidāl married, the average marriage age had gone up, her husband, like many other men from the village, was working in Kuwait, she was allowed to keep the dower herself and her material standard of living was considerably higher. Whereas Tāhiyya's life trajectory was still exceptional for a girl from Al-Balad, where only a very small number of girls had gone to university, for rural girls in general this was becoming more common.

The main trend in rural women's access to dower property is that they gradually started to receive an increasingly large share of the dower themselves. In Al-Balad, from the late 1950s on, the bride was no longer given one-third, but one-half of the dower, and by the early 1970s most brides, like Imm Nidāl, received the whole prompt dower. A father would not take anything, and in a few cases might even add to it (Rosenfeld 1980: 207 argues the same for the Lower Galilee). With the disappearance of the father's share, exchange marriages also became less common, as the main 'benefit' of this type of marriage had been that no father's share had to be paid.[9] Also, exchange brides were now often given the same as in the case

---

[9] Between 1961 and 1981 about 10 per cent of all marriage in Al-Balad were exchange marriages (n = 40).

of regular dower marriages. If Imm Rushdī, married in the late 1950s, argued that she had received less than the usual because she was married through an exchange marriage, women exchanged in the 1970s emphasised that they had received a dower similar to that of other brides.

### The urban poor: female rights and male debts

Among the urban poor, the divergencies between the text of the marriage contracts and social practice took a different form, as the following two cases indicate.[10] Describing her marriage, Imm Hilmī, from the old city of Nablus and married in the early 1940s when she was twenty, stressed that she was married 'because of poverty'. She had not seen her husband, who was about fifteen years her senior, before marriage, and he had not seen her. 'In the past people used to be very strict', she said. 'Once he came to the house to fit the wedding ring, but my mother took the ring from him, and put a piece of thread around my finger to show the size.' The dower did not impress her. 'The day of the signing of the contract he gave 45 PP as prompt dower, which was a very small sum at the time', Imm Hilmī recalled. The amount registered as deferred dower she did not remember. When I asked her what she was actually given she said: 'From the dower they bought me a pair of bracelets of 25 PP, further I only received a small chest in which they put my clothing.' Soon problems arose. Because her husband was an orphan they were married in the house of his mother's sister. 'She had a small room', recalled Imm Hilmī, 'where we were to celebrate and then we would return to his house. We stayed there two days, three days, and then he said that he had no petrol burner to cook on, no plates to eat from and no lamp. As it turned out, he had wanted me to stay with his aunt until he had bought these necessities.' But her mother did not agree, 'because there was another man living there', Imm Hilmī explained. 'They quarrelled and he took the mattress, the quilts and the pillows and brought me to his house. My mother then lent him some money and brought him a pan, a lamp and the other things we needed. She told him to pay it back when he had worked.' Her husband went to work in a village as a stone cutter. 'He stayed away a full month and when he returned he gave the money to my mother', Imm Hilmī concluded.

The experiences of Imm Ahmad, married around 1935 and also of lower-class background, were somewhat different. As her father had passed away when she was about seven, she was also raised by her mother, but was apprenticed to a seamstress. At a very young age her mother had already promised to give her in marriage to a distant maternal cousin. 'All

---

[10] On marriage transactions in Nablus in the 1920s, see Jaussen (1927).

sons his first wife bore him had died very young, so he needed a second wife', said Imm Ahmad, adding laughingly, 'she gave me to him instead of marrying him herself. I was married to him when I was about twelve, he was much older, about forty.' Imm Ahmad's prompt dower was 50 PP, the deferred dower was the same, but as she said, 'I did not receive much as he was a poor man and already in debt. What he gave me at the marriage ceremony my mother had lent him, and I had to return it the next day.' So, Imm Ahmad did not receive gold, but the groom had given her clothing and a sewing machine. After the wedding she moved to his village, where she lived in a room next to his family. Eight years later they would return to Nablus.

These two cases illustrate some contrasting elements in the marriage arrangements of lower-class women. Imm Hilmī probably married a man who could not offer her much because she was, by Nablus standards, already older. Not only in the rural areas, but also in the city many girls were married by the time they were eighteen; they could also be considerably younger, as in the case of Imm Ahmad. In particular in poor households it was important for girls to marry as there were hardly any opportunities for women to provide for themselves. One of the few possibilities was to work as a seamstress, but Imm Hilmī's eyes were too weak to learn sewing.

Both Imm Hilmī and Imm Ahmad received less than the minimum dower requirements. Imm Hilmī was married to a man who was already older and had virtually nothing. Her low prompt dower was used to buy her some gold and clothing and she was given a chest to put her things in. Her mother had insisted that she should live by herself, but her husband was not able to buy the essentials to run a household. Imm Ahmad was married as a second wife to an older, poor man from a village, a maternal relative her mother had a close relation with. The dower recorded was average, but she did not receive it, either in gold or in cash. Her husband had only provided her with clothing and a sewing machine and had taken care of the very basic household goods in the village where they went to live. Different solutions were employed to cover up that the groom was not able to fulfil his obligations. When it became clear that Imm Hilmī's husband would not be able to provide the essential household goods, she herself did not give him her gold, but her mother helped by lending him some money for the sake of her daughter. It was not uncommon that a man was not able to pay the whole prompt dower. If his wife (and her family) agreed, he might give her a promissory note for the remaining part. In the case of a relative he might be excused for part of the dower, such as happened in the case of Imm Ahmad, with her mother lending her gold for the marriage ceremony.

Whereas rural women received often less than the amount specified in the contracts because of the 'father's share', lower-class urban women did so because the groom was unable to pay the full amount. The summaries of court cases show that in dower cases urban women, in contrast to women from the villages, did not turn against their own kin, but sued their husbands. In the villages, men of insufficient means would regularly resort to exchange marriages and remain in their father's house, even if it consisted of only one room. In the city, on the other hand, it was uncommon for the bride's father to keep a substantial part of his daughter's dower, so exchange marriages had little material benefit for the groom. In addition, in the city demands for housing were higher, and household goods usually were not home-made, but purchased in the market. If stipulations were inserted in the contract – and that was virtually done only in the city – these often concerned housing conditions.[11]

Usually, however, an urban woman would litigate for payment of that part of the prompt dower she had not yet received only if her husband had left her without any source of livelihood. In virtually all court cases, she demanded at the same time maintenance (*nafaqa*) and in some cases suitable lodging (*maskan shar'ī*). In 1936, for example, D. from Nablus city raised a complaint against her husband stating that she wanted the 10 PP he still owed her from her prompt dower. Yet, the main intent seemed to have been that she wanted maintenance and suitable lodging, for when he promised to provide her with both she withdrew her demand for the 10 PP.[12] Just as in Imm Ahmad's case it often happened that a woman did not receive her prompt dower in full, but if her husband treated her well in other respects, she would not turn to the court, for marriage was too important. Poor women were confronted with the dilemma of either claiming their dower rights and, as a result, forcing their husbands into debt and being blamed for that, or allowing them to postpone payment, and perhaps forgo it. Many opted for the latter. Not wanting to jeopardise their marriages, they preferred to relinquish some of their material rights, convinced that this would morally strengthen their position within the family.

The marriage arrangements of Imm Ahmad's daughter and grand-daughter illustrate the historical shifts amongst the urban poor. Imm Ahmad had seven sons, who worked as drivers, builders and industrial

[11] After household goods this was the second most common stipulation in the marriage contracts in the mandatory period. Usually, the bride would stipulate that she was to live separately, and not to form one household with her husband's family. In other cases, urban women marrying rural men registered that they would live in the city of Nablus.
[12] MN, sijill 7?, case 26, p. 86, 1936.

sewers (three of them in Jordan), and two daughters. In 1953 her eldest
daughter, Imm Saʿīd, who was thirteen, was married. Imm Ahmad
emphasised that it had been her mother (the girl's grandmother) who had
arranged this marriage, 'even though the girl's father was against it', she
stressed. 'He had already more or less promised her to her paternal cousin
[*ibn ʿamm*]. But a young man, who was living near my mother saw her and
asked my mother to arrange the marriage and so she did.' Imm Ahmad
recalled that her daughter's dower was registered as 100 JD prompt, 150
JD deferred and 100 JD for household goods. 'But her husband had
nothing', she added. 'He was an orphan and had gone to Iraq to earn
money, but that was not sufficient. So I gave her some of the gold I had
earned with sewing.' At that time, Imm Ahmad was still living in a rented
house and her son-in-law rented a room underneath them. When, shortly
before the occupation, Imm Ahmad's husband bought a piece of land to
build on, he and his wife also moved. 'We gave them part of it, which he
could pay off in instalments. They lived with us because his parents were
dead', she said. All in all Imm Ahmad was content; 'he turned out to be a
good man, he worked as a driver and has built a house', she reflected.

Imm Saʿīd in turn had two sons, one a teacher, the other a tailor, and
four daughters, all married with very similar dower arrangements. Her
second daughter, Salwā, for example, married in 1980, but not without
problems. 'Her father had already given his word to one of his relatives
from the village that she would marry him, even before she knew about it',
Imm Saʿīd said. 'But when she saw him, she did not want the marriage
because he had a speech defect. Her eldest brother then approached his
paternal uncle and asked him to intervene, arguing that it was not fair to
his sister. It was a very difficult situation but in the end the marriage did
not take place.' Soon afterwards Salwā, almost fifteen, was married to a
friend of her sister's husband, a twenty-eight year old tiler and went to
live in an apartment above her in-laws, which her husband had furnished.
The dower was recorded as 700 JD prompt, 1000 JD deferred and 1000
JD for household goods. At the engagement her husband gave her a
bracelet, a necklace and a ring; her dower gold consisted of three heavy
'pear' (*injāsa*) bracelets.

The marriage arrangements for Imm Saʿīd, married in the early 1950s,
show that in those days poverty was still an important element. Married
very young, her recorded dower was average but, as had often been the
case in the mandatory period amongst the poor, her husband was not able
to pay the full amount. Yet, she was allowed to keep the gold her mother
had provided her with, as her mother had earned enough as a seamstress
to buy these for her. Even though in the 1970s and 1980s there were
also women who refrained from taking their full dower as their husbands

were not able to pay it, amongst the Nablus urban population this had become less common than previously. Imm Ahmad's granddaughters, for example, all received their dower. Urban grooms have become able to pay the dower more often because abject poverty has largely disappeared, and the dower has generally become less of a burden for grooms to pay (as will be discussed in section 5.4).

### The camps: traditions and poverty

Most refugee women, whether they were living in Nablus or in the camps, went through a sudden and rapid process of impoverishment and dispossession, which influenced both their marriage arrangements and their perceptions of these. Imm Muhammad from Jaffa was married in 1950, shortly after they had fled to the East Bank; her mother had already passed away and shortly thereafter her father's female cousin (*bint ʿamm*) had also died there. 'Her son came to my father and asked him to give me in marriage to him', Imm Muhammad said, adding, 'I did not know anything about it until my father told me "I have given you to so-and-so in marriage, because his mother has died. If you marry a relative you can also take care of us."' Several times Imm Muhammad emphasised that she had not wanted this marriage. 'I was only sixteen years old and he was much older, but I no longer had a mother to defend me.' Under these circumstances, shortly after the 1948 disaster (*nakba*) and the family still in mourning, there was little joy and Imm Muhammad hardly received any gold at the engagement. 'Our engagement period only lasted eight days and then his father and grandmother came to take me. My father did not ask much because my husband's mother had just died and he no longer wanted the worry of his daughters.' From her dower she bought four 'twisted wire' (*mabarīm*) bracelets, costing about 50 JD at the time. Back in Nablus living conditions were difficult and they soon moved to Balata camp where, as Imm Muhammad said, 'we spent some years in tents until a small room was built for us.'

In Imm Muhammad's marriage contract, a prompt dower of 90 JD was registered, yet as was common amongst the poor, her husband was not able to pay her the full prompt dower when they married and he was allowed to pay the remainder later. Considering herself married young at sixteen, her point of reference probably was Jaffa rather than Nablus. Also, her registered dower was not very low by Nablus standards. Still, had she married in Jaffa before the *nakba*, it is likely that a larger amount would have been registered for her, that she also would have received more gifts and that she may well have received the full amount. In fact, Imm Muhammad was still comparatively well-off. Shortly after the *nakba*, poverty forced many refugee families to arrange highly disadvantageous marriages for their young daughters. The old widow from Haifa, for instance, who rented the dilapidated old room from Imm Hilmī in the old city, had received hardly anything when she was married to a man, more than twenty-five years her senior. As her father had already died, her brother was her marriage guardian; he kept most of her dower 'to feed his wife and children' and only gave her some clothing.

If circumstances were a bit less harsh, the influence of the particular background of the refugee women could be reflected in the nature of the dower, especially the first years after the *nakba*. Refugee women settling in West Bank villages often emphasised the differences with their home village. One of them told me how in the West Bank village where they went to live it was common for a father to keep half the prompt dower himself. Yet when she was married in 1950 her father did not do so, as in her village of origin this had not been approved of. There a father would give the whole prompt dower to his daughter and, if he was well-off, he would even add to it. Although refugee women may have idealised the past, many coastal villages had indeed been more urbanised, which may well have influenced the nature of dower payments there.

Gradually dower practices in the camps became hard to distinguish from those of the Nablus urban poor, as the marriages of Imm Muhammad's daughters indicate. Her second daughter Bāsima, for example, was twenty-two years old, when in 1979 she married an unrelated man from bedouin background from the same camp. Whereas she received only a watch, a ring and a dress at the engagement, the prompt dower of 600 JD registered in her marriage contract did not differ from that current amongst poorer urban women. As dower she was given a relatively large amount of gold – three 'pear' (*injāsa*) bracelets worth 550 JD – probably because her husband built her a very simple house; the other 50 JD she spent on kitchen ware.

### The urban elite: the virtues of presenting gifts

Amongst the urban elite the relation between the contracts and the payments was different, as is indicated in Imm Shākir's description of how she was married in 1947, when she was nineteen years old and had just finished high school. 'Actually, I would have preferred to continue my education', Imm Shākir recalled, 'but my mother objected. She had missed me very much, because I had been away from home, at a boarding school, for a long time.' About her marriage she said: 'Our marriage was traditional, it was a family marriage. My husband was the son of a friend of my father. He had seen me in the street, but we had not talked together before the marriage contract was signed.' Imm Shākir had not been very eager to marry, but felt the pressure of her family. 'My family said, "as you wish", but of course, that was not what they really wanted; they considered him a very good match.' In the marriage contract they registered 1,000 PP as prompt dower and 1,000 PP as deferred, of which she did not spend anything, as all she needed was given to her. 'When we were engaged my future husband had already given me a lot of gold, some heavy bracelets and six thinner ones. My father put the dower in a bank account for me and my own family paid for clothing and household goods, that is how it was common with us. My father gave me a cupboard and everything else that belongs to a bedroom', Imm Shākir explained.

The story of Imm Shākir illustrates that dower practices amongst the wealthy followed the prescriptions of the 1917 OLFR: the dower was intended for the bride herself and she did not need to use it to buy gold, clothing or furniture. It is true that it was not uncommon for a woman to receive a few pieces of gold from her *fiancé* at the engagement, but she would still buy most of her gold from her dower. Urban elite women, on the other hand, received all their gold as gifts from their husbands (and fathers) in the form of a supplement to the dower. Also with regard to household goods the practices of the wealthy differed from the common pattern. If in the city it was usually the husband who had to bring the household goods, Imm Shākir received her furniture from her father. And, of course, he did not use part of his daughter's dower to buy it, as was the case in the rural areas. So, amongst the wealthy the whole dower was intended for the bride herself, while in addition she would receive many gifts from husband and kin. For the younger generation a token dower was often recorded.

## 5.2     The token dower: a plethora of meanings

### The contracts: an invention of the modernising elite

It was in the mid-1960s that a significant change occurred in registering the prompt dower. In a few contracts, instead of a regular sum of money, a very low amount, such as one, five or ten JD, ten silver dirham or one gold lira was registered. The contracts indicate that highly educated male professionals were the first to pay such a token dower; in the early 1960s the most commonly mentioned occupation of these grooms was engineer.[13] If registering a token dower had incidentally happened previously,

---

[13] The urban samples of 1960 and 1964 show that in five cases a token dower was paid (5.6 per cent of all sample contracts; n = 90); three grooms registered their occupation as engineer, one as free professional and one as driver. All, except the driver (who married his paternal cousin, *bint ʿamm*), registered also a very high deferred dower, varying from 500 to 700 JD.

from mid-1960s on it signalled the beginning of a new trend. In the 1970s the percentage of contracts with a token dower increased rapidly and, by the mid-1980s, a token dower was registered in almost half the urban contracts; thereafter there was no further increase. By then it no longer was only the professionals, but also men with more common occupations who did so, although labourers were still under-represented.[14]

While initially the registration of a token dower was an urban phenomenon (professionals usually lived in the city), beginning in the mid-1970s, villagers also started to record a token dower. By the mid-1980s, such a dower was registered in about one-third of the village contracts, often by a groom who was a trader, employee, teacher, skilled labourer, or who was self-employed.[15] In the camps it was only from the early 1980s on that the token dower became more common, and recording such a dower has remained more limited in scope than in the city; a token dower was registered in less than one-third of all camp contracts, a percentage similar to that of the poorer urbanites. From the mid-1980s on, the percentage of contracts with a token dower hardly increased in the villages and camps.

*The elite model: gifts rather than obligations*

Women's dower stories also indicate that the token dower is the invention of the modernising elite. If Imm Shākir had received a large sum of money as dower, her daughter's marriage arrangements were different. Having finished junior college at the American University in Cairo, she married in 1976 in Amman. 'A number of men had asked her but she refused them and chose a husband herself', her mother said, who obviously was pleased with her daughter's choice. From a prominent urban family, her husband had studied business administration in the US and then held a top position in a bank in Amman. With regard to her dower, Imm Shākir stressed that her daughter had 'not taken a dower'. As she said: 'His family gave her gold and diamonds, a ring with a three carat solitaire and other items, not a dower, only gifts. But his father insisted on registering 10,000 JD as deferred dower for her. We did not demand that, but so it happened.'

In the 1950s a high prompt dower was still usually recorded for brides

---

[14] In the 1980s, 35 per cent of those who gave 'labourer' as their occupation registered a 1 JD dower, while the average was 44 per cent (sample years 1980, 1984, 1987 and 1988; n = 207).

[15] A token dower was recorded relatively rarely by rural workers, students or farmers. There were, however, also considerable differences between villages, not linked to occupational status.

from wealthy families, although there was already a strong emphasis on gifts rather than on the dower itself, with in-laws and kin attempting to outdo each other in providing the bride with anything she may need. Some of the women who had married at that time already downplayed the importance of the dower in comparison to the gifts they had received, arguing that a regular dower was recorded only 'in order not to go out of tradition'. The rise in token dower registrations beginning in the 1960s can be seen as a culmination of the importance of voluntary gifts over registered obligations, with the bride's father stating that his daughter did not need a dower, as he himself would provide her with everything, which the groom and his kin understood as an invitation to do the same. The brides often fully agreed with the registration of a token dower, which they considered as an expression of modernity. Receiving gifts rather than a dower suited girls who by then were often well-educated, usually in a Westernised institution, which may have been conducive to them equating the dower with 'the sale of women'. Khawla, for instance, told me how in the early 1970s when her brother asked her whether she wanted a dower she had indignantly answered him with: 'Am I a donkey that he has to pay for me?' And in financial terms, these women would not lose much if a token dower was recorded, for they still received expensive jewellery and other valuable gifts at their engagement and wedding.

### Rural and lower class women: taking a chance

But not all women for whom a token dower was registered were wealthy. Even if amongst rural women and the poorer sections of the population a regular prompt dower was usually recorded, more recently a sizable minority has started to write a token dower. For example, from the early 1980s on recording a token dower became rapidly more widespread in Al-Balad. Already in 1981 Hanān had married with a 1 JD dower, and when Tāhiyya married in 1984 it was self-evident that a token dower would be registered for her.[16]

Yet, such a token dower could lead to serious problems, as is illustrated by the case of Amānī. The eldest of nine children in a poor Nablus family, she married Salīm in 1983, when she was twenty. Her father had worked for a long time in Israel and then had opened a small shop. Salīm's family, of refugee origin and living in a rented house in the old city, was not much better off. His brothers had regularly been imprisoned for long periods of time. He had dropped out of school and gone to work as a builder in Israel.

---

[16] In fact, Al-Balad was one of those villages where a token dower was very frequently registered. Between 1981 and 1988 this was the case in 77 per cent of the contracts in the sample (n = 31).

When I talked with Amānī about her dower arrangements, she had been married about four years. Refusing to stay with her in-laws any longer, she was living with her two little sons in a small, dark shed in the old city, her husband only worked irregularly, and she had just sold one of her heavy gold bracelets.

Amānī herself called her marriage 'traditional'. After leaving school at fifteen, she took a course in hairdressing and went to work in a hairdresser's shop, where Salīm's sister used to have her hair done. 'She liked me', Amānī said. 'Then his family came to our house, and asked for my hand. They were to come back another time, but the next day Salīm and his two brothers were imprisoned for eighteen days and they were excused. After their release my family went to visit them, as we always do when someone is let out of prison. They visited us again and a relation was established between us and them.' Shortly afterwards the contract was written and four months later they were married. 'His family had wanted it sooner', Amānī stressed, 'but I wanted to get to know him better. I did not object to marriage, because people here talk quickly if a girl is not married young.' It was agreed that they would register a prompt dower of 1 JD, a deferred of 1,000 JD and Salīm would bring everything for the house (*taqm bayt kāmil*).

'The problems started', Amānī recalled, 'when it became clear that his family did not realise how expensive the 1 JD is. If a 1 JD dower is recorded, this means that the groom has to bring everything, gold, clothing, a bedroom, household goods, that is my right. Salīm had helped his elder brothers to marry, but they did not support him. At the engagement he gave me a bracelet and a necklace. As dower I only received 6 thin gold bracelets [*sahab*] of 30 JD each and a wedding ring, and later it turned out that two of these bracelets were borrowed from his sister! So the dower gold was only about 180 JD, that is very, very little. Then there were also problems because my father had taken the money people had given me at the wedding [*nuqūt*] to buy things for me, as is usual. He bought me a 'pear' [*injāsa*] bracelet of 200 JD and household goods, as Salīm had only bought the bedroom. My father, brothers, mother and sister had also given me gold. But because my father did not give the *nuqūt* to Salīm's family they refused to arrange for the lunch the next day, which is always offered to those who have given *nuqūt*.'

When her sister married a few weeks later, her family, as Amānī said 'did not make the same mistake', adding, 'the people put the blame on the family, on my father for not guarding the dower of his daughter. This time everything was recorded in the marriage contract.' Her sister's prompt dower was 1,500 JD, the deferred 2,000 JD and household goods were also registered. 'Her dower gold alone was four heavy *injāsa* bracelets, six thin *sahab* bracelets and some smaller pieces, earrings, rings and so on', Amānī stressed, 'Do you see the difference?'

Amānī's family had taken a chance registering a 1 JD dower. While the lower classes often regarded the token dower as a status symbol, the bride's family may also expect to receive more gifts than a regular dower would have brought. For this reason a groom might actually prefer to record a regular dower, to avoid the (unlimited) expectations of the bride's family; a token dower generally was considered to be 'expensive'. By registering a token dower, poorer women did, however, as the case of Amānī shows, take a risk. For this strategy might backfire if the bride did not receive what she and her family had expected; and if only a token dower is recorded, she would not even be able to excuse her husband from making the full payment, as her 'power to give' would be gone.[17]

### Class and conviction

In other cases, a bride's personal convictions might induce her to downplay the material side of the marriage. Women and their kin sometimes mentioned ideological reasons to explain their preference for a token dower. Those of a strong religious conviction often cited the prophet's *hadīth*, 'The lower the *mahr*, the greater the blessing' (*aqallu-hum mahran, aktharuhum barakatan*).[18] If these women often had a token dower registered in their contracts, this did not necessarily influence the nature of the gifts they received. Women of a leftist persuasion regarded the dower as a relict of past times, like the sale of women, and supportive of the class system. In particular, if they married a lower-class husband, they might indeed prefer not to receive much. These were the sentiments ʿAbīr, the wife of Salīm's five-year-older brother Nāfiz, expressed. ʿAbīr's father had worked as a mechanic for twenty years before he was able to start his own small garage. Nāfiz, having left school in order to enable his elder brother to finish his university studies, had taken up any job he could find. He worked in a bakery, as a builder in Israel, as a driver, had a small sewing workshop and so on. Nāfiz and ʿAbīr met in 1976 through his elder sister; they held similar political views and both Nāfiz and ʿAbīr are ex-political prisoners.

When ʿAbīr started telling me about her marriage arrangements she stressed that although she and Nāfiz had met for the first time in 1976 they

---

[17] Neither would she be able to turn to the court to demand the amount she had expected as dower. For this reason, the Jordanian ministry of religious affairs had sent out a circular to the shariʿa courts asking them to discourage people from registering a token dower. Yet, as the registrars told me, people did what they wanted anyway, and because it is not legally forbidden to register a very small amount, there was nothing they could do about it.

[18] The *hadīth* refers to the formal tradition relating deeds and words of the Prophet.

were only married in 1982. 'Marriage is a very serious matter, you have to be really convinced of each other. Nāfiz first had to build himself a future, and I wanted to finish my studies', ʿAbīr explained. For a long time they would only greet each other, but not sit together. 'It happens so often in university that a boy and a girl become close; everybody knows it, but when they have taken their degree, each goes his own way,' said ʿAbīr. 'That has a negative influence on the girl, for nothing remains hidden in Nablus. From one side of the mountain to the other, everybody knows about it and she will be able to marry someone only from another place.'

When ʿAbīr had taken her BA, Nāfiz came to her father to ask her hand. ʿAbīr recalled that she had been very nervous about it, but Nāfiz had played it well and had already built up a relation with him. Her father agreed in principle, but told Nāfiz that ʿAbīr herself would have the last word. As a student ʿAbīr had refused all men with the argument that she first wanted to take her BA. When her father asked her opinion about Nāfiz she told him she wanted to think it over. In ʿAbīr's words: 'The next day I agreed but under the condition that I would be allowed to dress as I liked, to study for a MA if I could get a scholarship and that I would be free to work if I wished to do so. In this way it was clear that we did not know each other.' Nāfiz agreed to the conditions – which were not put in writing – and the men settled the dower as a 1 JD prompt dower and a deferred of 1,000 JD, although Nāfiz offered to register 2,000 JD. 'I did not want a high dower', ʿAbīr repeatedly emphasised. 'The best thing is when a man and a woman build up the house together. Even according to our traditions a small dower is best. The high dower pushes the most politically conscious men to leave the country to marry a woman who does not demand a dower, and the girls here remain unmarried. For not all men are able to pay a high dower, and it is the poor who suffer. And after all, what is the use of gold if the marriage is not happy?' Nāfiz rented a house and furnished it. 'I took only a little bit of gold', Abīr said, 'gold is not important to me.'

If a woman knows the man she is to marry and is convinced of him, she may not care much about her dower, feeling that gold means little compared to a good husband, her partner for life. Under such circumstances, she may well prefer a token dower. And if her family insists on registering a regular prompt dower, she will first attempt to set it as low as possible, and then ask her husband to buy her only small gifts.

### A question of trust

If a regular dower is paid, the groom has to trust the bride's father to hand over the full prompt dower to his daughter or to spend it for her benefit. This can lead to problems, as happened to the widow Nuzha, whose father attempted (in vain) to prevent her second marriage by demanding a very high dower of 4,000 JD prompt, 2,000 JD deferred and 2,000 JD household goods. Nuzha had intended to return most of the money to her husband, but when her father suspected this he refused to give her the dower. As a result she ended up living in a house with hardly any furniture and had very little clothing as she herself had no money to buy these and her husband refused to do so after having gone into debt to pay the dower.

In token dower marriages, on the other hand, trust of the bride's kin in the groom is the central issue. If the wealthy could afford to display their trust in the groom, for the lower classes the risks were greater. Even if a daughter herself would prefer to refrain from demanding a dower, her family might want to register one to guarantee her future. And if they did write down a token dower, trust was the key word. This became evident in the discussions about the dower of Zāhir, the eldest daughter of a large family, originally from a village near Jaffa, living in Balata camp. Her family has a history of nationalist activity. Both her mother and her father had close relatives martyred, her brothers and her mother's sister had spent time in prison and Zāhir herself had been placed under town arrest.

When studying at the local Al-Najah University, she met the man she later married, Khālid, a well-known political activist from another camp. Yet, although Zāhir was well-educated, from a politically active family and convinced of her husband, a prompt dower of 2,000 JD and a deferred of 1,500 JD were registered when the marriage contract was recorded in early 1988. 'Although my father and brothers had agreed to the marriage, my mother resisted the idea for three years', Zāhir explained. 'She would have preferred me to marry a doctor or an engineer. Having had a very difficult life herself she wanted me to have it easier.' When indeed, a doctor from a village came and asked her in marriage, Zāhir herself refused. 'He knew less about politics than I did, and was not familiar with the life in the camps, with town arrests and so on', she stressed. 'I was afraid that this might lead to problems.' It was only when her brothers were imprisoned and her mother saw that they had similar problems as Khālid, that she agreed. 'They convinced her by pointing to their own situation', Zāhir said. Discussing the dower, Zāhir stated emphatically that she had not wanted a dower, not even a deferred dower, but there was not much she could do. 'My family insisted. I tried to have as little gold as possible for the engagement; I was given gold for about 300 JD and my mother complained that everyone talked about how little I was given . . . '

Zāhir's mother justified why they had demanded a regular dower by comparing Zāhir's marriage to that of her eldest son who was marrying at the same time 'without dower'. 'He is marrying one of our neighbours', she said. 'The girl's family did not want a dower (only a token one) because we have lived here together for over thirty years. We know them and they know us. They know that we will bring everything for the bride, that we are not stingy. But we had only seen Khālid's family twice, we do not know them well, we only know the boy. We were afraid that if we asked for gold and clothing for our daughter they would say "that is much", so we wanted a regular dower.' (Actually she had asked her husband to register household goods as well for 1,000 JD, but he did not do that). Discussing what they would do with the dower, Zāhir mother's said: 'We will take the 2,000 JD, and buy her gold for about 1,000 JD, and clothing for 300 or 400 JD, as she likes, the rest we will put in the bank for her.' Then focusing on the groom, she added, 'Also, he is a student, he has no job. So we said, we will take the money as a guarantee for our daughter and we will bring her whatever she wants.'

The token dower, then, has different meanings for various categories of women. Especially in the earlier years it was an indicator of high status, the invention of the modernising elite which could express trust without needing financial guarantees. Gradually, less prosperous families might also take a chance and register a token dower to gain in status and perhaps hope to receive more gifts than a regular dower would have brought them. In other cases, a girl's personal and political convictions could play a role; if convinced of her husband, she might opt for a token dower, as this would facilitate the arrangements of the marriage, the material side of it being less of a consideration.

In gender terms, however, registering a token dower means taking a risk. Instead of the groom having to trust that his wife's father will not keep part of the dower himself, the bride and her family have to rely on the groom and his family to bring the gifts that were required and desired. Rather than relying on her father, the bride has become dependent on her husband. It is true that she may well receive more than expected, but the groom's side exercises control over the nature of the gifts, and women are no longer able to attempt to strengthen their position by refraining from demanding the full dower, as no such dower has been registered.

## 5.3    Household goods and gold

*Registering household goods: low status and distrust?*

In the late mandatory period, household goods were already registered occasionally in urban contracts either as a supplement to the prompt dower or as marriage stipulation; often a cupboard with mirror, costing 50

PP to 60 PP was recorded.[19] After a new marriage registration form was introduced in 1951 with a separate heading to record 'addenda' (*tawābiʿ*), registering household goods under this heading rapidly became more widespread. By the mid-1950s, this was the case in more than half the urban contracts. Sometimes only the value of a set of household goods (*taqm bayt*) was written down, in other cases the items were described in greater detail. In 1964, for example, the contract of a twenty-four year old shoemaker with a sixteen year old girl recorded household goods consisting of a cupboard of 50 JD, a bed with mattresses of 50 JD and a dressing-table with two drawers and six chairs of 50 JD.[20] Over time, household goods were registered even more frequently; in the 1980s, this was the case in about three-quarters of the urban contracts.[21]

Whereas the token dower was introduced by the elite, the urban lower-middle classes took the lead in the registration of household goods. In the Jordanian period, men with a high-status profession, such as doctors, pharmacists and engineers never recorded these, traders and teachers did so less frequently than the average, while labourers did so relatively often.[22] The better-off, and even lower-middle-class women themselves, told me time and again that registering household goods was improper; it was done by the poor, who have no trust in each other and need to provide security for their daughters. They argued that in their own case it was self-evident that a husband would bring his wife the best furniture available. Yet, the contracts indicate that registering household goods has gradually moved up the social hierarchy, although the elite still avoid the practice.[23] In 1984, for example, a twenty-five year old teacher marrying a seventeen year old student registered addenda of 2,000 JD, consisting of a formica cupboard (500 JD), two beds with mattresses (500 JD), a set of armchairs (500 JD), a refrigerator (300 JD) and a washing machine (200 JD).[24] As a result, among the middle categories, a 1 JD prompt dower is

[19] In particular in the later mandatory period women regularly had stipulations inserted. In 1944, an estimated 10 per cent of all urban contracts contained stipulations, with about two-thirds of these concerning household items; in the villages stipulations were rare.

[20] This in addition to a prompt dower of 150 JD and a deferred dower of 200 JD; MN, s. 331, no. 160348, 1964.

[21] As in the case with the prompt dower, the value of addenda also increased rapidly in the 1970s, with a limited decline in the 1980s.

[22] The absolute numbers for each category are, however, low. The average for the years 1956, 1960 and 1964 was approximately 57 per cent; for high-status professionals (n = 6) it was 0 per cent; for teachers (n = 8) 37 per cent, for traders (n = 11) 35 per cent, and for labourers (n = 11) 69 per cent.

[23] In the period 1968–1980, the percentage of marriage contracts which included household goods was 23 per cent for engineers, doctors and lawyers; 58 per cent for teachers; 60 per cent for traders; and 85 per cent for labourers. In the 1980s it was respectively 60, 66, 70 and 88 per cent.

[24] This in addition to a prompt dower of 1 JD and a deferred dower of 2,000 JD; MN, s. 637, no. 118814, 16/3/84.

commonly accompanied by household goods recorded as addenda. In 1988, the increased emphasis on registering household goods in the contracts expressed itself further when, for the first time, 'in cash' (*naqdan*) was added to a set of household goods (*taqm bayt naqdan*). This indicates, on paper, greater control by the bride and her kin as the groom is then to pay a sum of money to them and they themselves will take care of providing household goods.

Such is the situation in the urban context. In the villages, however, registering addenda was uncommon until the 1980s and thereafter it did not exceed 40 per cent of the contracts. Also, in nearly one-third of these village contracts with addenda not only household items but also gold was recorded under this heading; often more than half the amount was to be spent on gold, with the exact weight written down. For example, in the 1980 contract of a twenty-eight year old contractor from a large village near Nablus with a twenty-one year old woman from the same village, a prompt dower of 1 JD and addenda of 2,000 JD were recorded, consisting of 21–carat gold bracelets of 254 grams (1,400 JD), a bedroom (300 JD; with the items mentioned in detail), eight velvet armchairs (200 JD) and a buffet (100 JD).[25] In these contracts the prompt dower was always a token one, yet as gold was, in fact, recorded, such dower registrations are actually more similar to recording a regular prompt dower.

Another major difference with the situation in the city is that in the villages the very same category of men which introduced recording a token dower also was the first to register household goods. The main reason for this is that in the rural areas registering household goods as addenda has a different meaning than in the city. Whereas urban grooms were expected to bring household goods even if these were not registered, this was not the case in the villages, where the bride was to purchase them from her dower. In Al-Balad, for example, a bride usually spent about half the dower on gold and the other half on household goods. Thus, whereas in Nablus recording household goods was regarded as a sign of distrust in the groom, in the rural areas writing these in the contract implied a real shift of obligations from bride to groom. Once this process gained momentum and registering household goods had become more widespread, even village grooms who did not record anything in the contracts may well have contributed to the costs of household goods.

In the camps household goods were also registered, but especially in the 1950s less frequently than amongst the lower classes in Nablus. The socio-economic situation of the camp population and the poor urbanites did not differ much, but their history was different. Many refugees were from peasant or bedouin background and may well have been used to the

---

[25] Also a deferred dower of 2,000 JD was recorded; MN, s. 546, no. 60168; 23/12/80.

bride, rather than the groom, bringing the furniture. By the late 1970s, however, the percentage of camp contracts with household goods recorded had equalled that of Nablus.

Whereas registering household goods has become increasingly common in the contracts, women's dower stories indicate that in social practice the implications of this trend have remained rather limited. Among the better-off, a bride would receive expensive furniture anyway, either paid for by her father or by the groom. Among those lower in the social hierarchy there often appeared to be little congruence between the amount registered and the household goods the husband brought. First, court representatives often registered household goods in set phrases, some quite consistently wrote these down in detail, while others usually only recorded the amount concerned. More important, a bride herself would often rather start with simple furniture than force her husband into debt. For Imm Muhammad in Balata camp in 1950, a cupboard with two mirrors worth 20 JD, and a mattress, quilts and pillow covers worth 10 JD were registered as addenda, while in 1980 her daughter Bāsima had a cupboard with four doors worth 200 JD, two wooden beds with mattresses and quilts worth 150 JD and a buffet worth 150 JD recorded in her contract. In 1953, for Imm Saʿīd from the old city of Nablus, the addenda consisted of a flat sum of 100 JD, while for her daughter Salwā 1,000 JD was registered in 1979. Yet, none of them received furniture to the amount recorded. Whereas in the mandatory period a bride (and her kin) might excuse the groom from paying the prompt dower at once, more recently grooms usually pay the full amount, but then may not have be able to bring the registered furniture. A lower-class woman is then again faced with a dilemma. If she demands her rights her husband may blame her for the debts he has to take upon himself and may not be able to provide for her. By giving up some of her rights and allowing her husband not to bring everything at once a woman might actually strengthen her position. The importance of registering addenda then may well be that it makes it visible that the bride has refrained from claiming her rights.

### Towards consumptive property

In whatever way the dower was registered, brides always received gifts, often the most valuable property they were ever to obtain. Over time the nature of these dower gifts has changed. In the mandatory period, when sufficient cash was not always available, some rural brides acquired productive property as dower. Although the norm at that time was that the dower should be paid in cash, at least until the 1940s it was difficult for rural men to pay the entire prompt dower in this manner. Instead, women of Imm Sālim's generation might obtain a piece of land, a few olive trees or a number of goats as part of the dower (see also Granqvist 1931: 119). Beginning in the late 1950s, this practice became less common, as more men worked for wages and cash became more widely available. In the city, on the other hand, productive property was never an important component of the dower property, except perhaps for smaller items such as a sewing machine. Admittedly, beginning in the 1950s, some middle- and upper-class women, in particular those who were professionally employed, put their prompt dower in a bank account or preferred to receive it as financial paper rather than gold. But in general, gold, clothing and household goods were the major gifts brides received as dower.

For most women gold was, and still is, the central element of the dower. By the late 1920s gold jewellery had started to replace silver (Weir 1989: 194). Most women in Al-Balad acquired their gold in the form of Turkish, and to a lesser extent, British gold coins, sewn together on a ribbon, which they wore as a necklace inside their dress (qilāda dhahab). Beginning in the late 1960s, in the village heavy gold bracelets such as the 'twisted wire' (mabrūma), 'pear' (injāsa) or 'snakes' (hayāya) bracelets became more popular, while in the city such bracelets had already largely replaced gold coins in the mandatory period. Although these bracelets were quite standardised, there were small variations in style and the value was not immediately visible, as there were considerable differences in weight. So, if gold bracelets were registered in the marriage contract, their weight was usually recorded.

Gold jewellery served both as a means to store wealth and as a form of security. Both gold coins (22 carat) and these heavy bracelets (21 carat) were an attractive investment; they required little labour, so when they were sold the losses associated with the costs of labour remained limited (usually less than 5 per cent). Gradually, however, the 'decorative' side of wearing jewellery has become more important. For the wealthy, gold jewellery had also previously been more an expression of status than a source of security. As Imm Shākir told me, she never sold her gold; her husband always bought her more whenever there was a new model on the market. During the mandatory period, the better-off were already beginning to buy gold jewellery decorated with diamonds, in addition to the heavy gold bracelets. In the Jordanian period, diamonds became increasingly popular, and those who could afford it began to wear smaller, but more exclusive pieces of jewellery, often imported Italian pieces that required many hours of highly skilled labour for their manufacture, or rings with a 3- or 4-carat solitaire, which after the occupation could also be bought in Israel.

From the 1960s, Italian gold became more fashionable among the less well-off in the city. In the 1970s, this was also the case in villages like Al-Balad, although to a lesser extent, and the 21-carat bracelets still made up the major part of the dower gold. Young brides liked the large selection of nicely made necklaces, bracelets, pendants, rings, earrings and so on. But as this Italian gold was only 18-carat and a considerably larger part of the price was made up of labour costs and import duties, it was less valuable as an investment, and selling this gold women incurred a considerable loss. In the later 1980s, Italian gold started to become less popular and two new trends developed. Some village brides turned to gold coins again. In 1989, the young brides I saw in Al-Balad showed me with pride the *qilāda* they had received on marriage consisting of thirteen coins, with the middle one placed in a large gold frame; these coins were not sewn on a ribbon, as had been common in their grandmother's time, but hung from a heavy gold chain. And amongst the urban lower-middle classes, the 'Indian set' (*taqm hindī*) was becoming popular, a set of 21-carat gold, either imported from the Gulf region or made in Nablus, consisting at least of a necklace and earrings, elaborately decorated with many small pendants and so on. Even if labour costs were higher than for the traditional bracelets, these were lower than in the case of Italian gold. While brides still like fashionable jewellery, they seem to be turning again to more secure types of gold.

Gold was and is central in the dower, but over time a larger part of the dower has begun to be spent on other items. Such changes are most pronounced in the rural areas. During the mandatory period, extended family households were common in the villages; the dower need provide only the furnishings of the bedroom. A good part of these household goods were home-made, such as the woollen mattresses, quilts and so on. The most important element bought in Nablus was a chest and in the later period a cupboard, in which the bride would keep her personal belongings. With a greater emphasis on the conjugal family and a higher standard of living, more household goods were required, and these were increasingly brought from the city. In the late 1970s, ready-made furniture, locally produced or imported, again mainly from Italy, such as complete bedrooms, chairs and tables for the guest room, were purchased in Nablus.

Patterns relating to refugee women depend on their particular background. Although cash was more readily available in the coastal villages than in the Jabal Nablus region, some rural women who married before the 1948 disaster (*nakba*) had received productive property as part of their dower, just as the women in Al-Balad sometimes did. Whereas in Al-Balad this was halted when cash became more widely available, refugees lost access to productive property because of the *nakba*. Still, in some cases the dower gifts in the camps were influenced by what brides were used to receive at home (except, of course, land). Imm Muhammad, for example, had a piece of material of 3 JD included in her contract in 1950, which was uncommon among the inhabitants of Jabal Nablus. The daughters of these refugee women, however, received dower gifts which were similar to those of the urban poor.

In short, whereas there are women who prefer shares rather than gold, and others have turned to 'better gold' again, dower gifts have tended to become more consumptive. Land, trees or goats are no longer given as dower, gold has become more 'decorative', and household goods have become a more central element of the dower.

## 5.4    The dower and houses: the 'devaluation' of the dower

Whenever I mentioned that I was involved in research on the dower, people would complain about the high costs involved in marriage, forcing men to postpone marriage for many years. Yet, the dower was often not the major obstacle; for many, it was the rising housing costs which had become the main burden.

This had not been the case during the mandatory period. When agriculture was the major source of livelihood, sons in landowning households remained largely dependent on their father until his death. Brides moved in with their in-laws and married sons remained in their father's house as long as he was alive; at most, an additional room would be built for the new couple. When migration became widespread and agriculture subsidiary to various forms of male wage labour, sons became less dependent upon their fathers and it became socially accepted, and often actually preferred, for the young couple to move into a house of their own. This might well be an apartment nearby or a new floor on top of the house of the groom's father, yet it was to be a self-contained unit with a kitchen and other facilities.

This led to changes in the nature of the dower. Gradually the bride's father has become less interested in taking a share of his daughter's dower, preferring that the groom spend his money on providing her with adequate housing.[26] As the average cost of housing has increased much more rapidly than the dower, building a house has become a larger outlay for the groom's side than the dower. When Imm Sālim married in the

[26] This argument has been developed by Rosenfeld (1980) when discussing dower developments in a village in the Lower Galilee. While elaborating on the changing relations between fathers and sons, he pays no attention to shifts in the gender division of labour and sees women both previously and more recently as 'propertyless' and subordinated (1980: 210).

1930s, building a room was often less costly than paying the dower; in the 1970s the expenses involved in building a house could easily be ten times the dower, as was the case with her second daughter, Imm Nidāl. It is true that women themselves also have a stake in their housing situation, both as this implied a greater autonomy *vis-à-vis* their in-laws, and in terms of convenience and status. Yet, in contrast to the dower, which belongs to the bride, the house is the husband's property.

Simultaneously, since the mid-1960s, fewer and fewer women sell their dower gold to buy land and livestock. In part this is the result of the social 'devaluation' of the dower. As land prices have risen much faster than the bride's share of the dower, women have less opportunity to buy this type of property. The three *dunum* of land Imm Sālim received in the early thirties were the equivalent of her bridal share of 10 PP. In the early 1980s three *dunum* would have cost at least 3,000 JD or about four times the value of the average dower. More important, however, is that the greater emphasis on men as providers and women as (unproductive) consumers in itself discourages independent ownership of productive property by women. Until the 1960s, acquiring dower gold often signalled the beginning of a series of transactions, in which village women bought and sold gold, cows, goats, and – to a lesser extent – land, depending on the market. Since the mid-1960s, however, it has become increasingly common for a woman to sell her dower gold to help her husband build a house, to set him up in a small business, or to help him with the initial costs of migration.

The above refers to the situation in the rural areas, where changes in the housing situation and in the gender division of labour have been most evident. But, in the city and the camps, housing expenses have also gone up rapidly. During the mandatory period, separate housing for the new couple was already demanded more often in the city than in the villages; since then it has become ever more common. Renting a house, which does not demand the large outlay of buying land and building a house, is more usual in Nablus city than in the countryside; even so, men in the city often say that one had better first look for a suitable house, before starting to look for a wife, and home ownership is an important goal in life. It is true that in the camps where occupancy rights rather than ownership rights change hands, houses are considerably cheaper than in the neighbouring urban suburbs, but even there a modest house may easily cost two or three times the amount registered as dower.

In contrast to women in rural areas, urban women during the mandatory period were already largely defined as non-productive and their actions with their dower gold were mainly limited to investing in their husband or children. Supporting her husband could mean helping him to start a business of his own, as Imm Saʿīd did by giving her husband her dower gold so he could buy a truck together with a partner. This was generally acknowledged and occasionally even registered as a loan from the wife to the husband. After some years Imm Saʿīd's husband indeed bought gold for her again. Women also sold their gold to help their husband with the costs of building a house. But as was the case in the rural areas, even if a woman contributed a substantial part of it, the house would not be registered in her name 'out of respect for her husband'. Only in the better-off urban households, where a wife's financial contribution was not needed, would some women turn their gold into financial paper. In the camps, some women also used their dower gold to open a store near their house or to become involved in small trade, which was no option for women in the city, where trade and shopkeeping were virtually exclusive to men. Investing in children usually meant selling gold in order to pay for their education in order to secure a better future for them. Sons were often the major beneficiaries, with a mother expecting them to take care of her in old age, although mothers may also support their daughters in this way. As educational facilities for girls tended to be more readily available in the camps than in the villages, camp women more frequently invested in their daughters' education than rural women.

In summary, housing costs have generally increased much more rapidly than the dower, and the social value of the dower has declined. Even the expensive jewellery common among the wealthy is only a small sum compared to what the groom's side is expected to spend on the new house. In the urban areas women, defined as consumers, have a long history of investing in their husband's property and their children. More recently, in the rural areas their labour has been 'devalued', they are increasingly seen as consumers, and have lost the partial control they had over productive property. Still, among those poorer households where the new couple either moves in with the groom's family or looks for cheap rental housing, the dower is still a major outlay.

## 5.5    The intifada: marrying 'in silence'

Many people regarded the intifada as a breaking point in dower practices. I was often told that especially where intifada casualties had been high and Israeli repression particularly strong (such as in the old city of Nablus, in the refugee camps and in certain villages, such as Beit Furik or Beita), local leaders had called upon the population to lower the prompt dower, because many men were unable to raise the sums required. Indeed, marriage contracts indicate that in the first year of the intifada the registered dower went down. They also show, however, that this process had already started in the mid-1980s as a consequence of the recession.

Why then did people perceive such a sharp break with the intifada? Part of the answer is that in the first months of 1988 people simply no longer held wedding festivities and only a small number of marriage contracts were recorded. As a result of the first demonstrations and waves of arrests, most families, in particular, in the old city and the camps, had a neighbour or a relative killed, wounded or in prison, and cancelled wedding celebrations. In addition, the very insecure economic and political situation discouraged the arranging of marriages. Only when people started to realise that the intifada would continue for the foreseeable future were marriages again arranged and weddings held. But these weddings were, as people said, conducted 'in silence'.

The general historical trend in wedding festivities has been towards commercialisation and less community involvement. Whereas until the 1960s weddings were public events, with whole villages and urban neighbourhoods involved, the wedding parties I attended in the mid-1980s were different. In the city these were no longer held at home, but in a large marriage hall, such as that of the Palestine Hotel, in downtown Nablus. Invitation cards were sent out, pointing out that a doorkeeper would be present, that only those invited could attend, and, sometimes, that children were not allowed in. Even though practice was considerably more flexible, this is a setting very different from the public community affairs marriage festivities used to be. The wealthy may even go to Jerusalem or Amman to celebrate, while those who could not afford to hire the Palestine Hotel would choose one of the cheaper marriage halls. In the villages most marriages, like Hanān's, were still celebrated at home, yet there community involvement was also decreasing and women were hesitant to attend if they were not personally invited.

Although the intifada did not lead to a sudden and sharp decline of the dower, it brought about a considerable reduction in wedding costs, which the groom also had to pay, while the bride's side often toned down their demands for housing. During the intifada, brides more easily accepted the idea of moving in with their in-laws 'for a limited period of time', which could well turn out to be longer than expected. With marriages held 'in silence' and Israeli goods boycotted, the groom's expenses went down considerably as he no longer had to hire the marriage hall, send out invitation cards, arrange for live music, and hand out a large number of drinks and sweets which often consisted of Israeli chocolate. In fact, the Palestine Hotel closed its doors for marriage parties and was rented by the UNRWA for their staff. While previously the beeping of car horns had been an expression of happiness at the end of the wedding party, in 1988 it had become a warning that the car was transporting casualties.

The material effects of the intifada on the costs of marriage are evident in the case of Samar, the eighteen year old daughter of Imm Saʿīd, whose wedding I attended in July 1989. Her husband, a seller of *falāfil* in the market area, was ten years her senior. Samar's brother, himself university-trained, had agreed with his father that education was no longer an important selection criterion for a husband. A seller of *falāfil* could have a better income than he himself was earning as a government teacher. Actually, he had also started to sell *falāfil* from his house in the afternoons, as teachers were paid only half their salary because of school closures. Samar's dower was about average for a lower-middle-class family. In 1988 they had agreed on 1,000 JD as prompt, 2,000 JD as deferred and 1,000 JD for household goods, but after the devaluation of the JD in early 1989 the prompt dower was raised to 1,500 JD, for after all the price of gold had gone up from 3.5 JD a gram to 10.5 JD. At her engagement Samar was given a matching set of gold jewellery consisting of a necklace, bracelet and earrings. Her dower consisted of six thin bracelets and three heavy 'twisted wire' (*mabarīm*) bracelets. Yet the groom's costs were relatively low. With the wedding held at home 'in silence' – the hosts took care that the music of the tape recorder would not be heard outside – only a small number of relatives, friends and neighbours were invited, there was no live music, and only locally produced sweets and sodas were handed out. So the costs for the wedding party were limited to under 100 JD. The groom had some land, but had not yet been able to build a house, and after the wedding the new couple moved into the rented apartment where the husband's elderly mother was already living.

Under specific circumstances, intifada weddings could, however, turn again into a community affair. If the groom had a history of nationalist activity, his wedding might turn into a political demonstration with large crowds attending. Young masked men would suddenly appear to recite poetry in honour of the groom, folding a Palestinian flag around the new couple and then rapidly disappear again before the army spotted them. In the camps, in particular, such weddings were quite common.

Although the increase of the dower had already stagnated in the mid-1980s, the intifada and subsequent economic decline further contributed to it, and the devaluation of the JD in January 1989 was often not fully compensated for by a rise in the recorded dower. Many men working abroad no longer returned to the West Bank in the summer months in order to get married. It is true that even before the intifada, with the recession in the Gulf States and increased repression in the occupied territories, they had already become more hesistant about doing so. Yet after the intifada it had become even more risky as they feared losing their jobs abroad if a curfew was imposed or the bridges to Jordan were closed. At the same time parents were more intent to marry off their daughters at a younger age, as there was 'nothing for them to do'. For many girls, education had been a major reason to postpone marriage, but with schools and universities closed there were no longer opportunities for them to get an education. There were also incentives to have boys marry earlier. Their parents might encourage them to marry to keep them out of trouble, expecting them to be less politically active and hoping that the army would be less inclined to arrest married men. Moreover, with educational institutions closed, boys started to work and save for their marriages at a younger age. As a result, while up until the intifada the average marital age of girls had gradually increased, thereafter it went down. A comparison of registered marital ages of girls in the mid-1980s and during the first year and a half of the intifada shows that the percentage of girls who were under 18 at marriage increased from 23 to 27 per cent in Nablus city, from 26 to 40 per cent in the villages, and from 21 to 34 per cent in the camps.[27] At the same time, it became increasingly difficult for older women to find a husband. Imm Muhammad's two single daughters, Fadwā, in her mid-twenties and Latīfa, in her late thirties, were lowering their demands further and further. Both were out of work, the small factory in which Fadwā had worked had closed down and Latīfa had been unable to find work as a teacher after she had returned from Saudi Arabia and had refused to work as an informer. Latīfa no longer demanded an educated husband, and told me she would be content to marry an elderly villager as long as she would not have to work on the land. Fadwā was actually thinking about becoming the second wife of an urban man. As they both said, there was now no market for 'older' women.

## 5.6     From dower to provider: ambiguities and contradictions

Turning to the central question of this chapter, what are the historical trends in women's access to property through the prompt dower? Longer-term processes indicate that the prompt dower has generally become less central in arranging marriages. Although to many women the dower is still the major medium through which they gain access to property, it has become less important in property transfers. In the

---

[27] These percentages are based on the sample of marriage contracts; the mid-1980s refer to data from 1984 and 1987, the intifada covers 1988 and the first half of 1989.

mandatory period the dower was the main sum the groom's side had to raise. Since then, housing has become increasingly important, and many men have been spending considerably more on providing adequate housing at or shortly after marriage than on paying the dower. And these houses are male property.

This process ties in with changes in the socio-economic structure of the area. Instead of being dependent on their fathers and living with them, as was the case previously, many younger men are no longer employed in household production, but have turned to wage labour. Simultaneously, women's labour in the rural areas is less valued, women are increasingly defined as consumers rather than as producers, and they have also *de facto* become economically dependent on their husbands. With kinship less important as social principle of organisation, the conjugal tie, rather than kinship relations, is emphasised. So, women have become defined as wives rather than daughters, as dependent on their husbands rather than on their kin.

This definition of women as dependent wives has had serious consequences for their access to property through the dower. As mentioned above, the dower has been socially 'devalued', the sums men pay to/for women have decreased relatively, while they invest more in their own property, housing. The appearance of the token dower has underlined the shift 'from daughter to wife'; it is no longer the bride and her kin who decide how to spend the dower, but it is the groom who provides her with gifts. And the character of dower property and gifts has changed. Previously, women were given, or spent their dower mainly on quality gold and sometimes productive property; more recently, gifts of productive property have virtually disappeared and gold has acquired a more decorative value. Moreover, women no longer sell their gold to buy productive property because independent female ownership of such property clashes with their definition as dependent wives. Rather, they invest it in their husbands' endeavours or their children's future. As a result, women not only have less access to property, but what they receive is also of a (potentially) less productive nature.

This process is not quite as unidimensional as it may seem. There are a number of developments in dower registration and practices which contradict or modify the developments mentioned above. While women increasingly have a token dower registered, at the same time registering household goods in the contracts has also become more widespread. In this way, some sort of a balance is achieved between indicating disinterest in the material side of the marriage (attempting to claim a higher status through registering a 1 JD dower) on the one hand, and including some legal guarantees on the other. In addition, the proportion of 1 JD marriages has not increased since the mid-1980s. And while over time the decorative side of gold has become more emphasised, in the later 1980s Italian gold has become less popular and there appears to be a renewed interest in gold coins.

Another point is that there are very real differences between women. Even if the dower has generally become less central in the organisation of marriages, this is not the case for all women to the same extent. After all, the contracts indicate that dower differentials between women are considerably more limited than social differentiation and the dower differentials have further decreased over time. It is true that differences between the dowers of women from various social backgrounds were greater in social practice, but these differentiations have also gradually decreased. As a result the dower is still considerably more important as a means to gain access to property for poorer women than for those from wealthier families. It is also the women from poorer backgrounds who often do not register a token dower and almost always register household goods. Even if they do not receive the full amount or decide to invest it in their husbands, at least it is still visible that 'they are giving'.

Finally, women also have various reasons to actively support or acquiesce in the fact that their control over dower property is limited. The dower is not only 'female property', but also part of the process of arranging marriages. For many women, losing control over their dower coincides with gaining a greater say in their marriages. They may well regard the person of the groom as more important than the dower, hoping to facilitate marriage arrangements by de-emphasising the material side of the marriage. Moreover, the nature of the dower also ties in with social hierarchy. Elite women (and later also women of the urban and rural lower classes), refrain from registering dower obligations as this means to them a rise in social status. On the other hand, some lower-class women are not interested in their dower property because they see the dower system first and foremost as reproducing class hierarchies. And to rural women, ownership of productive property often coincides with a very heavy workload rather than control over their own labour. For these women, a lighter workload and a higher social status may well be seen to compensate for reduced access to productive property.

# 6 Repudiation and widowhood: the deferred dower

The deferred dower is very different from the prompt dower as a mechanism for women to gain access to property. Women are entitled to receive the deferred dower only under specific conditions, namely if they are repudiated or widowed. This means that relatively few women can claim their deferred dower and that they do so only at a later moment in their life cycle.

In this chapter, the trends in registering a deferred dower are discussed first. The marriage contracts, which are always registered if part of the dower is deferred, indicate that gradually the deferred dower has become more important than the prompt.[1] This discussion looks at the relation between the written texts of marriage contracts and social practice in order to interpret what this means to the women concerned. The case summaries show that women did turn to the court to demand their deferred dower, but divorcees and widows are not proportionally represented. While many more widows than divorced women are entitled to the deferred dower, over two-thirds of the court cases were raised by repudiated women. Why is this? And what happened to those who did not turn to court? Did they receive their deferred dower automatically, or did they refrain from claiming it at all? These questions will be addressed in the following paragraphs.

## 6.1 The contracts: the increasing prominence of the deferred dower

Whereas the registered average prompt dower was and is rather similar in urban and rural contexts, there were great locational divergencies in deferred dower registrations during the British mandate. In the city, not only was a deferred dower recorded in virtually all marriage contracts, but it also gradually became the most important part of the dower in monetary terms. If in the 1920s the deferred dower was equal to or higher than the

---

[1] My analysis of historical changes in deferred dower registrations is based on the same sample of marriage contracts as mentioned in chapter 5, note 1.

prompt dower in less than one-third of the contracts, in the 1930s this had increased to almost half, and by the 1940s this was the case in three-quarters of the contracts; in 1940 the average (rounded off) urban dower was 60 PP prompt and 80 PP deferred. More so than in the case of a high prompt dower, registering a high deferred dower was a characteristic of the wealthy or those striving for a higher status. In a contract in 1940, for instance, a man from a prominent family, registering his occupation as 'lawyer and property owner' recorded for his bride from an equally well-known family a prompt dower of 200 PP and a deferred dower of 500 PP.[2] The amounts registered as deferred dower in the city were more divergent than in the case of the prompt dower, with the relation between the top and bottom 20 per cent of the deferred dower of women marrying for the first time being a good four and a half to one (prompt: almost three to one).[3]

In the rural areas, on the other hand, during the British mandate a deferred dower was registered in only one-third of the contracts and the amounts recorded were considerably lower than in the city; a deferred dower of only 30 per cent of the total dower was common. In 1940 the average rural dower was 50 PP prompt and 20 PP deferred (if registered). Recording a deferred dower was more widespread in larger villages which were close to the city and where agriculture no longer was the only source of livelihood.[4]

During the Jordanian period in the city the deferred dower became ever more central in the total dower. In the 1960s, the urban deferred dower was virtually always higher than the prompt dower, averaging 210 JD prompt and 340 JD deferred in 1964. Simultaneously, differentials between the top and bottom 20 per cent increased a bit further to five to one. As previously, the amount recorded was positively related to the higher-status occupations of the groom, while often a relatively high deferred dower was also registered if the groom worked abroad or lived outside the West Bank. In 1964, for example, a prompt dower of 300 JD and a deferred dower of 1,000 JD were recorded for a twenty-two year old Nablus woman who married a dentist from Gaza.[5]

At the same time deferred dower registrations in the rural areas started to become more similar to the urban model, with an increasing number of contracts including a deferred dower. Whereas in 1952 a deferred dower

---

[2] MN, s. 111, no. 73771, 15/12/1940.
[3] If the contracts of remarrying women are included it was eight to one (compared with the prompt: four and a half to one).
[4] In villages such as Asira Shimaliyya, Burqa and Sebastia a deferred dower was recorded much more often than in, for example, Qusra or Aqraba. In Al-Balad, a small village with few men working outside agriculture only in 16 per cent of the contracts a deferred dower was recorded.        [5] MN, s. 339, no. 176542, 3/10/1964.

was recorded in 39 per cent of the village contracts, by 1964 this had gone up to 68 per cent, with skilled labourers, the self-employed, drivers, teachers and employees serving as trendsetters. Still, in only about one-third of the rural contracts was the deferred dower equal to or higher than the prompt dower; in 1964, the average rural dower was 170 JD prompt and 110 JD deferred. And the differentials between rural women were considerable, the top and bottom 20 per cent relating as almost ten to one.

In the camps, the deferred dower was in some respects similar to that of the poorer urbanites while in others it mirrored the specific background of the refugees. Although a deferred dower was virtually always registered, it was usually a smaller percentage of the total dower than in the city; in 1964, the average camp dower was 140 JD prompt and 80 JD deferred. The enormous differences among the dowers of refugee women, in particular in the first years after the 1948 disaster, seem to tie in with their divergent backgrounds.[6] The deferred dower of a refugee woman of urban origin was often considerably higher than that of a woman from a rural background. In 1952, a worker born in a village near Jaffa, for example, registered for his bride from the same village a prompt dower of 72 JD and a deferred dower of 2 JD, while in the same year a worker originally from the city of Jaffa itself registered a prompt dower of 100 JD, a deferred dower of 100 JD and addenda of 100 JD.[7] In the coastal areas, as in the Nablus region, recording a deferred dower had probably been less common in the countryside than in the cities.

During the Israeli occupation, the villages and camps continued to follow urban patterns. From the early 1970s on, a deferred dower was registered in all marriage contracts, and in the villages and the camps the deferred dower also became higher than the prompt. The differences between city, villages and camps decreased further, and everywhere the average amounts increased rapidly. This increase was phenomenal especially from the late 1970s; between 1976 and 1984 the deferred dower in the city went up from 840 JD to 2,710 JD, in the rural areas from 510 JD to 1,980 JD and in the camps from 490 JD to 1,530 JD. Thereafter it more or less stabilised and in 1988, the first year of the intifada, the average deferred dower was 2,780 JD in the city, 2,190 JD in the villages and 1,400 JD in the camps. Even though social differentials within the various locations remained notably larger than was the case with the prompt dower, these also diminished; in the city and the camps the relation between the top and bottom 20 per cent was a good three and a half to one,

---

[6]  In the camps the relation between the top and bottom 20 per cent was twenty-two to one. Whereas because of the small number of cases these data are not reliable, they do give an indication of the magnitude of the differences.

[7]  MN, s. 188, no. 4765, 27/7/1952; MN, s. 188, no. 4755, 29/6/1952.

in the villages over four to one. In general, it was and still is the same category of men who write a high deferred dower: men with a high-status occupation, who sometimes also live abroad.[8]

In the contracts, then, the deferred dower has gradually become more important than the prompt, while both locational and social differentials have decreased. What are the practical consequences for women's access to property? Has the deferred dower indeed become an important source of property for women? Do the smaller differentials imply that the deferred dower is especially important for women from the lower classes and rural areas? These issues will be discussed in more detail. Firstly, though, two divorce stories help contextualise the deferred dower within the process of separation.

## 6.2    Dissolution of marriage: the stories of Imm Mahmūd and Rihāb

Not all divorced women are entitled to the deferred dower. If a woman is unilaterally repudiated (through talāq) or if she has a legally valid reason to ask the court to dissolve the marriage (through tafrīq ) she can claim it. But if a woman wants a divorce without litigation, her only option is to have her husband repudiate her for a consideration (khulʿ). She then usually has to give up her deferred dower and other rights, such as maintenance during the period she has to wait before she is allowed to remarry, and her husband has to agree to the divorce.

Imm Mahmūd and Rihāb had both been divorced when I talked with them in 1988 and 1989. Repudiated by her husband through talāq, Imm Mahmūd turned to the court to demand her deferred dower. Rihāb, on the other hand, renounced her rights to the deferred dower. She preferred to end the marriage quickly through khulʿ, rather than raising a court case against her husband. What strategies are involved here?

### The story of Imm Mahmūd

I met Imm Mahmūd, a twenty-one-year-old village girl, for the first time in the summer of 1988 in the girls' orphanage, where she was living. Her three-year-old daughter and son of five had been placed in another orphanage and she herself was working long days as a garment worker. Tired from work, worried about her children and in a situation of a great

[8] But from the mid-1970s on the correlation between higher-status professions and a high deferred dower was modified to some extent; in a few cases, men with a better profession registered a relatively low deferred dower. The numbers are, however, too small to assess whether this is the start of a new trend.

insecurity, she sought solace in religion. Interested in my research because of her own experiences and indignant about the way in which her family, her in-laws and society as a whole had treated her, she told me the story of her divorce.

Born in the village of D., to the east of Nablus, a village very similar to Al-Balad, Imm Mahmūd was the second daughter in a family of two boys and five girls. Her father only had a few *dunum* of land and was employed as a janitor at a local institution. Her eldest brother who was sixteen had left school early and was working as a labourer in Israel. Her mother had taken care of the land of her own family for a long time as all her brothers were abroad. But when they needed money and decided to sell the land, they did not give her anything.

At fourteen Imm Mahmūd was taken from school and a year later, in early 1982, she was married. 'A distant paternal relative had come to ask me in marriage', she explained, 'and, of course, at only fifteen I could not say I wanted or did not want. So, I was married and we moved in with his family.' Soon, however, Imm Mahmūd ran into problems with her mother-in-law. 'She had five daughters and all the time they complained about me to my husband when he came home from work, telling him that I did not work with them', she said. And there was something else which made things worse. Imm Mahmūd's prompt dower had been 1,000 JD, which her father had used to buy her two gold 'pear' (*injāsa*) bracelets of 450 JD, a necklace with a heavy pendant of 150 JD and some smaller pieces. As Imm Mahmūd explained, at that time her in-laws had told her father not to bring the furniture as she and her husband were still living with his family. 'They said that it would be better if he brought it later. But then they started talking, "Why did he not bring the furniture? True we did not want it now, but he should have given us the money back!"'

By the time that Imm Mahmūd was four months pregnant her in-laws apparently no longer wanted her and sent her back to her own family. 'Even after I gave birth to a son', she recalled, 'they did not care about us and did not give me maintenance.' At first, she said, she had remained patient. But when her son was seven months old she felt she had no other choice but to go to the court to demand maintenance for him. She was very small and not able to breast-feed, yet her father refused to give her money to buy milk for the baby. It was a very difficult time for her. 'I could not convince him', she recalled with sadness. 'My father said, "the child has family, I have no obligations towards him, I raise my own children and that's it."' When the court summoned her husband about the maintenance, he got so annoyed that he repudiated her and had the court send her the divorce notification. 'In villages, divorce is, however, considered a serious matter', said Imm Mahmūd. 'Mediators came and the judge also tried to mend our relation, saying that the little boy would be the one to suffer. In the end my husband took me back and promised to provide separate lodgings [*bayt shar⁽i*].' With this she referred to her legal right to live in a dwelling separate from her in-laws. Indeed, her husband rented a house in the village and put everything in it that was required. But as Imm Mahmūd pointed out, 'Renting a house always leads to problems with the owners of the house. So I said to him, "take the gold, use it to build a house for me." '

At first things looked a little better. Although her husband only spent half of the gold to buy cement and building materials, using the other half for himself, he did start to build a house. Three months later, however, as Imm Mahmūd pointed out, 'He again listened to his mother and went to eat with his own family; he only came to our house to sleep.' This continued after she had given birth to her second child, a daughter. The situation further deteriorated when her husband, having gotten into a very serious fight with some distant cousins, had to spend a long time in hospital and then almost one year in prison. 'While he was ill, my in-laws again sent me back to my family and did not give me any money', Imm Mahmūd recalled. 'My father got very annoyed as they are actually much better off than we are.' Her father-in-law owned a lot of land and her brothers-in-law were well-educated and held good jobs. Her husband himself was a skilled builder, yet, as Imm Mahmūd said, she hardly saw any of his money as he gave it all to his mother. After she returned to her father's house, Imm Mahmūd found herself in a very difficult position as her father did not want her to keep the children with her (at the time the boy was three and the girl was one year old). When we talked about her family Imm Mahmūd time and again emphasised with indignation how her father had put pressure on her to remarry and to send the children back to their father's family. But she had consistently refused to do so. 'Why should I marry? I already have offspring', she argued.

Yet Imm Mahmūd was well aware of the problematic situation she found herself in. She knew very well that people in the village would consider it shameful for a woman to work for money but she felt that because of the children she had no other option. This was brought home to her when her son had fallen ill. In her words: 'He almost died. When I asked my cousins and uncles, none of them wanted to help me unless I would give up the children. I also went to my brothers-in-law, to my father-in-law, but they all refused. When I saw that no one was able or willing to help me, I realised that I had to trust my own hands. I said to myself, I will go and work.' About twenty years old by then, Imm Mahmūd went to Nablus, as in the village there was only share-cropping and no wage labour, 'so you have to wait for a year, until the harvest, to get anything'. She first worked for one month in a diaper factory, but she had to spend half her wage on transport back and forward to the village. When she heard from one of the girls she worked with that she may be able to go and learn sewing at a centre run by the department of social affairs, she went there and was indeed accepted. Financially it worked out. 'During the six months course they give you a small sum of pocket money and some flour, rice and so on, which I gave to my father', she explained. 'I still had the money of the first month of work and two months later I started working in the afternoon as a finisher in a sewing workshop, which gave me another 20 JD. I even bought a second-hand sewing machine in instalments for 5 JD a month.' But there was the problem of the children. 'When I started the course I promised my sister that if she took care of them I would pay her back later, 10 JD for every month. But that did not work, and my father did not allow me to leave the children at his house. What could I do? I had to take the children with me to the centre, but then it was difficult for me to learn, as they wanted to drink, to sleep and so on. So, I turned to the department of social affairs and said, "please, help me, their future depends on my learning."' Her children were then placed in an orphanage.

The day after Imm Mahmūd finished the course, she went to work in a sewing workshop, starting with 40 JD, which was to increase every month. Yet transport remained a problem. When the department of social affairs allowed her to stay in the girls' orphanage for free, if she would help there in the evening with some work in the kitchen, she agreed. She also had to change jobs and started to work in the orphanage's sewing workshop. When five months later the intifada started, there was no longer a market and the orphanage workshop was closed. It took some months before she was able to find a job in another workshop.

Faced with many problems, Imm Mahmūd still held some hope for the future. 'Of course it is very difficult, my children are elsewhere and I do not have freedom here', she acknowledged. 'But at least they are taken care of and fed. When I have saved some money I hope to open a house, even if it is only one room. Then I can bring my children together and we can be a family, a happy family. I will support myself, and spend money like any other woman with children.' When I asked her why she had not turned to the court to claim maintenance for herself and the children, she said she did not like to do so. 'My husband knows he has children, that he has a wife, and according to Islam he ought to support them. If he does not do that, do I have to go to the judge so he will tell my husband that he has a wife and children?' Yet her objections were not only emotional, she also expected few material benefits. 'If I raise a case in court, I will have to come and go, to leave my work and will lose money. If I work this will bring me money, that is easier.'

When a year later, in the summer of 1989, I talked again with Imm

Mahmūd she had changed her mind and had decided to turn to the court. With increased Israeli repression and the numerous curfews there was often no work at all and she had experienced how difficult it was to save anything from her low and insecure wages. She wanted her husband to either pay marital maintenance or to officially repudiate her, so she could claim her deferred dower and other rights. It was not easy. 'My husband was angry when I turned to the court to ask for maintenance for myself and the children', Imm Mahmūd said. 'But who would pay for us? I would have to continue working forever under these circumstances, with the children in an orphanage.' Her husband then repudiated her again. When I asked her with whom she had gone to the court she said that she had done so by herself. 'So neither my father nor anyone else would become involved. Then problems would only spread and no solution would be possible', she explained. 'I first went to the judge to ask for information and told him about my case. He said that I had made a big mistake. If I had come immediately, then I would have had rights to maintenance for the last $3\frac{1}{2}$ years! Well, I do not care about that. All I wanted was to know my position, whether he would have to pay or not.'

When she officially filed a case, two months after her waiting period was finished, the court summoned her husband, but he did not show up. As it was a day with incidents, the judge thought that he may not have been able to come so he summoned him a second time. 'Then he showed up with a lawyer', Imm Mahmūd said. 'I did not have a lawyer, how could I pay for one? His lawyer brought all sorts of arguments forward, that I had left my husband while he was in prison, that he had no money, that we were staying in an orphanage and thus did not need any money. The judge told me not to speak, he would speak for me. He was astonished that a mother was working to raise her children, while her husband was still alive and able to work, but refused to support his own children.' The session was adjourned. 'First they said he would have to pay 60 JD', Imm Mahmūd vividly recalled, 'but later, because the lawyer kept talking and talking, they reduced it to 12 JD a month for me and $4\frac{1}{2}$ JD for each child.' The court also ordered her husband to pay her the deferred dower, and the maximum compensation for arbitrary repudiation (talāq taʿassufī), the latter amounting to the equivalent of her maintenance for one year, that is 144 JD, to be paid in six monthly instalments. 'I had given him no reason for a divorce', Imm Mahmūd stressed. 'When the judge asked him whether he had reason for repudiating me, any reason, he said he did not. So he was immediately ordered to pay compensation for arbitrary repudiation as he so clearly admitted himself that he had no reason at all.' Imm Mahmūd was, however, confronted with the problem of implementation. 'I only received the maintenance because he was imprisoned and they found out that he still had to pay it. But it does not matter, this judicial order is valid for twenty years.'

Her relation with her own family improved a bit. 'They accept the reality. My father does not speak or ask any more, since he sees that I have money.' Imm Mahmūd emphasised that she had received very little from her husband. 'I had given him the prompt dower to build a house, but he does not acknowledge that he used my money and the house is on the land of his father, so it is in his name. When he no longer asked about me, I even sold our wedding ring and bought my daughter earrings instead.' Even though the situation had become very difficult with the intifada and Imm Mahmūd had been out of work for about two full months she had managed to save some money. Working for different workshops and in Ramadan in the village she put away about 170 JD. From this money she bought gold. 'Once you put your money into gold, you do not spend it like cash', she pointed out. 'And gold is much better now that the JD has lost so much of its value.'

In spite of her family's pressure and the difficulties she had faced Imm Mahmūd still did not want to remarry, although she recognised her uncertain position. 'If I knew that my husband's family would take good care of the children, I might return the children to them and not take maintenance, but remarry. That would be in my interest, for a woman needs a house of her own. But his family does not want the children.' Turning to the example of someone who recently came and asked her in marriage, she also indicated that she was afraid to be taken advantage of. 'When I was in the village a divorced man from Jenin asked me in marriage, he wanted a wife to raise his child, but he did not want my children, so, of course, I refused. Even if I had no children, I would not have agreed, as there is a good chance that he would only marry me to take care of his child, not as a partner for life, and that is wrong.'

### The story of Rihāb

When I met Rihāb in 1988 she was employed in the kitchen at the same hospital where her mother, a widow, was already working as a cleaner. She was one of four girls in a poor, rural landless family with seven children. Her brothers and sisters were all married. Her eldest brother had been working in Jordan before the 1967 war and was not allowed to return to the West Bank. Her two other brothers were living in the village, one of them a labourer in Israel, the other unemployed and largely supported by his mother after having spent some years in prison. Rihāb herself had wanted the divorce, so she told me. As she was very withdrawn and obviously much affected by what had happened, it was her mother who told me extensively about how the divorce had come about.

'Three years ago when she was twenty, we married Rihāb to a man from a refugee camp, a teacher', she said, 'but after she moved in with his family, she soon discovered that he always listened to his mother; he gave all his money to her and did everything she wanted. Rihāb was not allowed to do anything without her permission and could not even take a piece of bread.' But it was not simply problems with her mother-in-law which led to the divorce. 'The main problem was that for a long time he had been in love with a woman from the camp', Rihāb's mother stressed. 'But his mother had not wanted him to marry this woman so he only married Rihāb because of the wishes of his family.' Rihāb had found out about her and even discovered the letters they wrote each other. As she lived nearby it was inevitable that the two women got into arguments with each other.

Soon after marriage Rihāb had become pregnant, but 'By the time she gave birth no one cared about her', her mother recalled, venting her anger. 'They did not come with her to the hospital where she had a caesarian, and did not even ask whether it was a boy or a girl. Imagine, even her husband did not show any interest in the child.' The situation worsened and it did not take long for Rihāb to become *hardāna* (offended and angry) and to move back to her own family with her little daughter. As her husband never came to ask for her, six months later they went to the court to arrange for a divorce. In her mother's words: 'We told the judge everything and Rihāb showed him the letters she had found. He then asked us whether we wanted to file a case about the deferred dower and the maintenance. We said we did not. We were not interested in the money, even though her deferred dower was 1,700 JD. We were not after money, but we wanted a future for our daughter. Had we raised a case it would have been adjourned for a month and another month and another month, and she would have to go to court and meet him there every time.'

But if they showed little interest in the deferred dower, they did not accept what had happened to her prompt dower. 'Her husband had sold her dower gold to start building a house', Rihāb's mother said. 'From her prompt dower we had bought her gold for 900 JD and she had no gold left at all. So we gave up the deferred dower and the maintenance, but we wanted the money of the prompt dower back to buy her gold again.' For Rihāb herself the fact that she lost her baby girl was the most difficult thing to bear. Her mother realised well the pain this caused. 'The little girl was only six months old when, in front of the judge, we gave her to his family. According to the law we were allowed to keep her, but we did not want that. Of course, Rihāb would have liked to raise her, but we convinced her.' Emphasising that this was in her daughter's interest her mother eloquently explained to me the future problems a woman from a poor family with a baby girl would find herself in. 'If the people know that she has a child with her, they will not ask her in marriage. A man would want to marry the mother, but not also take care of the girl, so we gave them the little girl in order that her mother could remarry. If she kept the girl and raised her, his family would take her back when she has grown up, and Rihāb would remain a servant in her brother's house. We would buy milk for the girl but his family would take her and her mother would suffer. Rihāb was, however, very, very upset after we gave the girl away and she became ill. Then I brought her here to work, to take her mind off this problem.'

In the summer of 1989, Rihāb's mother told me how, soon after I had left in 1988, Rihāb was indeed remarried to a distant maternal relative in Jordan, who had recently repudiated his wife after a brief marriage. He had first asked Rihāb's eldest brother in Jordan whether he would allow him to marry her. After consulting with her mother and other brothers, and in the end asking Rihāb herself, her brother had agreed. Within a few days Rihāb left the West Bank, was married and moved in with her husband's family in Amman. A high deferred dower of 3,000 JD was registered 'because her husband had already been divorced', her mother said. The prompt dower was 2,000 JD but she only received gold and clothing for about 1,000 JD, for he still had to pay off his first wife's deferred dower, and also had to support his family. Her mother hoped that by the end of the year they would move into a small house of their own.

## 6.3   Repudiation on the husband's initiative: unilateral talāq

In 1983 Imm Mahmūd had been repudiated once and taken back again. In 1988 she was finally repudiated when she completed the waiting period. What is the law concerning talāq and how has this changed through time?

According to Hanafī law, a husband had the unlimited power unilaterally to repudiate his wife through talāq. If he pronounced talāq before the marriage had been consummated the repudiation became operative immediately. Otherwise, he could revoke a single talāq until the end of the waiting period – usually three menstrual cycles; for post-menopausal women three calendar months and for pregnant women until delivery – when the repudiation became final. A third talāq, however, would not only become irrevocable (final) immediately, but would also make it impossible for a man to remarry his ex-wife unless a third party had married her in the meantime. A woman could be repudiated irrevocably at once if her husband pronounced a triple talāq.

As a woman's rights were very limited, repudiation could be particularly injurious. An irrevocably repudiated wife had to leave her husband's house and was entitled only to the deferred dower and maintenance during the waiting period; if the marriage had not yet been consummated she was entitled to half the dower. She retained custody (*hadāna*) over her sons until they reached the age of seven and her daughters until they were nine years old, when they were to be handed over to their father. During this period her former husband was obliged to pay maintenance for his children, a 'caretaker wage' (*ujrat hadāna*) to their mother and if they were still being suckled also a 'suckling wage' (*ujrat irdā*ᶜ). If a woman remarried she immediately lost her custody rights.

Certain protections gradually were introduced against the most problematic aspects of repudiation. The 1917 OLFR no longer considered valid a repudiation uttered in a state of drunkenness or under compulsion (Anderson 1951c: 274). The 1951 JLFR reform declared conditional *talāq* void if intended as inducement to do something or a threat to abstain from an act. It also abolished triple *talāq* pronounced in one session, classifying all *talāq* as revocable, with the result that the marriage dissolved only after the waiting period had passed without the husband taking his wife back (Anderson 1952: 201).[9] This reform was intended to discourage divorce on the spur-of-the-moment, as the repudiated wife had to spend the waiting period in her husband's house. The effects of repudiation for the wife were also mitigated to some extent, at least on paper. The 1951 JLFR extended the age limit of child custody to nine for boys and eleven for girls; the 1976 JLPS increased these further to the onset of puberty. The same law (art. 134) also introduced compensation for arbitrary repudiation (*talāq ta*ᶜ*assufī*), giving a wife the right to ask for a maximum of one year's maintenance if her husband had repudiated her without valid reason. Thus, the major tendency of legal reform has been to underline the importance of the conjugal tie and the mother/child relation.

How does this compare to social practice? Even though there are no legal impediments, unilateral repudiation is not common. Whereas for the earlier years official registration of *talāq* is not very reliable, as a *talāq* pronounced out of court was – and still is – valid, legal reform has induced more men to register *talāq* in court.[10] In the 1960s and 1970s there were on average only forty registered repudiations for every one thousand mar-

---

[9] Unless the *talāq* had taken place before the marriage was consummated, was in exchange for a consideration from the wife (through *khul*ᶜ), or was the third of three *talāq*. Then it was immediately irrevocable.

[10] According to the 1917 OLFR, husbands were already obliged to register *talāq* with the shariᶜa court, yet if they did not do so this had no legal effect. The 1951 JLFR went further in stating that a husband could only substantiate his claim of having divorced his wife through registration, while a wife was allowed to bring any adequate evidence (Anderson 1952: 201).

riage contracts and by the mid-1980s this had decreased to twenty-three per 1,000.[11] And the number of final repudiations was considerably lower, as in the years concerned an average of 29 per cent of these repudiations were registered in court as revoked.

It is hard to say whether the deferred dower is a major deterrent to arbitrary repudiation, but it is evident that the reverse is not true, at least not in the villages. During the British mandate, registering a deferred dower was not common in the rural areas, but few women were repudiated. According to Granqvist less than 5 per cent of the women in Artas had been divorced (1935: 269). A man was reluctant to repudiate his wife, as this would not only mean that the dower he had paid would be lost, but also that he would again have to pay a dower for a new wife (1935: 284). So the *prompt* dower served to discourage repudiation. This is similar to what elderly women in Al-Balad told me. In a fit of anger a husband might send his wife away, but soon he would feel obliged to bring her back, as her labour was crucial both in the household and in agriculture, and he could not afford to pay a dower for a new wife. In their eyes divorce was something for the rich urbanites.

Women themselves generally do not regard a high deferred dower as a major disincentive to *talāq*, for, as they say, no matter how much money is registered, this will not keep a husband and wife together: 'if a man does not want his wife he will get rid of her at whatever cost'. Rather they consider the deferred dower as financial security for the divorced woman. This begs the question whether repudiated women indeed receive their deferred dower. In the 1970s and 1980s, 37 per cent of the women who were finally repudiated litigated in court to claim their deferred dower.[12] This suggests both that a considerable number did not receive the deferred dower automatically and that they were willing to fight for it.[13]

[11]  The first number is based on data concerning the sample years 1964 and 1976; the latter on 1984 and 1987. Of these repudiated women 36 per cent was from the city, 42 per cent from the villages and 21 per cent from the camps. As a very rough estimate of the locational distribution of the population is one-third urban, a little over half rural and about 15 per cent from the camps, this means that rural women are underrepresented and camp women overrepresented.

   Repudiation here does not include *talāq* for a compensation (*khul'*; see next section). Other authors (such as 'Ayyush 1985) put both together, which is problematic in discussing women's access to property as in the case of *khul'* women give up the deferred dower.

[12]  The sample years are here 1976, 1984 and 1987. As women may wait for years to claim their deferred dower, those litigating are not necessarily the very same women finally repudiated in these years. Yet in many cases women turned to court within a few months after being repudiated.

[13]  This was the case for women from various locational backgrounds. In the sample years 36 per cent of the women turning to court to claim their deferred dower were urban, 43 per cent rural and 22 per cent from the camps; this roughly coincides with the occurrence of final repudation. The major exception is the year 1988, the first year of the intifada, when no women from the camps made a court claim.

Moreover, when it became possible to claim extended maintenance on the ground of arbitrary repudiation (*talāq taʿassufī*), a considerable number of finally repudiated women did so; in the mid-1980s, almost one-third of them turned to court to claim extended maintenance.

Whereas the deferred dower was particularly important for poorer women, higher-class women also occasionally turned to the court if they did not receive the deferred dower or the maintenance they were entitled to. In 1940, for example, M. sent her lawyer to court, one week after she had been irrevocably repudiated, to demand her deferred dower of 50 PP and other rights. When the court wanted her to take the oath, her lawyer claimed that she was not able to come to court as she belonged to the *mukhaddarāt* (women who strictly follow seclusion). She was allowed to take the oath at home and won the case.[14] So, following the rules of seclusion did not stop women from claiming their rights. More recently women from prominent families also sometimes litigated in the court. In 1976, A., for example, with the help of a lawyer, raised a complaint against her husband Dr B., who had repudiated her for the third time, demanding her deferred dower of 600 JD. He argued that she had no right to the deferred dower as she was working. The court, however, pointed out that this was not a valid argument and ordered him to pay her the deferred dower and the costs of the lawyer.[15] In general, however, in the case of the better-off, both parties tended to be interested in arranging a quiet separation rather than a public fight, the husband would be able to afford to pay the deferred dower and the wife and her family did not need to press the matter. A woman from a wealthy background may also have resources of her own, which makes claiming her deferred dower less urgent.

As was the case with the prompt dower, poverty was often a major incentive for women to request the court's intervention. A finally repudiated wife is required to leave her husband's house and usually returns to her own family, unless she has an adult son with whom she can live or has a house of her own. As the maintenance stipend for herself and the children and the caretaker wage are far too low to live on, she usually becomes financially dependent on her own family unless she has an independent source of income. Imm Mahmūd, for example, only obtaining 12 JD for herself and 4½ for each child, received a monthly 'income' of 21 JD, at a time that 80 JD was seen as a very low wage for a man with a family. Returning to a needy family, a poor woman frequently is pressed to remarry as soon as possible, often, if she has children, against her will. To her the deferred dower often represents a large sum of money that may

---

[14] She was also awarded daily maintenance of 25 piaster for herself, 15 piaster for her son and 10 piaster custody wage. MN, s. 8/88, case 48, p. 203, 2/4/1940.

[15] MN, s. 21/189, case no. 183, p. 292, 13/9/1976.

strengthen her position *vis-à-vis* her own family. At the same time, an impoverished husband may face grave difficulties in paying the deferred dower. The impact of poverty is evident from the case summaries in which men point to their difficult financial situation and offer to pay in instalments. When in a case in 1936, for instance, a repudiated woman with a five-year-old son demanded her deferred dower of 15 PP, her husband was allowed to pay it off in thirty months.[16] Although such details are not always recorded in the post-mandatory period, in most cases a relatively low deferred dower was registered, pointing to a lower-class background. In the 1980s payment of the deferred dower in instalments was still common, as the women concerned told me. A poor refugee woman living with her five children in Balata camp, married in 1968 and repudiated in 1985, was entitled to her deferred dower of 300 JD. Her husband offered to either pay 200 JD in cash, or 10 JD every month in instalments. Determined to get her rights, she chose the second option. Actually, men often bargain about the deferred dower by offering to pay a smaller sum in cash. Another woman from the same camp, married in 1984 and repudiated two years later after she had demanded maintenance and separate lodging, went to court to claim her deferred dower of 1,000 JD and household goods which had been registered at 500 JD. Her husband first refused to pay anything, and after a lot of coming and going to court in the end agreed to pay her 750 JD at once if she would renounce any further rights. This she did.

While women frequently turned to court, it was not easy for them to obtain their entitlements. As sessions were often adjourned, they needed the patience and support of their relatives and time and money to travel to the court. Once in court they had to fight attempts to bargain down the deferred dower and to lower the monthly instalments. They also had to face the problem of implementation, a major incentive for many women to settle for a lower cash sum. In particular in times of political tension few cases were brought to the shariʿa court as implementation involved the support of the civil (Israeli-run) administration. This was a major reason why in 1988 no women from the camps turned to the court. Finally, a man, wanting to repudiate his wife, might actually make her life so miserable that she would opt for repudiation for a consideration (*khulʿ*) renouncing her rights to the deferred dower. In fact, *khulʿ* was more common than unilateral repudiation, in particular in the 1980s. If in 1964 there was one separation through *khulʿ* for every one final *talāq*, in 1976 it was 1.6, in 1984 3.3, in 1987 3.5 and in 1988 it had reached an all time high

---

[16] She also was entitled to 600 fils a month as maintenance during the waiting period for herself; 200 mils for her son; and 100 mils as caretaker wage. MN, s. 7?, case 140, p. 147, 1936.

of 4.4. What is the legal and social context in which *khul* separations have become so popular?

## 6.4    Separation on the wife's initiative: *khul* and *tafrīq*

There are two ways in which women actively may seek the dissolution of marriage. The first is a *khul* divorce, which allows a woman to be irrevocably repudiated by her husband in return for a financial consideration, usually her renunciation of claims to the deferred dower and maintenance; this form of divorce requires the husband's compliance. If, on the other hand, a woman wants a divorce without her husband's consent and without having to give up her rights, she needs a legally valid reason and has to ask the court to dissolve the marriage (*tafrīq*). Hanafī law recognised *khul*, but made *tafrīq* virtually impossible. It did, however, allow the wife to stipulate in her marriage contract that if her husband committed certain acts, such as marrying another wife, she then would be divorced.

With legal reforms the grounds for *tafrīq* gradually were expanded. The 1917 OLFR allowed a woman to ask the court to divorce her if her husband had deserted her without providing maintenance or if he had become afflicted with a grave disease making her remaining with him injurious to her (Anderson 1951c: 272).[17] The 1951 JLFR extended the grounds for *tafrīq* to failure of a husband to provide maintenance, to the absence of a husband of known whereabouts even if maintenance was provided, and to a long prison sentence (Anderson 1952: 202ff.). In addition, the same law (art. 21) also explicitly allowed for the insertion of the husband's delegation of the power of *talāq* to his wife as a stipulation in the marriage contract.

One form of *tafrīq*, already incorporated in the 1917 OLFR, allowed either a wife or husband to ask for dissolution of the marriage on the grounds of 'discord and strife'. This had specific property consequences as the wife was not automatically granted her deferred dower. In such a case the court would first appoint arbitrators. If they were not able to reconcile the couple and the responsibility for the discord lay with the husband the court would divorce them, with the wife retaining all her rights. If, on the other hand, the wife was regarded as responsible the court would impose a *khul* divorce, requiring the wife to renounce her dower and maintenance rights. In this case a man could repudiate his wife

---

[17] When maintenance was provided the situation was more complex. If the husband could not be contacted and nothing was heard of him for four years, he was assumed dead and his wife had to follow the waiting period of a widow. In a situation of war one year was sufficient (Anderson 1951c: 281).

against her will *without* having to pay her the deferred dower. If the arbitrators found both spouses to blame then the deferred dower would be divided in fractions reflecting their respective culpability, for example, two-fifths and three-fifths or one-quarter and three-quarters.[18]

In practice, a woman's ability to leave her husband often depended more on her relation with her own kin than on her juridical position. Most commonly a woman who felt ill-treated by her husband or his family would return to her father's house 'in a state of anger' (*zaʿlāna*) and remain there as an 'offended and angry' (*hardāna*) wife. When her husband sent mediators to try to convince her to return home, as was commonly the case, she might place conditions on her return. For example, when Amānī, who had only received six, thin gold bracelets as dower and, to make things worse, had to return two of these to her husband's sister, became *hardāna* and her husband asked her to return, she put as a condition that she receive two bracelets and be housed separately from his family. So it happened. If mediation did not solve the problem, the *hardāna* wife often sued for maintenance and suitable housing, and the husband then tried to have her declared 'rebellious' (*nāshiza*) in order not to be obliged to maintain her and to pressure her to return. In fact this made it possible for a woman to get a divorce against her husband's wishes as she could then claim 'discord and strife' (see also Antoun 1990: 42).

As a *zaʿlāna* wife usually returns to her own family, her position *vis-à-vis* her husband depends on the support she receives from her kin. In particular among the poor it may be difficult to provide her with living space and maintenance. In the case of Rihāb an important reason to opt for a *khulʿ* divorce was that she really had no place to return to. Her mother was living in the dormitory for hospital cleaners, while her virtually destitute brother was living in a small two-room house in the village with his wife and children. If a woman had many children the situation could be even more complicated. When I was staying with Imm Muhammad in Balata camp, her daughter Bāsima came to her father's house in anger, because her husband refused to go to work, had sold half of the UNRWA rations and did not bring any food home. While her mother was very annoyed about the situation and encouraged her not to return to her husband's house, she did not want Bāsima to bring her five small children. With great indignation she told me that years ago her

---

[18] The 1951 JLFR only gave the wife the right to turn to the court for such a divorce, but in the 1976 JLPS the husband regained this right again. The 1976 JLPS also allowed the husband to apply to dissolve the marriage if his wife was afflicted with a disease preventing consummation of the marriage or causing injury to him. Both of these reforms were justified on the ground of the 'equality between spouses' (Welchman 1988: 873).

daughter-in-law had returned to her own kin in anger, leaving her four children behind for her to take care of. Leaving children with their father (and his mother) puts strong pressure on him to mend his ways and beg his wife to return, but it is emotionally very taxing for her. Bāsima returned home the same evening for the sake of her children. Yet, there was also another reason that Bāsima was only half-heartedly supported, as her sister put it. While a woman's kin tend to feel responsible for her in the case of marital problems if they have arranged the marriage, this is less so if a girl has 'chosen' her husband herself. As Bāsima had to some extent married against her family's wishes they were less motivated to support her; they felt that, as she had wanted the marriage, she also had to bear the consequences.

The question remains whether the legal reforms which gave women more options to obtain *tafrīq* have effects on women's access to property. Did women indeed increasingly turn to the court to ask for *tafrīq*? It is true that during the mandatory period women had very few valid grounds to request *tafrīq*. Still, there were women who initiated a separation, as, for instance by demanding the court's confirmation of their husband's repudiation. These often were triple repudiations that the husband regretted but could not revoke, while the wife insisted on dissolving the marriage. For example, in 1928 a woman came to court to have her repudiation confirmed. She argued that her husband had sworn that she would be triply divorced if he played cards or backgammon, drank alcohol, or roamed the streets. When he did indeed play cards, she immediately left for her brother's house. Her husband responded that he would never have taken such an oath as he played backgammon daily, and asked the court to reject the claim. The wife, however, brought witnesses, and as he had already publicly admitted that he played backgammon daily, the court confirmed that his wife was irrevocably repudiated.[19]

Whereas the legal reforms gave women additional grounds to raise a *tafrīq* case, the actual number of women litigating in court remained limited; in the 1960s, 1970s and mid-1980s there were on average only ten cases of *tafrīq* for every one thousand marriages.[20] The two most important grounds for *tafrīq* were absence of the husband and, increasingly, 'discord and strife' (in which case, as noted, women do not automatically receive their deferred dower and other entitlements).[21] In

[19] MN, s. 3/68, case 82, p. 149, 1928.
[20] The years concerned are 1964, 1976, 1984 and 1987. Of the women turning to court to ask for dissolution of the marriage through *tafrīq* 29 per cent was urban, 48 per cent rural, and 23 per cent from the camps.
[21] In 1952, shortly after the 1948 disaster, absence of the husband and his inability to pay

addition, the number of contracts in which a husband delegated his right of divorce to his wife remained very limited.[22]

In the 1960s, 1970s and mid-1980s there were on average 4.5 *khul* separations for every one *tafrīq* case.[23] Why do women apply for a divorce through *khul* more often than through *tafrīq*? In the past women did not only have very few legally valid reasons to request *tafrīq* but one particular type of marriage, that is exchange marriage, also encouraged separation through *khul*. The women involved in an exchange were not only to receive the same dower, but if one marriage broke up, the 'exchanged' woman also was to leave her husband. Such a double divorce was usually arranged for through *khul*, with both women renouncing their entitlements. Exchange marriages, however, have become increasingly less common, while this form of *khul* may well be initiated by the husband rather than the wife. On the other hand, more recently one particular development has encouraged *khul* separations. It is a commonly accepted solution for a divorce after the marriage contract has been signed but before the marriage has been consummated. With especially in the city, longer engagement periods and more contact between 'groom' and 'bride', such *khul* separations have increased considerably.[24] In other cases an important reason for a woman to opt for *khul* rather than for *tafrīq* (even if she has a legally valid reason to raise a case) is because then a separation can be arranged for rapidly, as Rihāb's story indicates. Her mother did not want her to have to go to the court time and again, but preferred her to give up her entitlements so she could remarry rapidly. The main impetus for a woman to seek *tafrīq* is if her husband is absent or refuses to consent to a separation (which makes it impossible to arrange for *khul*), while not having to renounce the deferred dower may also be an important consideration, especially for poorer women.[25] Once granted a

maintenance were the main reasons. For the period 1973–1983 'Ayyush (1985) gives a total number of 185 cases for the Nablus region; 40 per cent of these are 'absence'; 33 per cent 'discord and strife'; and 14 per cent 'inability to pay the dower or maintenance'.

[22] The delegation of the power of divorce to the wife was included in about 0.1 per cent of the marriage contracts in the sample years, and only in approximately one-quarter of the contracts in which such a stipulation was included, the delegation was not limited to a specific action on the part of the husband (for instance, his marrying another wife or a prolonged absense of the husband). Moreover, implementation was problematic, because it was not clear whether or not the husband could revoke this *talāq* (Welchman 1988: 874).

[23] The years concerned are 1964, 1976, 1984 and 1987.

[24] In the Jordanian period (sample years 1952 and 1964) 17 per cent of all *khul* separations took place before consummation, in 1976 this had increased to 38 per cent and by the mid 1980s (sample years 1984 and 1987) to 54 per cent. This is mainly an urban phenomenon.

[25] Comparing the number of *tafrīq* cases with *khul* separations after consummation of marriage, *tafrīq* has become relatively more popular; if in 1964 there were 3.6 *khul* separations for one *tafrīq* case, in 1976 it was 3.4; in 1984 1.5; and in 1987 2.8.

separation, these women would, however, face the same problems of implementation in regard to the deferred dower as women repudiated through *talāq*.[26]

## 6.5    Widows: claiming as the exception

As the material situation of a widow differs fundamentally from that of a repudiated woman, only few widows, as compared to divorcees, turn to the court to claim their deferred dower. Before her husband's estate is divided amongst his heirs (including the widow), the deferred dower must first be paid to her. The manner in which widows act in regard to their deferred dower is very similar to their attitude towards inheritance. If a widow has at least one son, she usually renounces her right to the deferred dower and allows her children to inherit the whole estate. On the other hand, a widow would not hesitate to claim her deferred dower if her late husbands' agnates were contending heirs (which is the case if he did not have sons), or if there were (children of) other wives who would share in the estate.

The summaries of court cases clearly show that during the whole period women litigated against such contending heirs if they refused to pay them the deferred dower. In 1928, for example, a Nablus woman, from a prominent family, raised a case against her late husband's brother. She argued that her husband had died nine years previously in Aleppo (Syria) and that she wanted her deferred dower of 50 French lira, before the estate was divided between herself, her fifteen-year old daughter, her husband's brothers and his sisters. The accused argued that he did not know about the death of his brother nor about the deferred dower. Witnesses confirmed his death and the widow took the oath about the deferred dower. The court decided in her favour.[27] In this case the widow turned to the court as she had no sons, so part of the estate would go to her husband's siblings. Widows also turned to the court if the contending heirs were her late husband's children from other wives. In 1940, for instance, a Nablus woman, with a lawyer, went to the court to raise a case against a son of her late husband, who refused to pay her the deferred dower. The estate was to be divided among herself and her two daughters, his two sons from his first deceased wife, his one son from his second deceased wife, and his three sons from a woman he had repudiated. She

---

[26] In 1988 there were again 4.1 *khul* separations after consummation of marriage for every one *tafrīq* case. The main reason was probably that the intifada encouraged a separation that could be arranged for rapidly, and people realised that under such circumstances implementation would be highly problematic.

[27] MN, s. 3/68, case 4, p. 80, 1928.

demanded her deferred dower of 10 Egyptian pounds, registered when she married in 1925, plus the inheritance share she was entitled to and the costs made for the lawyer.[28] The widow also won this time. Cases brought more recently by widows are still similar. In 1976, for example, a Nablus woman, with a lawyer, litigating against a son of her husband and his second wife, demanded her deferred dower of 300 JD. Her husband's son argued that she had renounced her rights to the deferred dower when her husband was still alive. Taking the oath that this was not the case, she won the case.[29]

Over time, the number of widows claiming their deferred dower has declined relatively. If in the mandatory and Jordanian periods over one-third of the deferred dower cases were raised by widows, since the Israeli occupation this has decreased to about one-quarter. It is likely that the main reason here – as in the case of inheritance – is demographical. Fewer women are widowed at a young age, finding themselves in a situation that they would be interested in claiming their rights.

### 6.6 The deferred dower: underlining conjugality?

Looking at marriage contracts, the most striking and immediately visible change is the increased prominence of the deferred dower. In the mandatory period such a dower was registered only in a minority of contracts. Gradually, this has not only become universal, but also the amounts recorded have become considerably higher than the prompt dower. In addition, the legal system has extended women's options to ask for separation (through *tafrīq*) without losing their deferred dower and has given them the possibility to claim compensation for arbitrary repudiation (*talāq taʿassufī*).

In property terms, does this mean that divorced and widowed women have more access to property? The divorce registers, the summaries of cases and women's stories about divorce and widowhood indicate that women commonly do not receive their deferred dower. If most women entitled to the deferred dower are widows, they are the ones who usually abstain from claiming it for the sake of their sons. Many divorced women also give up their deferred dower because they are separated through *khulʿ*; in fact the number of *khulʿ* separations is on the increase compared to registered final repudiations. And a considerable number of women who are repudiated through unilateral *talāq* do not receive their deferred dower automatically, but have to go to the court to claim their rights and

---

[28] MN, s. 8/88, case 4, p. 173, 1940.
[29] MN, s. 21/189, case 264, p. 346, 21/12/1976.

then face the problem of implementation. So, while the deferred dower has become more central in the contracts and women have more options to turn to the court, in practice relatively few women obtain the deferred dower.

Registering a high deferred dower is often regarded as an expression of modernisation, protecting women against arbitrary repudiation. Women themselves do not show such a trust in the deferred dower. As they say, if a man really wants to repudiate his wife he will do so anyway and attempt to get away with not paying the deferred dower, or he may 'convince' her to accept *khul*. Still, registering a deferred dower does emphasise the importance of the conjugal relation, but in a particular way. For, as has been argued, the prompt dower can also be interpreted as a disincentive to divorce; a man will hesitate to repudiate his wife if he is not able to pay the dower for a new wife. Yet with younger men having greater access to cash and the gradual 'devaluation' of the prompt dower, this does not work any more. The shift to registering a high deferred rather than a high prompt dower underlines conjugality in a highly specific sense: women are seen as needing property in the event of divorce and widowhood rather than when marrying. This ties in with the greater emphasis on husbands as providers and the lower valuation of women's labour: a woman does not need property when she marries but when she returns to her father's house, as a compensation for her family taking in an 'unproductive' woman. In the rural areas, the shift from prompt to deferred dower has been greatest, as it is there that the shift in 'defining women' (from 'valuable' to 'burdensome') is most evident. Women themselves also emphasise the need of having resources of their own after divorce. In particular, poorer women with young children, like Imm Mahmūd, are interested in the deferred dower, as they hope that it will strengthen their position *vis-à-vis* their own kin, so they can refrain from remarriage. For wealthier women, on the other hand, the status aspect of registering a high deferred dower as an indication of modernity is more central, even if in practice it does not really work as a disincentive to divorce.

## A note on dower property and anthropological theory

Returning to anthropological conceptions of the *mahr*, how are these notions related to the developments in the Jabal Nablus region?[30] As has been examined in chapter 4, Goody defines the *mahr* not as bridewealth paid *for* women, but rather as a specific type of dowry ('indirect dowry') paid *to* women. Thus, he stresses women's property rights in societies

[30] Part of this discussion has been previously published as Moors (1991b).

where a *mahr* is paid. The empirical material presented here strongly supports this point of view; for many women in the Jabal Nablus region, the *mahr* is indeed a major source of property.

Yet at the same time, defining the *mahr a priori* as an indirect dowry intended for the new generation and as very different from bridewealth (which forms a circulating fund) is problematic. It is true that such an interpretation is supported in Islamic law, which explicitly states that the dower is intended for the bride herself. But social practice has been different. Although at present brides generally receive the full dower themselves, this was not always the case in the rural areas. In the past a village bride's father only gave part of the dower to his daughter and the father's share functioned as a (limited) circulating fund. In other words, there can be important differences between the law and social practice; depending on its social, locational and historical context, the *mahr* can have both bridewealth and dowry aspects.[31]

Differentiating between bridewealth and dowry, Goody also argues that women receive a dowry in hierarchical agricultural societies where women are seen as heirs to property, marriages are strictly controlled, and status considerations are important rather than women's involvement in agriculture. Considering the changes that have taken place in the rural areas of Jabal Nablus, there are some interesting contradictions between Goody's theory and local practice. In the Jabal Nablus region, the *mahr* has gradually lost its 'bridewealth aspects' and has indeed become more akin to an indirect dowry, with the bride's father giving the whole dower to his daughter and sometimes even adding to it. In Goody's terms, this would go hand in hand with greater access of women to property, less female labour in agriculture and stricter control over marriages. Yet developments in the Jabal Nablus region have been very different. The empirical material shows that women indeed receive a larger share of the prompt dower, but at the same time the social value of this dower has diminished, the gifts have become more consumptive and women tend to have less control over it. Also, women's agricultural work has increased relatively (compared to that of men) and women have more rather than less say in the arrangement of their marriages.

The main problem is Goody's disregard of the specific historical context of the *mahr*. For the meaning of marriage and the dower in the

---

[31] A related problem is Goody's ambiguity as to who is to receive the *mahr*. He regards (indirect) dowry both as the bride's property and as part of the conjugal fund under the control of the husband. Such an indifference to the gender of the recipient, or rather such an implicit assumption of male domination, is remarkable as for Goody the main point of dowry systems is that property is transferred to both men and women (divergent devolution). If in the case of an indirect dowry it is the husband who is really in control, there is no such transfer at all.

rural areas in the 1930s is very different from that in the 1980s, and this ties in with shifts in the way in which women are conceptualised. When production was mainly directed towards subsistence, kinship and marriage were crucial for the transfer of property and the allocation of labour. This changed when agricultural property became less central and (male) wage labour more important as a source of livelihood. While women's relative labour input in agriculture has increased, their labour is less valued and they have become defined as dependent wives rather than as productive daughters. This expresses itself in the social devaluation of the prompt dower and the greater emphasis on the deferred dower. Women have less control over dower property and the prompt dower has indeed become closer to a sort of conjugal fund with the husband more often in charge of buying the dower presents and women no longer using it to buy productive property, but rather preferring to 'invest' it in their husband. And when they do so, they indeed become economically more dependent on their husbands.

A similar disregard for changes in the meaning of the dower to women is evident in the work of other authors who discuss the *mahr*. Kressel and Rosenfeld, who both address the implications of the increase of the bride's share amongst Palestinians in Israel, come to divergent conclusions. In Kressel's view (1977: 447) the greater share the bride receives is an indication of her greater freedom, while Rosenfeld (1980: 210) sees the continued existence of a bridal share as an indication of women's ongoing subordination. Whereas also in Jabal Nablus women receive a greater share of the *mahr* themselves, the situation is more complex than the terms 'increased freedom' or 'ongoing subordination' suggest. There the disappearance of the 'father's share' has generally coincided with brides having both more limited access to and control over dower property and greater influence in marriage arrangements.

*Part III*

# Paid labour and property

After focusing in part I on inheritance and in part II on the dower, the central theme of part III is women's access to property through paid labour. In the preceding chapters I have referred many times to the increased importance of male wage labour but usually the women whose stories I have presented were not employed. In the following chapters, considerable space will be devoted to women's labour stories, which were generally more extensive and detailed than their inheritance and marriage stories. Many women demonstrated their ability in analysing the gendered nature of the inheritance and dower systems, yet except under problematic circumstances, they did not elaborate extensively on their own experiences, as arrangements were largely made for them, not by them. In the case of paid labour this was different. For women working outside the home, their employment was not only a central element in their day-to-day life, but as female paid labour goes against the grain of a system in which men are defined as providers, women often felt the need to talk at length about their motivations.

In debates about Arab women in the labour force some have argued that there is a culturalist bias, with women's low participation in paid employment blamed on 'the "conservative nature" of Islam' (see Hijab 1988: 74) or 'the seemingly inviolable laws and traditions of Islam' (see Hammam 1986: 158). With regard to Palestine, however, this is not the case; the major focus has been on the impact of the Israeli occupation on women's work. While the Palestinian women's movements and progressives in general assume that women's participation in wage labour has (potentially) emancipatory effects (Hiltermann 1991a: 148; Warnock 1990: 117), they also consider women the most exploited sector of the Palestinian labour force. The literature points to the increase of women's participation in the labour force after occupation both as an effect of labour scarcity (due to male migration) and the negative impact of economic dependence which makes it imperative for women to enter the labour force (Hiltermann 1991a: 26). The main emphasis is on the integration of women's work in the capitalist system and in particular on

151

its advantages for the Israeli economy. Samed (1976) has argued that Israeli employers benefit both from women's unpaid labour which allows them to pay lower wages to their male workers, and from the even lower wages they can pay women workers (also Warnock 1990: 126). Rockwell (1985) and Siniora (1989) have shown how the ultimate benefits of women's low wages in the local subcontracting workshops in the occupied territories accrue to the Israeli producers. Hindiyyeh *et al.* (1991) have pointed out how women street vendors, however marginalised, are nevertheless integrated in the capitalist process.

This emphasis on external determinants and the 'working of the system' ties in with those strands of feminist theorising which focus on the effects of macro-economic processes on women's work and underline the importance of women as a 'reserve army' of labour for capitalism (Beneria and Sen 1981; Leacock and Safa 1986). Admittedly, in the case of Palestine it is hard to overestimate the impact of external factors. Still, such approaches run the risk of making women workers appear as puppets on a string, rather than as knowledgeable actors. Little space is left for the impact of local structures and strategies of individual actors on processes of change. This makes it hard to understand why some women work for money while others do not, and how certain women take up specific positions in the labour market. To start answering such questions an approach is needed which addresses both structural constraints and women's agency, and which also pays attention to women's participation in higher-status and better-paid employment.

In the following three chapters 1 will discuss several interrelated aspects of women's access to labour: the fields in which women were and are employed and how the organisation of these occupations has changed, under which circumstances certain categories of women became involved in specific types of paid work, and the workings of gender in women's access to labour and in the labour process itself. Chapter 7 and chapter 9 are each in a sense the mirror image of the other. In the former the focus is on poor, illiterate women, often widows from the rural areas and the refugee camps, who stressed that they had no option but to go and work for wages in low-status occupations. The latter concentrates on the higher-status professions, in which at least initially mainly single women, often from the better-off urban families, participated because they were glad to do so. In chapter 8, on the other hand, historical shifts in one specific sector, garment production, are looked at in depth, with particular attention paid to the way in which gender ties in with the organisation of the labour process itself. In the last section I will return to the central question: namely, the extent to which women's access to labour has given them access to property.

# 7 Poverty, labour and property

The hospital close to where I was staying during the summers of 1988 and 1989 turned out to be an excellent location for meeting poor female wage labourers. Most of the women whose stories are presented in this chapter worked there as cleaners. Although their labour stories differ, they had all started working because of financial need. The girls were from impoverished families, the married women had spouses who were unable to provide for them, and the widows and divorced women had been left to their own devices to earn a living. Whereas rural women who had previously worked as agricultural labourers considered hospital cleaning an improvement, for those women from the camps who used to work in Israel, it was usually a negative choice to which they had to resort, since working in Israel was no longer possible after the intifada.

In this chapter, the focus is on two major fields of employment for poor women: agricultural wage labour and domestic service or cleaning. Processes of historical change have had major implications for these types of work. First examined are the wage labour of women, often poor rural widows, in dry-farming agriculture and the circumstances under which some of them have turned to institutional cleaning. This is contrasted with the very different work of refugee women in irrigated agriculture in the Jordan Valley on the one hand, and the work of domestic servants in the private houses of the better-off Nablusi on the other. Following this is a discussion of the particularly contested position of women who have turned to working in Israel. Finally, the focus shifts from labour to property, and the questions of whether and how poor women in low-status employment have gained access to property.

## 7.1    Poor rural widows: charity or toiling

*The labour story of Imm Khalīl*

Imm Khalīl loved to talk about her life. In the summer of 1988 I met her for the first time in the cleaners' dormitory after she had finished her shift

153

and had said her prayers. In her early sixties, from the village of M., she slept at the hospital and only went home at the weekends, leaving Thursday afternoon and returning Friday before dark. Although she was clearly in favour of strict gender segregation, she was broad-minded enough to reassure younger cleaners whenever they were upset because people had been talking about them. She had gone through difficult times, yet it was with pride and self-confidence that she started her labour story with 'I have been working from the day I was born'.

As the first-born in a virtually landless family of seven girls and two younger boys with her father working as a share-cropper, she had soon become involved in agriculture. 'We had to, we were many girls', she recalled. 'I was seven when I went with my father to work on the land.' Helping with planting, weeding, and harvesting wheat and barley, and picking olives were all activities Imm Khalīl remained engaged in until she was married at about twenty. Her husband was a poor distant paternal relative, who had been sent away from home at fifteen after his mother had died, his father had remarried and he had got into problems with his father's new wife. Taken in by Imm Khalīl's father and working with him, he was allowed to marry one of the daughters. It was to be Imm Khalīl, as she was his age, was understanding and would bring order in his life. To earn the money for the dower and the wedding costs he went to work in a British army camp in Haifa, where Imm Khalīl joined him soon after the wedding. Unfortunately after living in the barracks for a few months, he was imprisoned and sentenced to three years in a complicated theft case. She then went back to the village.

There Imm Khalīl returned to agriculture. 'I went to live in my father's house and worked again with him on the land and also for the people,' she recalled, adding with pride, 'some days I even made the trip from the village to Nablus twice on foot, carrying yogurt [laban] for those who wanted to sell it in the city.' When in the late 1940s many new houses were built, she also got involved in building. 'The boys would fill the baskets and the women would carry these on their heads up the steps for the men who built the domes', she said. 'They paid the women 4 qursh, but I got $4\frac{1}{2}$ because I was young and strong and my husband was in prison.' Imm Khalīl did not recall how much the men earned, but assumed that they must have made considerably more, as they were the ones who were building the arches and vaults. She used her wages to fix up the room her husband had rented previously.

After her husband was released he first worked as an agricultural labourer, and later as a well digger and stone cutter. Imm Khalīl then no longer worked for the people. With her husband present there was no need to and she also had to care for the children, seven in total. Still, sometimes she would help him by taking care of the plastering (*shīd*), when he was hewing out cisterns in the rocky ground. Then suddenly, in 1973, 'when he was finally working on a cistern for his own house', her husband died of a heart attack and Imm Khalīl, at that time in her late forties, was left a widow with the four younger children still at home. Her eldest son, married for some years, had gone to Jordan before the Israeli occupation and was not allowed to return. The second one was only recently married and on his way to work in Libya. Imm Khalīl realised she was not to expect much of them. To stress this she said: 'As my eldest son could not come to the funeral of his father, his wife came instead. She arrived two days after his father had been buried and brought me 20 JD. I said, "thank you very much" and I bought her olive oil to take with her to Amman.' In this way she immediately paid back part of the 20 JD and showed her son she did not count on his help.

Neither did she want to become dependent on her relatives. As Imm Khalīl recalled, 'The first one to send me something was my paternal cousin [*bint ʿamm*]; she gave me two *ratl* of wheat [about six kilos]. How much does that help you? I looked and saw there were worms in it. I said, "my dear, thank you very much, but I cannot accept it." The other relatives were waiting to see whether I would accept or not; if I had done so, all of them would have sent me something. They were already collecting money. When I heard that they had brought together 100 JD, my husband's brothers, my relatives, my mother's relatives, I went to the one who had collected it and told him, "thank you very much, but I cannot accept what you have collected". He asked, "why not?" I told him, "no, the one who cannot eat from the work of his own hands is not human. I will not accept wheat or money."'

Imm Khalīl, perhaps as the eldest in a large and poor family with many girls and only two young brothers, had developed a strong personality. When her mother died, she had been the one who had found her father another wife, arranged the marriage and even negotiated the dower. She definitely did not like the consequences of accepting charity. 'You know, I have seen what happens if you accept', she explained. 'There are widows waiting for such gifts, they wait for the money they are given at the end of Ramadan [*fatra*], for religious alms [*zakāt*] and so on. But when she and her husband's brother's wife [*silfa*] have an argument, that one will scorn her, she will tell her, "you have raised your children on charity, on alms." I said, "that never." If you tire yourself and work with ten fingers you will eat with five; you will die honourably.'

So, in order to avoid such problems she went to work in the government hospital in Nablus, where a woman from her village was already working as a cleaner. With small children at home she went from the village to

Nablus and back every day and gave the money to her daughter-in-law who was taking care of them. Having started with 45 JD, at the end she was earning some 65 JD, but in Israeli currency, for it was a government hospital. This left her with about 40 JD after subtracting the costs of transportation. She worked at the same job for six years, until she received a letter from her eldest son in Amman, urging her to quit work. 'He thought it was a shame that I was working in the hospital while I had three sons, three young men. They were ashamed that their mother was working as a servant in the hospital.' With her son threatening her that, if she continued to work there, he would no longer know her, she decided to resign. 'Money does not give peace of mind', she said, yet it was obvious that she had not wanted to give up working.

The next few years Imm Khalīl stayed in the village with her three daughters and youngest son. As it turned out, and as she probably had expected, her two eldest sons only sent her money for two months, and she again had to find a way to earn a living. 'The eldest sent me 30 JD and the younger one sent me 30 JD and thereafter nothing at all. I did not want to live as a pauper, so I went to work for the peasants, for my brothers-in-law, for my father's brothers, harvesting wheat, pulling out vetch, picking olives and so on.' Comparing agricultural labour to the work she had done in the hospital, the former came off much worse. 'Working on the land was very hard work, much harder than in the hospital and I made very, very little money. And when I asked for my wages they would say, "I do not have it, wait till the olives are sold", and so on.' When I asked her whether her sons did not object to her working in agriculture, she explained: 'No, my sons did not see it as shameful that I worked on the land, they were all our relatives in the village; they only did not want me to work as a servant, as a *khaddāma* in the hospital in Nablus.'

In the end she got fed up with the situation and in 1984 decided to go and work in Nablus again. 'I stopped listening to my sons, to anyone. I had three daughters to take care of, they were not yet married then', she argued. Occasionally the eldest son still attempted to get his mother to quit, but as he had not supported her, his arguments were weak and she did not respond. 'This year, when I visited my eldest son in Amman he said, "Why don't you stay with me, and send them a letter that you resign, then we will go on the pilgrimage to Mecca [*hajj*] together." But I said, "I do not listen to you, as long as I can walk I will not quit work."' As Imm Khalīl aptly pointed out, her two eldest sons were both labourers, one with seven children to take care of the second one in the village with six; she really could not expect them to also provide for her.

In Nablus she went to work in a private hospital, where she could eat and sleep because, with her children grown up, there was no need to go

home every day. This meant, however, long working days, from 6 a.m. till
2 p.m. and from 4 p.m. till 6-30 p.m. When I talked to her she was earning
65 JD, which she thought was not too bad, 'because I only go to the village
one day a week, so I have little costs'. Most of the money she had spent on
marrying her youngest son a year ago. 'I was the one who paid for
everything for his wife, for the gold, the clothing, for everything', she
underlined. 'At that time I even worked extra hours at night, to enable
him to marry and I took a loan from the hospital, which I have already
paid off. He had been in prison for some years and had not saved
anything.' But Imm Khalīl did not only pay for her sons. After one of her
daughters was divorced, she was also planning to buy gold for her, 'for her
future, you never know, if she does not marry it will help her'.

When I asked her whether she felt that people were talking about her
because she was working, she said: 'It is not shameful for a woman to
work, if people talk that is no problem. We are old women, we work for
our families, not to put the money in a bank account.' But she strongly
emphasised that she would never go and work in Israel. 'We would never
do that, never. Only the girls from the camps work there. In the villages
their brothers would not allow them to go. We only work in the hospitals,
for the peasants, in the houses of Nablus women, for respectable doctors
with a good reputation. You know, if a man is late, if there is a curfew, you
do not have to be afraid. But a girl, what will happen to her? We care for
her honour, her honour is expensive, we do not care about the money.'
Yet working in the houses of the better off Nablusi, she felt, was also
shameful. 'These people, they have many visitors and they go on trips, to
the beach and so on and the girl will go with them. I do not like it when a
girl mixes with men. A girl is like a glass, if it is broken, it is finished. If
someone says I saw her talking with a young man, that is a disaster for her.
Later, if her children and those of her husband's brother have an
argument, they will say, "go away, your mother is a servant, she has
served in the houses and went here and there . . ." That is very difficult.'

Actually, Imm Khalīl was generally opposed to younger men and
women working together. 'Between you and me, working in the hospital is
also not good', she said. 'It is mixed, there are young men, it is as with
petrol and fire, should you bring them together? Then the fire will burn
. . . The same with a man and a woman.' For older women, it was,
however, in her opinion, no problem, and she often told me about how she
joked with the younger men working at the hospital. 'I am an old woman,
it cannot bring my reputation down', she emphasised. 'The male nurses
like to make jokes, that it is no problem, I will joke with them. Even if I
was undressed no one would distrust me, because I hold my head in my
hands [am in control], and if I talk I weigh my words on a golden scale, I

know what I am doing. And if there is a curfew and there are no visitors with the patients, I will make them tea and wash off their heads, and they call me mother. But a young girl, no, never, she cannot stretch out her hand to him, she has to be very, very careful.'

A year later I talked again with Imm Khalīl. The hospital administration was at that time implementing a new policy to retire all those over sixty. Some of the cleaners were content, because they could stop working and would receive compensation, 70 per cent of their monthly salary for every year they had been employed, and would also obtain money from the savings fund. Yet, Imm Khalīl felt she was still strong and would have preferred to continue working. She was not very optimistic about her living conditions back in the village, having to move in with one of her sons, and she had not yet made up her mind what to do with the money. Once she told me, 'I will receive about 550 JD. I will keep 50 JD with me and the rest I will put in the bank, you never know when you will need it. Then I will tell my sons, I want the one in Amman to pay me 15 JD and the two who are here also 15 JD each, this will give me 45 JD a month. I am not stingy and I do not like poverty, and my daughters are married to strangers, to men from neighbouring villages, so I do not want to visit them empty-handed and I have to pay for transport to visit them.' At other times, she seemed to consider helping her sons to build another room, which would also be to her own benefit. 'They are waiting for the money I will receive', she said. 'They are talking about wanting to build me a room. We have little space at the house, when I go home I have to sleep in the guest room. They want to build a small room behind the house, that is also good for when my daughters come to visit me. Now they cannot stay overnight, but have to return home with their husbands, because there is no space.' She did, however, remain hesitant. 'But you never know when you need money, you may fall ill or something.'

### Poverty and agriculture

Many cleaners in hospitals and other institutions are, like Imm Khalīl, from the rural areas. Their lives have invariably been characterised by poverty. Even if technically they had a male provider – a father, husband or son – he was often not able to maintain the household, and the women also had to work outside the house. Before coming to work in Nablus these women had frequently been working in agriculture. When Imm Khalīl grew up in the 1930s it was common for women in peasant households to work on the land. Amongst the peasantry women's work was crucial; only in the households of large landowners or of shaykhly families did women not go to the land but adhered to the rules of seclusion.[1] There was a certain division of labour based on gender, with men ploughing and threshing and women weeding, transporting the produce and processing the grains and the milk, but this gender division was not very strict and many tasks, such as harvesting, were done both by men and women.

The participation in agriculture of women such as Imm Khalīl, whose father was virtually landless, went further than the usual. In the 1920s and 1930s, share-cropping was one of the few ways rural landless men could make a living. In such households, labour was even more central as at least half the crop was to be returned to the landowner. In some share-cropping contracts it was even explicitly stated that the cropper would receive a share of the harvest in exchange for his labour and that of a woman (Graham-Brown 1980: 49). Croppers were obliged to provide female labour to water and feed the animals, to sieve the wheat on the threshing floor and so on (Dalman 1964 II: 148). In particular, in households with many daughters and only younger sons, such as Imm Khalīl's, it was self-evident that the girls would go and work on the land from a very early age on.

Compared with the labour stories of other cleaners, Imm Khalīl's circumstances had not been particularly difficult. Many of these women were not only from landless families, but had also lost their father or mother when they were still very young. Without a mother to protect her or a father to provide for her, such a girl stood a good chance that a rather disadvantageous marriage would be arranged for her. Imm Hassan, for example, in her mid-fifties and from the same village as Imm Khalīl, had lost her father – a fighter against the British, hanged by them in 1936 in Acre – when she was only a few years old. Her mother who only had one daughter, remarried and left her in the care of her paternal uncle. He forged her birth certificate and married her when she was twelve with his son for a very low dower.

Often the husband was not only poor but he might also be many years the woman's senior, which increased her changes of being left a widow with small children. These widows would find themselves in a particularly difficult situation, at the end of the line of receivers. Even for those who had previously not been involved in agriculture, this was often the moment to go out to work. Imm Hassan also did so soon after her husband

[1] For detailed information about women's involvement in agriculture see Dalman 1964 II and III. About the women from *dār al-shaykh* in Al-Balad it was said that they rarely went outside, and if they did so they wore their ʿ*abāya* (a cloaklike wrap, covering them from head to toe) also nearby the house, largely concealing their faces with it (Nimr 1975 I: 165). Also after many of the shaykhly families were impoverished these women would still adhere more strictly to seclusion than the peasant women.

was killed in a bus accident on his way to work in Israel. Leaving her in her late thirties with four sons and one daughter to care for, she never received any compensation and her father-in-law only gave her 5 JD a month. 'You will always be a pauper and remain a beggar if you have to depend on your relatives', Imm Khalīl had stated eloquently; Imm Hassan fully agreed with her.

While in share-cropping households women were highly involved in agriculture as part of household labour, women 'without working men' – usually women with a disabled husband or widows with small children – might find it difficult to perform all the tasks involved and worked more often as wage labourers, paid either in money or in kind (also Dalman 1964 III: 60). Like many other rural women, in times of hardship Imm Khalīl always returned to working in the fields. When her husband was imprisoned, she worked for the peasants. When in the 1970s her sons did not want her to continue working in the hospital, she again turned to agriculture after they stopped sending her money. The only other major type of work some rural women were involved in was building. In particular in the 1940s when there was a lot of building activity, poor women could make some money by carrying stones and water for others.[2]

Both in agriculture and in building women earned very little. Women's restricted freedom of movement made it difficult for them to find work elsewhere and low women's wages were socially accepted as the legal obligation of men to maintain women defined them as economic dependents. So, picking olives in 1922 women were paid ten piasters plus food, while men received fifteen piasters plus food (Graham-Brown 1982: 147). In the mid-1920s at a Dutch archaeological excavation near the village of Balata men earned twelve piaster and women and children six piaster (Böhl 1927: 18). Also more recently women's wages in agriculture – their involvement in building has virtually stopped – are still considerably lower than men's.

Gradually agricultural labour has become less important for the landless as a source of income. In the Jordanian period some of these men found work on the East Bank or in Kuwait. But it was in particular after the occupation that many male agricultural labourers left their work on the West Bank and went to work as labourers in Israel. With the rising standard of living and, later, the increased access to education many rural women also stopped working in agricultural wage labour. Between 1972 and 1984 the proportion of agricultural wage labourers in the female labour force went down from 24 per cent to 11 per cent (CBS 1973: 719; 1986: 908). And for those who were dependent on their own hands to earn

---

[2] Elsewhere women were also involved in embroidery on a commercial basis (see Weir 1989). Yet this was not the case in Jabal Nablus.

a living, there were other options. Some, like Imm Khalīl and Imm Hassan, went to Nablus to work as cleaners.

### From agricultural labour to institutional cleaning

This was not an easy step for any of them, either in terms of the logistics involved, or in terms of the reactions of their fellow villagers. There was a social stigma attached to working as a cleaner outside the village. While Imm Khalīl was quite matter-of-fact about going to work in Nablus, even she had to face the problem that at a certain moment her sons no longer accepted their mother working as a cleaner. It was both the nature of the work and the fact that it was outside the village that mattered, making their failure to provide for their mother visible to all. In the case of younger rural women, the fact that they would be working in a much less gender-segregated environment outside the control of the village was deemed particularly problematic, as this in itself was regarded as threatening the integrity of the village community. The dangers of gender mixing continually reappeared in Imm Khalīl's views on women's work.

If for Imm Khalīl both her age and the fact that a number of women from the village were already working in the Nablus hospitals plus her personality made it relatively easy to go and work in town, for others it could be very difficult. After Imm Hassan had heard about work opportunities at the hospital, she did not dare to go by herself, so her mother went with her to register. When she was accepted she waited another two or three days before she had gathered enough courage to go to Nablus. Imm ʿAbdulrahīm, from the village of N., also found it very hard to start working outside the village. After her husband had died shortly before the Israeli occupation, leaving her in her mid-twenties with four children, she had no source of income. Her father's brother had taken the land she had been entitled to, while she had spent her dower when her husband was wounded during the flight in 1948. After his death she first worked in agriculture for a long time. As she emphasised, at that time she did not even know that it was possible for a woman to find work outside the village and to earn money. In the mid-1970s, the UNRWA helped her to find work as a cleaner in the nursing school in Nablus but she found that very difficult as only one other woman was working outside the village. 'When I first went to work at the school, I kept crying, I felt the walls pushing on me, my head was throbbing while I worked. I was not used to it, I was embarrassed. I was criticised very much.' Yet through time her feelings and opinions about work changed. 'People said "it is shameful". But why is it shameful?' she reflected. 'If it is honourable work, and you stick to your honour, and you bring a little money by tiring yourself, by the sweat of your brow, why do they tell us that working is shameful? No, work is not shameful, it is shameful if you sit and need the people, while you are able to work.'

This change in perception was not only the result of her increased work experience with various institutions, but also the political activism of her children played a role. In the 1970s her eldest son had been imprisoned for five years, which had left her in great despair during the first years, but had increased her self-confidence greatly after she came into contact with other mothers of political prisoners. 'If you had seen me then, the first time, all of us, his brother and sisters, me and his wife, we were all sitting together, doing nothing, thinking, worrying. Then many other women came to the prisons to visit their sons. They asked me how long my son had to sit. I said "five years". They said, "how lucky you are!" This one said "twenty years", another one "ten years", again another one "twelve years."'

Yet, if politics had brought her into contact with many people from outside the village and enhanced her self-confidence it also made it imperative for her to continue working. Imm ʿAbdulrahīm was well aware of the economic consequences of her children's political activity. 'After the occupation there were people who did not care about politics, they only worked and brought money, they did not help the Arabs and they did not work against them. Then there were the collaborators, they have large houses and cars at the doorstep, they went way up. And the nationalists, they were destroyed. They go into prison more often than they are out of it. But if your honour goes it will not return.' When I talked to her in 1988 her youngest son had just been sentenced to six months administrative detention. When I talked to her again in 1989 her daughter had been shot in the back, the bullet narrowly missing her backbone.

Once a rural woman had decided not to heed the censure of the community and to go to work in Nablus she was faced with other obstacles, first of all, how to get to the city. Transport to many villages was erratic and expensive, often in cars and delivery vans, only leaving when there were enough passengers. So women would commonly prefer to 'eat and sleep', staying in the cleaner's dormitory, where they had a bed, and part of a cupboard to keep their clothing, towels, tea kettle and cups, and some food. Yet, women with small children or a disabled husband at home did not have this option. As a result many cleaners came from the larger villages not too far from Nablus, and even then they might spend over a third of their wages on transport costs.

For women with smaller children, the central problem was who would take care of them in their absence. Imm Khalīl gave her wages to her daughter-in-law in order that she would care for the children. Imm

Hassan had put her infant daughter in the girls' orphanage, but this affected her so much that her husband's brother's wife (*silfa*) offered to keep an eye on the children while she was away; she herself came home every day after work and then baked bread and prepared the food for the next day. To emphasise the extreme work load of some of these women, Imm Khalīl related to me the story of a widow from her village, who had started working in the hospital after her husband had a stroke, and had become paralysed, bedridden and incontinent. For ten years, until he died, she had worked eight hours daily at the hospital, then returning home to take care of him and her four children.

So, if conditions were so difficult, why then did these rural women take the step to go and work as a cleaner in an urban institution? As Imm Khalīl's labour story indicated, there were considerable advantages working as a hospital cleaner. Even though she made long days, she still considered cleaning to be less demanding than agricultural work. More important, however, was that the job was stable and the wage secure. Most agricultural work is seasonal, and one of the better paying jobs, picking olives, even has a two-year cycle. In addition, working in their own village, often for relatives, made it difficult for them to press wage claims. As cleaners in the hospital, on the other hand, they were employees of an institution which had regulations about wage levels, seniority, vacation days and so on. It was work you could depend on.[3] Even though the beginning wage was low, there were regular increases, and women with seniority might earn more than a beginning government teacher; some of the elderly women made wages of over 150 JD a month. That women reached such a relatively high wage was due to the fact that there was one pay scale for men and women.

It is no surprise, then, that with the intifada and the rapidly growing unemployment amongst men, there was some pressure on women's access to institutional cleaning. When in 1989 all women over sixty were retired, they were in part replaced by men. With the universities closed and the labour market contracting further, even university students were willing to take on this job. And for washing the laundry, which had been exclusively women's work, machines were brought in and young men were hired. Still, it was not possible to replace women by men on a large scale; due to the norms of gender segregation, in the women's wing of the hospital only female cleaners were employed.

Before turning to the history of cleaning I will first contrast the work of

[3] It needs to be stressed that the women I talked to were employed in a non-governmental hospital. While in the (Israeli-controlled) government hospitals wages may be higher, employees could easily be fired for political reasons. It is unlikely that women from families with a history of nationalist activity would have been employed in government institutions in the first place.

rural women in dry-farming agriculture with that of refugee women in irrigated, market-oriented agriculture.

## 7.2    The camps: making ends meet

*The labour stories of Imm Sāmir and Fadwā*

Women from the camps were also involved in agriculture. Fadwā, Imm Muhammad's daughter, started working in agriculture when she was still at school, going to the Jordan Valley with her neighbour, Imm Sāmir, who at that time was responsible for a number of girls from Balata camp working there. In the summer of 1989 I talked with Imm Sāmir. Although she preferred to elaborate on her children's achievements, she related her labour story to me, pointing to the great changes refugee women have experienced.

Imm Sāmir was originally from Al-Auja (Jaffa region), an area where many settled bedouin, such as her family, were living. Her father had about 20 *dunum* of land, growing wheat and barley, and also vegetables like cabbage, cauliflower and spinach. The first major change in her life came when she was married. She had been spoiled very much in her father's house, she told me, as she was her mother's first child after four years of marriage and it took another four years before the next child was born. After she was married at fourteen she found herself in a very different situation. She had to work very hard with her husband's family because she was the first daughter-in-law in a large household and her mother-in-law was very domineering.

Whereas the heavy work load of a daughter-in-law was usually seen as temporary, part of a woman's life cycle, the 1948 disaster (*nakba*) was to have long-lasting and irreversible negative consequences. First the family fled from the coastal areas to Qalqilya, where her husband went to work in the orange groves, then to Rafidia, to the north of Nablus. By then Imm Sāmir had three children and had spent all she owned. When they were still in Al-Auja she had sold part of her dower gold (of her dower of 20 PP her father had bought her gold coins) to buy some live-stock. 'The people said to me, "you are working all the time with the cows of your in-laws, bringing them water, milking them, why don't you buy a cow yourself?" ' So she did, but when they fled everything was lost, and she had to sell the remainder of her gold to buy food and to pay for the treatment of her son when he had a severe eye problem.

By the time they reached Nablus they had nothing left. 'We went to look for work', Imm Sāmir told me, adding with emphasis, 'yes, me too; we had nothing. After the *nakba* I have always worked, until the intifada.

We started working in road construction.' When I interrupted her asking whether men and women had been working together, she said, 'There were separate work groups for men and for women, but we did the same work, I worked like a man! We filled in the roads with the stones we carried, I worked on the road to the Ittihad hospital, to the ʿAin camp. We earned the same, maybe 10 *qursh*. I did this for three or four years.' To my question why she had stopped she answered 'it became shameful', adding after my probing, 'they stopped employing women for this type of work and the municipality brought only men in'.

Then she went to work in agriculture in the Jordan Valley, picking cucumbers, eggplant, tomatoes, watermelons and so on. 'Men, women and children worked in the Jordan Valley. A man came with a car to pick us up at Balata camp, and later I became a *muʿallima*, the one responsible for fifteen to twenty girls to go and work there', Imm Sāmir said. For a while her husband held an UNRWA job, distributing rations, but it did not pay very much and he was frequently ill. He stopped working when he accompanied his two daughters who had become teachers, to work in Saudi Arabia. As one of them pointed out to me, it was her mother who had always worked, not her father.

The driving force in Imm Sāmir's life had been to ensure her children a better life. A large part of the money she earned was spent on their education. 'I wanted them to learn, to finish school', she told me repeatedly. 'My mother-in-law said to her son, "take them from school and let them work. Do you want them all to become teachers?" But I did not react to that. She had not wanted her own children to learn and she did not want mine to. But I have sent them all to school, both my sons and my daughters. I was the one who worked, the children did not. I only took them with me to the Jordan Valley in the school vacations, so they would see how tiring it is to work, and realise that it is much easier to go to school.' Indeed, only her eldest daughter did not finish school. Her other two sons and four daughters are all well-educated. With little professional employment available on the West Bank they all live abroad, either in Amman or in Saudi Arabia.

Fadwā, Imm Muhammad's daughter, elaborated further on her work with Imm Sāmir in the Jordan Valley. She had started working there when she was about twelve. 'Some of the old women worked most of the year in the Jordan Valley', she recalled. 'They did not only pick vegetables, but also did the planting, cleared the land and so on. In the summer vacations they asked school girls if they also wanted to come and work there with them.' Fadwā went with Imm Sāmir. 'A man, the owner of the land, or his agent, would come to the camp and pick us up', she said. 'We would start working before the sun was up, at four or five in the morning, and work till about twelve, because it gets very hot in the Jordan Valley. The older women picked the vegetables, they were experienced and knew best how to do this. The girls arranged the boxes and carried these to the cars. We worked five or six days and then the agent came to Balata, to the house of the *mu'allima*. He had registered how many days we had worked and called us to pick up the money.'

The girls earned much less than the elderly women, but other benefits were also important. 'Of course, the older women took more. But we did not only go there for the money, but also because they would give us vegetables. Had we sold all the vegetables that might have given us more than our wage.' Fadwā was not sure how much men earned, because their work was different. 'They do not have men picking vegetables, only women. Men cannot do it, they cannot bear to carry, to pick and to bend down, they have no patience. Only for oranges and lemons they take men, because it is high up in the trees.' She was convinced the men made considerably more.

The family kept some of the vegetables for home consumption, some was sent to friends and relatives, and if any remained this was sold. Fadwā was allowed to spend part of the money she earned on her school expenses. 'When we went back to school after the vacations, we had money for the schooluniform, the books and the notebooks.' It had been Fadwā herself who had wanted to go and work. In the beginning her parents were against it. 'They were afraid that people would see me and start talking. I told them, "All the girls go, I will be careful and not sit at the window, so people will not notice me." And I left the vegetables with someone and only brought them home after dark, so no one would see me. Nowadays it is no longer such a problem, about three-quarters of the girls have done this work. I worked because if I wanted something I had to keep asking, if I needed a book for school I would ask my father and he would say "tomorrow." The next day I would tell him that the teacher asked me to bring the book, and he would say "tomorrow." The third day he would say, "I have bought flour, I have no money left."'

Fadwā did not take her final exams because she had fallen ill. She attempted to go to nursing school, but her health was still bad, and neither was she physically able to return to work in agriculture. In the end she found a job as an assistant in a charitative clinic in Nablus, working from eight until anywhere between two and four. 'I registered the patients, and did simple things, such as renewing the bandages, giving injections and so on. I did this for some years. But I only earned 40 JD a month, and I had to spend about 15 JD for transport and maybe another 10 JD on food, if I worked late. So, that left me at the end of the month with only 15 JD. If I bought a skirt or anything I had nothing left to give my parents. It simply was not worth it.'

Then a friend suggested that she come and work with her on a small commercial farm, where yogurt and cheese were made by machine, work she had also previously done in the school vacations. Fadwā went there. 'First the owner offered me 40 JD and I refused. Then he said, "If I give you 50 JD, will you agree?" I agreed but only if they would take care of transport. After five months I asked for a raise, because there was much work. He agreed and gave me 60 JD and every year I got a raise, so in the end I was earning 90 JD. That was very good, because I had no transportation costs, and we could eat there; we only brought bread with us, and we ate cheese and the vegetables of the farm, and he gave me extra to take home with me.' Part of her wages, about half, Fadwā gave to the household. 'When I was earning 50 JD I gave 20 JD to the house, I put it in a cupboard, and if my father or mother needed it they could take it. The rest I saved and I bought gold, eleven thin bracelets of 50 JD each. I do not wear them, they are hidden for my wedding, then I will not have to spend much of my dower on gold.'

When I talked to Fadwā in the summer of 1988 she had not been working for some months. There was hardly any work at the farm, because the Israeli authorities had forbidden transport to Gaza, the major market. Yet Fadwā expected to return to her job soon. It did not turn out that way. As she told me the following year, a few months later she had been fired, receiving 180 JD as compensation for the three years she had worked there. It was very difficult to find another job. Even if she had wanted to she would not have been able to work in the Jordan Valley again. From the beginning of the intifada the local activists had warned people not to work there. 'They stopped anyone going there. There are many Arab landowners in the Jordan Valley, but also Jews, who have taken the land from the Arabs', Fadwā explained. 'We mainly worked for Arabs, but occasionally also for the Jews and sometimes an Arab would have leased the land from a Jew who had taken it from the Arabs and we worked for him. The activists think that people who go and work there may be working for the Jews, so they do not allow anyone to go there.'

When I asked her whether she had thought about working as a domestic worker in Nablus, she first compared this work with agriculture. 'Agriculture is better than working in the houses. It gives you more money and you can take your freedom. No one tells you, "do this", or "do that". They only say, "you have to finish this piece of land today". And you are with friends, you can have fun, more than when you work for a woman in her house. That only gives you 50 JD a month. The Nablus women agree amongst themselves not to pay more. Or you get 5 JD a day, like we made in the end in agriculture, but then you have to work very, very hard. They do not treat you well, not like a sister who comes to help them.'

Yet, neither did Fadwā want to be dependent on her eighteen-year old brother, the only earner in the household, regularly detained and working irregularly as a day-labourer. She had tried to make some money through a partnership with him raising chickens on the roof of the house and through petty trade. Yet, she frequently disagreed with her brother's 'investments', as he not only wanted to raise chickens, but was also spending the money to buy and sell pigeons. Neither did the petty trade she was involved in, give her much income. She would have her brother buy maybe fifty large bottles of shampoo, which she then sold in Balata with a small profit. Or she asked a friend from Egypt to bring twenty house dresses, some of which she put in a store in Balata, the owner taking a small cut, while she attempted to sell the rest herself. But with most people out of work, competition was fierce.

### Refugees: the new agriculture and other irregular work

The 1948 disaster (*nakba*) was a dramatic break in the labour stories of elderly refugee women, with the peasant and bedouin refugees losing their land and often also their live stock. During the first years of the *nakba* many of them had to sell their gold, commonly the only valuables they had brought with them, to make ends meet. Once everything had been spent, men, women and children all had to contribute to the household income. Out of sheer necessity many women did any work available during these first years. So Imm Sāmir was employed in urban road construction, which was very different from the rural construction work village women, such as Imm Khalīl, had been involved in. Women with small children and without 'working men' were in a particularly difficult situation. A friend of Imm Sāmir, for example, repudiated in the early 1950s when they were still living in tents, recalled vividly how she had to leave her small children by themselves to make some money by doing all sorts of odd jobs, such as carrying water for other camp women. Even in the camps not all were equal.

After the situation had 'settled' to some extent, and the UNRWA provided rations, tents (and later one-room dwellings), medical care and education, attempts were made to return to the 'normal' pattern of the male provider. As Imm Sāmir said, the municipality no longer employed women for road construction. Yet in many individual households things did not work out this way. Often women's work remained crucial, as is evident in the following example. Imm Mas'ūd, also living in Balata camp, had never been on particularly good terms with her husband, who was ten years older. He was a driver, but as she said 'one year he worked, three years he did not'. So, in the late 1950s, when she had four children, she decided to sell the gold she still had in order to open a small grocery shop. After school her young sons would stay in the shop, while she went to Nablus to bring groceries from the wholesalers. She also started trading in cows and goats on a small scale. As so many women in the camps, she did this all, as she said, to support her children and to give them the chance of education. And she succeeded. While she was trading in cows, her sons and daughters went to teacher training college. Once they were employed she stopped working.

Agriculture was, however, the major type of work refugee women were involved in. The Jordanian period saw a rapid growth of larger-scale, market-oriented production of vegetables and citrus in the Jordan Valley. Much of the labour was supplied by the refugees from the large camps in that area itself, yet also many of the Balata camp refugees went to work there, either as share-cropper or as day-labourer. After the Israeli occupation, development of Arab agriculture in this area was halted, with large tracts of land confiscated for Jewish settlements. There was, however, still some demand for labour from Balata camp, as during the 1967 war a large number of refugees from the Jordan Valley camps had fled to the East Bank. Whereas most men preferred working in Israel over the drudgery and humiliation of working as agricultural labourers for the large landowners of the Jordan Valley, such work remained an important source of income for the women from the camps.

Women's work in this market-oriented agriculture was very different from that of the rural Nablus women who generally worked for people from their own community, often their relatives. The latter had to operate within the constraints of the kin economy, and their work was often hard to distinguish from 'helping relatives'. In addition, their employers, would indeed have problems paying their wages, as dry-farming agriculture was largely directed towards subsistence. In the case of refugee women employed in irrigated commercial agriculture, labour relations were very different. Landowners would often send an agent who would in turn contact one of the older, experienced women from Balata camp, such as Imm Sāmir, who then would ask girls to come with her to work. The girls had no idea how much the agent made, but were convinced that he took a large cut of the pie. Still, as these refugee women were unambiguously defined as workers, they usually would earn more than village women working in dry-farming agriculture.

It is true that employment in irrigated agriculture was also largely seasonal, but for the women involved it was an important source of income, and it could make the difference between living on charity, having to ask for everything, and some autonomy and self-respect. For Fadwā it meant that she was able to go to school with dignity and self-confidence, feeling respectable and without being scorned by her teachers. To Imm Sāmir it gave the possibility to have her children learn against the wishes of her in-laws. Moreover, as these women were not only paid in cash, but also in produce, they could strengthen their own position in networks of relatives, neighbours and friends by giving them some of it. In general, secondary benefits, such as receiving food at work and having transport taken care of, could be quite important, as Fadwā's comparison between working at the dispensary and the commercial farm indicated.

The intifada brought agricultural day labour in the Jordan Valley virtually to a standstill. The national leadership had advised workers in the Israeli settlements to try to find other employment, but had not forbidden such work outright.[4] Yet, local activists strongly discouraged work in the whole Jordan Valley and stopped the vans going there. The few other opportunities left for women were either small trade or home production, the latter actively encouraged by the intifada leadership. On many rooftops people had chickens, while they also grew vegetables and occasionally raised goats. Yet feeding them could be expensive. In addition, many people had become involved in petty trade, girls often attempting to sell hairpins, shampoo, simple custom jewellery, vegetables (brought by a male relative from the wholesale market) and so on. But with so many people out of work, this was becoming very competitive, and in no way a stable source of income.

## 7.3    The stigma of serving: the destitute

*The labour story of Imm ʿAdnān*

Imm ʿAdnān had been working for four years as a cleaner in the hospital when I talked to her in the summer of 1989. She already knew about my research as we had met previously when I visited her neighbours in Balata camp. Although she first scolded me for not visiting her then, she was very friendly and cooperative in explaining to me the work she had done. As it was the tenth day of a curfew it was not very crowded in the hospital and she sat down in the kitchen to tell me about her labour history.

Imm ʿAdnān was in her mid-forties, a refugee from settled bedouin background. Her parents were from a small village near Jaffa, where her father had a little land, growing wheat, cucumbers, potatoes, and some grapes, while he also worked as a labourer in the citrus plantations for the

---

[4] The national leadership refers to the UNLU (Unified National Leadership of the Uprising), a pro-PLO committee set up in the occupied territories shortly after the start of the intifada. One of the main ways in which it communicated its positions was through the distribution of leaflets, issued as numbered communiqués.

Jews. Imm ʿAdnān recalled him telling her that in those days everything had been different; 'they were better then, it was as if we were the same people', he had often said.

When they had to leave the village with the fighting in 1948, the family first went to Qalqilya, and then on to Nablus, settling in Balata camp. At that time her father was no longer able to work. 'He was an old man. So, we, the girls, had to work, because we had nothing', Imm ʿAdnān explained. 'Our father could not bring us food. I was the eldest of four girls and two boys. Could we have let our mother go and work for us?' It was at this point that Imm ʿAdnān, who generally was a cheerful person, showed some bitterness. ʿAnd we have remained toiling up until today, our lives have been drudgery', she added.

While still very young, Imm ʿAdnān was sent to Kuwait to work as a housemaid. 'I do not know how old I was, I needed papers to go to Kuwait, but I had no birth certificate, so I had to go to a doctor and I remember he raised my age in order that I could get papers.' The people she went to work for were from a small West Bank town; both the husband and the wife were working in Kuwait as school directors. Having travelled there with them by plane Imm ʿAdnān stayed for nine months and then returned over land to spend the three months' summer vacation on the West Bank. It was not easy being separated at such a young age from her family. 'In the beginning I cried a lot, Kuwait was far away from where we were living and I was homesick.' But after some time she got used to it. When I asked her how much she earned, she said she did not know. 'My mother took half the yearly wage before I left, and then the second half after I returned. I only went and came, I did not ask. But I am sure that it was cheap, very cheap, because there was not much money and we were in need; we had left our country and had no money.'

The third year Imm ʿAdnān did not want to return to Kuwait with the family she was working for. 'I was tired of it, bored, fed up. I simply did not want to go. So, they took my sister instead. But they did not like my sister as much as me, because I obeyed them, and my sister did not get along with them. She only went for one year.' Then they made Imm ʿAdnān go back one more year, but thereafter she refused to continue working there. 'I said, "I will not stay here". It was not bad there, but I was tired of it. I felt as if I was locked up, imprisoned, and I could not go anywhere. I had been entrusted to them. They had written a paper that no harm should befall me. I was a girl and they had to protect me, they could not let me go by myself to the store or anywhere.'

Back in Balata camp she was soon married to a paternal relative, who had repudiated his first wife. Imm ʿAdnān guessed she was about eighteen when she married. Her prompt dower was 160 JD and no deferred dower was registered. Her father took the money and brought her gold, two 'pear' (*injāsa*) bracelets and eight gold Turkish (*uthmanlī*) coins. When I asked her whether she had sold her gold, she said, 'No, I never sold any of the gold. I had also brought a very nice bracelet from Kuwait. The people I worked for had been very good to me and had given me presents, money, which I saved and then they paid part of the bracelet and I paid part of it. In the Nablus market the jewellers wanted to buy it from me, but I did not agree. I want to save it for my daughters or my daughter-in-law when ʿAdnān marries.'

Her husband first worked as a labourer on the plantations in the Jordan Valley; when after the 1967 war there was no work at all, he sat for a while and then went to work in Israel, in construction, until he could not do this any longer. 'For over ten years he has not been able to work', Imm ʿAdnān said, explaining why she started to work again. 'He was ill, had an operation and is an old man now. So, I went to work and I am the one who feeds them.' When she began working she had five daughters and one son, her youngest daughter not yet in school. She had heard about work through her sister who was already working in the houses in Nablus. One day her sister told her that a relative of the woman she herself was working for had asked her to bring Imm ʿAdnān to come and work once or twice a week. So she did and when this woman asked her to work for a monthly wage, she agreed. Imm ʿAdnān said: 'When I started working for the people it was difficult, I was embarrassed and felt very uncomfortable. Slowly I got used to it. I stayed with them because they liked me very much and I obeyed them, I did as they wished. I stayed with them a long time. In the beginning I did not earn very much, but at the end I made 80 JD, and sometimes more, if they wanted me to stay longer or to work on Fridays. They also gave me extra money if another child was born and when their son returned from the United States, and at the religious feast they gave me clothing for the children.'

When this family moved to the United States, Imm ʿAdnān had to find another job. She asked for work at the hospital and was accepted. When I talked to her she was earning 107 JD a month. 'It is not enough', she said. 'Every day I have to pay 2 IS ( = almost 1 JD) for transport to Balata and we have to pay everything from my wage, water, electricity, food and clothes for the children.' Yet, she preferred the work in the hospital over that in the houses. 'You have more freedom, in the houses you are hemmed in. They might tell you "do it this way or that way" and you are not able to speak back, that would have been shameful and they would say, "if you do not like it, go away". But here I can talk back.' In answer to my question whether she had ever thought about working in Israel she simply answered that her husband would have repudiated her had she done so.

Even so, 'the people talk', said Imm ʿAdnān, 'about why I go to work and so on. Well I need the work, so what can I do? I worked when I was a girl and I worked again after I had the children. Then they got used to it, they know my husband is old, that it is necessary. That is life, there is no other option.' Yet if she started working as a young girl in order that her mother did not have to go, she herself did not want her daughters to do the same. 'I never went to school, we should have gone shortly after the *nakba*, but there were no schools, so we did not go. But my daughters have gone to school.' She also saw education as central for the future of her son. 'And ʿAdnān took his secondary school diploma, we want him to learn a profession, but there is nothing now. We wanted him to go to teacher training in Ramallah or at the Al-Najah University, but these are all closed. I do not want him to become a day-labourer, I want him to learn a trade.'

### Working as a khaddāma

Domestic service is strongly despised. When Imm Khalīl expressed her son's annoyance at her work in the hospital she said, 'He was ashamed of his mother working as a *khaddāma*, a servant.' It is this association of hospital cleaning with 'serving' which makes it suspect. Both the hospital administration and the women themselves use the English term 'cleaner' to refer to their occupation, and the women who work as domestic servants for the Nablus elite used expressions such as 'working for the people', 'working in the houses' and so on, rather than the term *khaddāma*.

That women shun domestic service has to do with the strong cultural emphasis on equality and autonomy, values Imm Khalīl expressed so emphatically in her labour story. Imm ʿAbdulrahīm also eloquently explained to me the importance of these values, by describing her reactions to the request of a man from a wealthy Nablus family, who had come to visit a relative in the hospital, and asked her indirectly whether she would not want to come and work for his family. Although, as she stressed, it was only a small household with all amenities available, and she would earn more, she had felt very uncomfortable and had told him that she was not able to go and work in the houses. Reflecting on this episode she said: 'I work in my own house why don't they do the same? You are the one who makes it dirty, so you ought to clean it. No one wants to give up her dignity [*karāma*], or would accept to be ordered around.' At that moment Mājida, a young politically active nurse from a camp, interrupted her saying, 'I support working whenever possible. It is wrong to remain sitting and say "I do not have"; working is good, also for your personality. But it is true, working in the houses is a very sensitive issue. You want to keep your dignity. Working in the houses you are seen as a *khādima*, not as a human being who works. But in the hospital and in other institutions they consider you as a worker [*shaghghīla*]. A worker remains independent, she works because she wants to work. But a *khādima*; they shout at her.' When I asked an elderly elite woman who referred to the woman cleaning her house as *shaghghīla*, why she did not use the term *khaddāma*, she said, 'We never talk about her as *khaddāma*, then it is as if she has to serve you, as if you are her master, that you are better, that you have deeper roots than she has. But a *shaghghīla* has set working hours, like an employee. She does her work and she goes; a servant has to come whenever you want. And the language used is different. A servant gets orders, "do this", "clean that", "carry this"; a servant is never finished, always has to be available.' Another elite woman, explaining why women preferred to clean in schools rather than in private houses, pointed out that 'Even if she only cleans in a school she can call herself employee [*muwaththafa*], she feels that she is not a *khaddāma*.' Indeed, many cleaners in institutions would point out that they were employees (*muwaththafāt*).

The emphasis on equality may well be even more outspoken among women than among men. After all, men are obliged to maintain their family and for that reason might have to suffer humiliation at work. In the case of women, on the other hand, working for money is neither legally required nor socially expected of them. And although the women who work as cleaners often have no other option and do so to survive, if they really get fed up they will withdraw from the labour market and return to dependence on kin or charity. During the intifada, with many households in a very difficult financial situation, institutions still complained that they had trouble finding female cleaners, while they had no problem finding men. Women strongly stress that what they want is respect. They are very sensitive to a condescending attitude towards them and would often complain more about the way in which they were treated than about their wages. As Imm ʿAbdulrahîm said, 'If somebody asks me something politely, in a friendly way, I will do whatever they want. But if someone wants to order me around, even if they gave me a bag full of money, I would not accept it. If the director does not answer my greetings and turns his head away, I will not return his greetings. He does not give me charity, I earn my money with my own sweat. He does not pay me out of his own pocket. If he respects me, I respect him.'

Whereas working for an institution everyone is an employee (and in that sense even men and women are equal) and hospital cleaners also underline the social and, with the intifada, the national aspects of their work, domestic service is regarded as the most difficult labour relation for women. Working as a servant continuously reinforces social hierarchy in a direct and unmediated way. Being ordered around, shouted at, without being able to speak back is what these women detested most. Many domestic workers criticised their employers for not cleaning their houses themselves and virtually expected them to partake in some of the work. The employers I spoke to always pointed out that they would help their cleaners, which, in some cases, they actually did. Perhaps Fadwā expressed best the importance of equality in her complaint 'they do not treat you like a sister'.

### The history of working in the houses

These sensitivities about domestic labour also ought to be seen in its historical context, the tradition among the wealthy of having slave women as domestic servants.[5] This relation between service and slavery was still vividly alive in the minds of the people. Some elderly elite women recalled their grandmothers in Ottoman times having black female slaves; one of them told me how her mother had virtually been raised by her grandmother's black slave.

When elderly wealthy women talked to me about their youth and how housework was organised during the mandatory period, they often pointed to the help they had at home. They would be very careful not to call these women 'slaves', yet in attempting to explain the labour relations to me they often described these as 'they were like slaves.' In those days it had not been uncommon for poor rural families to offer a son or daughter in service to wealthy urbanites for a certain amount of money and a set period of time. Some elite women elaborated on how their family had cared for such a girl 'as if she were a daughter' and how she had refused to return to her own family once she had realised that 'they had sold her'. Many of these 'servants' were from the Jordan Valley. Poor urban women, on the other hand, tended to avoid domestic service.

If in the mandatory period it was women from the rural areas who worked as servants, this changed when after 1948 the refugees came to the West Bank. The refugee women, in dire need, often went to work in the urban households of the better-off. Some of them did so as living-in help, but many also as day cleaners. In contrast to rural women, who had to face the problem of transportation, they were able to travel daily as the camps were located at the edges of the city. As a result the pattern of 'selling girls

---

[5] In eighteenth-century marriage contracts of girls from well-off backgrounds, slaves were sometimes included in the dower (Tucker 1988: 170). For the position of female slaves in nineteenth-century Egypt, see Tucker 1985: 164ff.

into service' took on another form. Whereas few rural women were still
'sold into service' in Nablus, some young girls from the camps were sent
to work in Kuwait, usually on yearly contracts. Many of them, like Imm
ʿAdnān, went to work there because their family was destitute, for this
work was generally despised. This was brought home to me when Fadwā
told me about Imm Sāmir's eldest daughter. If her younger brothers and
sisters were all educated, the eldest, as Fadwā said, 'had sacrificed her
future for their sake, working for years in Kuwait as a housemaid'. This
was something Imm Sāmir herself, who had not hesitated to discuss her
own work in road construction with me, had never told me about. Yet,
poverty was not always the only incentive. Imm Rubhī, also living in
Balata camp, underlined that in her case family circumstances were also
important. Explaining how she went to work in Kuwait in the early 1960s
she said: 'Many girls were working there at the time. I wanted to go
because my mother had died and my father had married another wife; she
made me work very hard and I wanted to leave.' And if Imm ʿAdnān was at
least allowed to keep the gifts she received, this was not so in the case of
Imm Rubhī. 'The money was given to my father', she said. 'In those days
the fathers took it, they liked money.' The pair of bracelets her employer,
a wealthy Kuwaiti family, had bought her at the religious feast, her father
also took away when she returned home to Balata camp, homesick, after
ten months working in Kuwait. She received the gold back when she was
married; as the women in her family still used to wear coins in those days,
her father sold the bracelets and bought her coins. But he then kept her
dower in order to pay the dower for a bride for her brother.

While working in the houses was quite common for women from the
camps during the Jordanian period, after the Israeli occupation many of
them gave up this type of work. With more employment for men available
in Israel, the standard of living increased sufficiently for their wives and
daughters to quit their cleaning jobs. To the dismay of their Nablusi
employers, some of the women who had no male provider went to work as
cleaners in Israel. As a result, wages for day cleaners in Nablus rose
considerably and in 1987 a cleaner could earn about 5 JD a day.[6] Although
in itself not very much, this sum compared favourably with the monthly
wages of 40–50 JD a starting hospital cleaner, garment worker or private
secretary might earn. Even so, the elite had trouble finding domestic
workers. They would complain that these women had forgotten their

[6] This amount remained more or less constant through 1988 and 1989, while the JD
devaluated considerably. Many camp women complained that the Nablus women were
taking advantage of the fact that with the intifada their employment opportunities had
become severely limited and working in the houses was one of the few types of
employment still available.

homeland and went to work in Israel not only to earn more, but also as work there was much easier. Still, in the end the employers agreed that what mattered most to women working in the houses was respect. But their interpretations of whether they were, indeed, shown respect could differ radically from the opinions of the cleaners themselves.

## 7.4 Crossing all boundaries: earning a living in Israel

### The labour stories of Imm Jamāl and Firyāl

Imm Jamāl, in her mid-forties, a neighbour and close friend of Imm Muhammad's daughter-in-law, was one of the first women who did not hesitate to discuss her work in Israel with me. When I met her in the summer of 1988 she was very distraught and immediately started talking about the problems she had been confronted with. Later she introduced me to her mother and younger single sister, both of whom had also worked in Israel.

Imm Jamāl's mother had actually been the first to work there. An elderly woman of over sixty-five, she was most matter-of-fact about her work in Israel. She was originally from the village of Kafr Saba. Her father had passed away when she was still very small and she had been raised by her father's brother. When she was twelve he had married her to a virtually landless distant relative, who worked as an agricultural labourer. Her husband had registered one of the two *dunum* of land he owned as her dower and had also given her some gold. When in 1948 they fled from Kafr Saba, first to Qalqilya and later to Nablus and Balata, she already had four children; Imm Jamāl was the eldest.

To Imm Jamāl's mother the flight from their native village was obviously the major break in her life story. 'You think life was then as it is now?' she exclaimed. 'In our village people did not work, they only worked the land. We grew wheat and watermelons and tomatoes and so on. In the past you took from the land and ate from it, they did not take money.' To her it was not so much the possession of land – they had owned very little – but being part of a community with the ability to feed itself from the land, be it through share-cropping or agricultural labour, that counted.

After the flight her husband worked again as an agricultural labourer, but now 'for strangers' in the Jordan Valley; later the whole family became engaged in share-cropping without much success. After the Israeli occupation her husband went to work in Israel, but when his health deteriorated, he stopped working and stayed at home. Then she herself went to work in Israel. 'It was two, maybe three years after the war that they started to register people for work in Israel', she said. 'All the women went to work there, my husband was ill and I still had three daughters at home. We had no men to pay for us, we had to fend for ourselves.'

At her first job in a fruit juice factory in Hadera, she only worked for four months. Then she found work as a cleaner in a hospital in Raʾanana. 'Work in the hospital is better, the wage is better, the work is much more quiet and you can move around', she explained. 'In the factory we sat at a conveyor belt and did not move. And our hands would get burned because they put stuff on the fruit to ripen it and that bites into your hands.' Imm Jamāl's mother remained employed in the same hospital for some eleven years. Then, sixty-five years old, she was retired, but she did not receive compensation, because she had not worked 'officially' but 'through an agent'. Explaining the difference to me she said: 'An agent brings the workers and takes the money; he gives us as he wishes. If you work officially you get the check from the hospital directly.' Apparently Israeli state institutions commonly worked with agents contracting unregistered (illegal) labour from the occupied territories.

For Imm Jamāl's mother, work had been important to be able to feed the family, but she had not managed to improve her situation much. 'From the work I did not even buy a dress', she emphasised. 'All of it is gone for the house. No, I did not build, it was just for our food and costs of living. We had no men to pay for us, we paid for ourselves and for my daughters. First things first.'

Imm Jamāl herself, having few personal recollections of the situation before 1948, showed much more reluctance about working in Israel than her mother. As the whole family was involved in share-cropping in the Jordan Valley, she never attended school. In the late 1950s, about fifteen years old, she was married to a man also originally from Kafr Saba. He worked as a plasterer in Nablus and the surrounding villages and they lived in Balata camp in the one room hut build by the UNRWA. When in 1973, after fifteen years of marriage, her husband died of a heart disease, she had to face the major crisis in her life. Left with four small sons and one daughter, the youngest only eight months old, she was confronted with a very taxing situation. 'I was five months pregnant and had only small children, but nobody came to feed us. My husband had no brothers and no father's brothers. Only his paternal cousins [awlād ʿamm] gave us something, three Israeli lira. "For the children", as they pointed out. But I did not want to take that, I was afraid it would lead to problems with their wives; they did not have much, and I did not want to take from it.'

Her own family, although unable to help her financially, did not put pressure on her to remarry. 'My mother felt sorry for the children', she explained. Dearly wanting to keep her children, Imm Jamāl was, however, faced with the problem that her husband had not left her any money 'not even enough to bury him'. So after she had spent her dower gold, she told her brother that she wanted to go and work. 'He said, "what, you want to work in Israel, what will the people say?" I said, "why do you say that, I want to work, I want to eat."' As her brother, who was in bad health and had a family of his own to take care of, was obviously not able to maintain her and her six children, Imm Jamāl did not heed his words and went to look for work. 'There were already women working in Israel, so I asked some of them to help me find a job. In the beginning it was very, very difficult. I felt myself very small when I went there. Everyone who saw me knew I was going to work, that is shameful. I wanted to hide my face, I felt very uncomfortable and was almost crying. But then many women went to work there.'

Imm Jamāl started working in a textile factory in Holon. But the pay was bad, so two years later she went to the labour exchange to ask for another job, telling them that the money she made was not sufficient for a widow with small children who want to eat. Ironically, she was then sent to work in a hospital in the village in which she had been born (renamed Kfar Saba in Hebrew). She worked there as a cleaner for fourteen years. Her work hours were from six in the morning until two in the afternoon, and she spent an additional two hours travelling to work and another two returning to Balata camp. About the work routine, she said: 'There were two women cleaning each ward, both Jews and Arabs. I worked for a long time with a Jewish woman from Yemen, we talked half in Hebrew and half in Arabic. In the end we (the West Bank women) made good money, we reached seven or eight million. But we did a lot of overtime, we often worked twenty-six days, and also on Saturdays. And when they had their feast, Pesach, they asked us to stay there overnight for four days to work in the evening too. But when we wanted one day off because it was our feast and our relatives would come and visit us, they shouted at us.'

Having started to work when the youngest was only eight months old, Imm Jamāl had not been able to take care of her children. They were virtually raised by her younger sister. It was to her that Imm Jamāl gave the money she earned. 'Part of my wages she spent on food and such things, and part of it she saved for me', she said, adding, 'she encouraged me to improve the one room we had. She suggested to have electricity installed and later we built another room.' A few years ago, Imm Jamāl further extended the house; when her neighbours moved, she bought one of their rooms and the kitchen for 1,000 JD. 'That was all from my work, I had the house built and I have married my sons', said Imm Jamāl to emphasise the importance of her work.

After taking care of Imm Jamāl's children for over ten years, her sister, at that time in her late twenties and still single, also went to work in Israel.

By then Imm Jamāl had already married her eldest son so his wife could take care of the household. 'I married him young, when he was eighteen, to my brother's daughter so with a daughter-in-law to do the housework we could open our own house', Imm Jamāl explained. Her two daughters she had taken from school in the fifth grade to help her sister with housework. 'They had to, could I work from four till four and also do all the work at home?'

After fourteen years of cleaning Imm Jamāl was increasingly bothered by her back and found that the overseers were becoming very difficult. This came to a climax when she got into an argument with one of them and, feeling abused, quit the same day, even though by resigning she might lose her rights to compensation. Then she went to work in a hospital in Petah Tikva where her sister was already working. That only lasted for a few months, until the beginning of the intifada. Then local activists strongly discouraged women from working in Israel, advising them to work in the local hospitals instead. After many women had been warned personally and a few had been physically attacked, Imm Jamāl left her work in Israel and went to work in the kitchen of a hospital in Nablus. But wages there were very low. 'Here you only take very little, there I made over 150 JD, here only 60 JD. Imagine, 60 JD, what is that for a woman with a family, who carries responsibility? And I also had to pay transport costs from it.' Also the work conditions were much worse. 'There is so much poverty here in the hospital and the wards are very full. In the kitchen there was not even ventilation.' After two months she left, as, in her words, 'it was not worth it'.

Comparing work in Israel with that in the local hospital there was something else she did not like. 'In Israel the doctors, the nurses and the cleaners were the same, and there were rules and regulations, you knew what you had to do and they did not make any differences between us. Here you are never done. They shout at you and if you sit down they ask "don't you have to work?"' If Imm Jamāl emphasised the patronising attitude the cleaners often encountered in the Nablus hospitals, this did not mean that there were no problems working in Israel. Pointing to the discrimination she had experienced there, Imm Jamāl said: 'Working in Israel was very hard. They wanted us to work three times as hard as the Jewish women and we earned less. And we had to leave home at four and returned at four. Then there could be a curfew and the soldiers would ask you where you had been, where you were going, from where you were coming, and we had to sit in the sun and wait and wait and wait.'

When I talked to Imm Jamāl in 1988 she was very tense and upset. She had become dependent on her sons to bring in money, who, because of the numerous curfews and strike days, 'worked one day and missed ten days'.

None of them had been able to set up an independent household. The wife of her eldest son had recently left the house 'in a state of anger', because her husband wanted to take a second wife, something Imm Jamāl strongly disagreed with. He did not love his first wife and felt his mother had forced him into that marriage. As five years ago her second son had been imprisoned for twenty years, Imm Jamāl was in fact dependent on the two younger ones, who each gave her 50 JD a month. One of them had recently married a girl Imm Jamāl originally disapproved of, but in the end accepted, as she did not want the same trouble as with her eldest son. To make things worse, her eldest daughter was living in such an impoverished situation with her three small children that they spent a lot of time at her mother's house. Adding to this the general strain of the intifada, Imm Jamāl was indeed under great stress. In the summer of 1989, when I visited Imm Jamāl again, her situation had further deteriorated, and she had sent her younger daughter to work at the local hospital.

If Imm Jamāl, her mother and her sister all had started working in Israel when they were older, some girls began working there at a very young age. Firyāl, for instance, twenty years old when I talked to her, had by then already worked for almost eight years in Israel. Her parents were from the Jaffa region, from bedouin origin, and she was the eldest of ten children. After she had gone to school for about five years, she was sent to work in Israel, aged twelve. 'It was because of the circumstances', she explained. 'My father was poor, he worked here and there, he had no skill, he was no painter, no plasterer or anything. And my mother did not like to ask this one and that one for money. So I said, it is better that I will go and work.' It is unlikely that Firyāl had much choice. Actually, her mother had worked in Israel, but she was in poor health, suffering from severe hypertension. So when the first child, Firyāl, was old enough to work, her mother stopped.

Firyāl first worked in a food processing factory in Ramat Gan, peeling grapefruits and breaking them into small pieces. Her young age was no problem. 'They pretended that I was older', she recalled. 'I wore shoes with high heels and a long dress and I started to work. Some girls were even younger than me. We all had to work.' After five years she left. By then she strongly disliked her work, a dislike which expressed itself through eating disorders. 'I had started to eat only salt and lemons, a glass of water with salt and lemon. I had become as thin as a little finger. My father was afraid that I would fall ill, and they sent us away.' Then Firyāl worked for about three and a half years in the same hospital in Kfar Saba where Imm Jamāl had worked. This work she liked better. 'In the factory you could not move, you had to stay standing and the machines were dangerous, you could get injured. In the hospital we could take a shower and change, the food was better and the wages also. There I made five million, and they gave us presents at the Pesach feast, that never happened in the factory.'

When I asked her why people said it was shameful for a woman to work in Israel, Firyāl said, defending herself, 'Look at my uncle's wife, she says it is shameful. First she worked there herself and then she says that about us. But everybody went to work there. If a girl does not have brothers who are working, and her father is the only one to work, then she helps her father a little. If our father works alone, that is not enough to raise us, to bring what is needed. It is necessary that we help our father. I do not know, but if a girl is honourable [sharīfa], if she goes and comes honourably, then no one is smarter than she is. When my uncle's wife said it is shameful, I told her, "Your husband pays for you. But my father, he has no skill, every day he works somewhere else."' Also Firyāl stopped working in Israel after the intifada when the local activists had ordered them to do so, and went to work in a Nablus hospital. This also influenced what she did with the money she earned: 'First I took the money and bought everything for the house, and clothing for myself. Now, that I have stopped working in Israel, I do not buy anything for myself; I have enough. We need the money for the household, for electricity, for water, for gas and for bread. My father cannot pay it all himself. He has tired himself for us, let us now tire ourselves for him. Who else would help my father? No one.' She expressed her impression about working in the local hospital in one sentence: 'Here they do not know how to say "thank you".'

### The discourse on gender and morality

As statements by Imm Khalīl and Imm ʿAdnān indicate, women's work in Israel is highly controversial. This was also brought home to me in my first attempts to locate women working in Israel. A close friend, a free-lance journalist from Nablus, whom I asked for help, told me about her own difficulties in interviewing these women. It had been a quite unnerving experience to her; their language was intermingled with an undertone of sarcasm towards urban women and some of them had virtually refused to speak to her. Women activists from the camp itself, who had been very helpful to me, were quite negative about women working in Israel and hardly had any personal contact with them. Only through my relation with Imm Muhammad in the camp and through the hospital was I able to meet them 'on their own terms'.

Male labour in Israel has also not been uncontested. In the first years of the Israeli occupation the rapid increase of men from the occupied territories going to work in Israel had set off a debate in the PLO on what stance to take on this issue.[7] When by 1973 about half the West Bank labour force was working in Israel, the question had more or less resolved itself. Their presence there was legitimised through arguments centering around the negative impact of the Israeli occupation on the West Bank economy and the obligations these men have to provide for their families. If in the beginning of the intifada the national leadership called upon workers to stop working in Israel, this position was soon modified and they were only requested to stay away from work on general-strike days (Hiltermann 1991b: 147). While in Balata camp local activists occasionally enforced general-strike days by preventing workers to go to their jobs, they never attempted to stop them from working there altogether. Women, however, were already strongly discouraged from working in Israel before the intifada. Once the intifada had gained momentum, local activists put those who had not 'voluntarily' refrained from going there under very strong pressure, including occasional physical violence. Although the intifada leadership never specifically asked women to stop working in Israel, neither were these local activists rebuked.

Why is women's work in Israel such a sensitive issue? The answers given point to how gender and morality are intertwined. It is true that higher-class Nablus women often simply followed the line of thought of their male counterparts who had lost their workers to Israel. 'These women go and work there and forget their homeland because the work there is much easier and they earn more', was a much given answer. Yet, arguments usually were more gender-specific. A woman was perceived to have less of an excuse than a man to go and work in Israel, as only a man is, after all, obliged to provide for his family. A young activist from a better-off camp family put this in a rather blunt way, stating: 'Women do not have to work there, they have men who can provide for them. And if they really are in need they can always turn to charity.' In such strong wordings few adult camp women would accept this, knowing from close experience how unreliable and painful dependence on charity could be. Yet, many did indeed distinguish between those who were 'really forced to go and seek work there', such as female heads of households, and those,

---

[7] Sahar Khalifa's novel *Al-Subbār* (1976; trans. Wild Thorns) elaborates on this theme. One of the main characters of the book is an activist returning to the West Bank to blow up the buses which transport workers from the West Bank to Israel. Khalifa vividly describes how such a perspective in fact strengthens the position of the Palestinian upper classes. While the wealthy themselves maintain trading relations with Israel, they criticise the poor, when they try to escape the exploitation and humiliation by their local employers, for going to work in Israel.

'whose fathers or brothers hang around all day, sit in coffeehouses or even drink alcohol, letting their daughters and sisters work in Israel'. The first category they would defend even if they themselves would not consider ever going to work in Israel. In the latter case the bad reputation of their male relatives also reflected on the girls themselves.

The commonly held view was not only that women had less valid reasons to go and work in Israel, but that they also put themselves into greater moral danger. Elderly women, such as Imm Khalīl, often expressed their dislike of men and (younger) women working together, as this might lead to romantic involvements. This ties in with the cultural emphasis on the need to curtail women's freedom of movement to avoid such relations, which were seen as undermining the social order. If women's work outside the village was often frowned upon and seen as a loss of control of the village, how much more compromising their labour in Israel would be, where Palestinians felt completely powerless? Here the integrity of the Palestinian community was at stake, with women's work in Israel signalling its potential destruction. As younger girls were seen as especially vulnerable, they were particularly condemned.

Yet not only the morality of women working in Israel was brought in discredit, their politics were also suspect, in particular, but not only, amongst activists. Often moral decay and collaboration were seen as two sides of the same coin. On the one hand, when I asked about the background of women working in Israel, I was often told that many of them or their relatives were collaborators. On the other hand, 'fallen women' were seen as easy targets for the Israeli authorities to recruit as informers. Zāhir, a well-educated activist, pointed out that the problem was not that men and women worked together in Israel, as she herself did so in Balata camp, but that 'these women would get into contact with men who were morally suspect, who would drink alcohol and use drugs, who might be collaborators and take advantage of them'. Rumours abounded about attempts of the secret police to place people in compromising situations to blackmail them into collaboration. Many variants exist. One very common rumour was that of young women going to a hair-dressing salon, being drugged and then photographed in compromising situations by collaborators in order to recruit them as informants.[8]

---

[8] In 1989 the written confession of an informer was widely available in Nablus. Recruited as a young boy by the Israeli secret service, he admitted that he had drugged and videotaped numerous girls in compromising situations to blackmail them into collaboration. Not willing to cooperate nor being able to bear the shame, one of these girls committed suicide and the case became publicly known as she explained her reasons in a note to her family. Some doubt, however, the authenticity of this account. See also Harlow (1990) for a comment on these themes in fiction.

*Working in Israel: the women involved*

Whereas some argued that women working in Israel were often from a 'collaborating background', my interviews indicate that many women working there were from ordinary nationalist families. In fact, it could well be the imprisonment of a son or brother which contributed to impoverishment, such as in the case of Imm Jamāl, making it imperative for them to continue working there.

Female workers in Israel always pointed to dire poverty as the incentive to go and work in Israel. Imm Jamāl stands as just one case of a poor widow with small children and no relatives to maintain her. Her mother is one of the less numerous cases of married women, working because her husband was unable to provide for the household. Firyāl is one of those young girls who went to work in Israel to help her family, often the eldest in a large household, having left school at an early age and functionally illiterate.

While poverty was an important motive, there are also many poor women who did not go and work in Israel. In the Nablus region location was an important factor, as virtually only women from the larger refugee camps did so. If for uneducated women from the villages it was already very difficult to go and work in Nablus, it was virtually inconceivable for them to work in Israel. In the camps, on the other hand, a larger number of men worked in Israel, and transport was available for women to travel in groups. One of the points the women themselves consistently emphasised was that it became easier for them to work in Israel once many women followed that course. This condition was met most easily in the larger camps.

Still, also in the camps poverty did not explain everything and there were different work patterns, tying in with generation, life cycle, family background and so on. To Imm Jamāl's mother, the flight had been the major disaster and working in Israel was not such an issue. Imm Jamāl had been very hesitant to go and work there and would never have wanted her daughter to take her place. Firyāl, on the other hand, replaced her mother when she was unable to continue working there. As in many families more than one woman worked in Israel, also the processual aspect plays a role. Once the first step was taken, it was apparently not so difficult to take the next, and the rewards could be considerable. For if in Israel these women were discriminated against both in wage level and in treatment as workers from the occupied territories, they were paid better and, according to many of them, treated better than in Nablus.

With the intifada women were not only prevented by local activists from going to work there, but also their own perceptions about this work changed to some extent. Some of the girls who were working at the local hospital after having been employed for a considerable time in Israel told me that it was indeed better to work 'for your own people'. While they perhaps did so to emphasise to me and other audiences that they were indeed good Palestinians, some of them had been strongly affected by the intifada and even girls from non-political families had become rapidly politicised. Khitām, for example, who had worked together with her sister for six years in Israel, experienced within the first six months of the intifada one brother being imprisoned, another brother shot and a third brother thoroughly beaten up in a nightly raid at their house. 'Before there were problems between us and the Jews, my friends said to me that work there was good and I went with them', she reflected. 'Then the intifada started, and when I saw the Jews beating my brothers, I stopped loving them like before. In the beginning I did not mind, I said that the Jews were good. But when they beat my brothers, I did not want to go there any more.' As arbitrary violence was one of the characteristics of army action, shooting with live ammunition into crowds could kill even collaborators or their relatives. Still, these girls resented their work in the local hospital. There was of course the wage differential. They often earned about a third of what they had made in Israel. Yet also important was the way they felt they were treated by the administration and staff. If women who had previously worked as domestic servants emphasised the freedom they experienced working for a local institution, these girls with work experience in Israel felt very much looked down upon by the local hospital staff.

### 7.5    Poor women, owners of property?

For poor, uneducated women from virtually propertyless households, paid labour was crucial in order to acquire income and sometimes property. Yet the local construction of gender interfered with their access to paid employment. Men's success as provider is fundamentally questioned if their wives, daughters, sisters or mothers work in lower-status jobs, obviously to earn a living.

Still, women work for money. In relating their labour stories, these women elaborated extensively on how they had no option but to go and work because of dire poverty. Married women or widows underlined that they had to do so in order to feed their children; single girls that they 'sacrificed' to help their destitute parents. In this way they underlined other elements central in their gender identity and, in fact, legitimised their actions by adhering to another central value, household autonomy. Whereas they never even hinted at wanting to be less dependent on their husbands or fathers, they did express, however, a strong dislike of having to depend on other kin or charity. Both Imm Khalīl and Imm Jamāl, for example, preferred to work rather than wait for the gifts of their own or their late husband's relatives. Girls like Firyāl, went to work so their father would not have to depend on charity, while Fadwā did so in order not be scorned at school. Sometimes, women actually preferred the less respectable types of work, rural women coming to the city as cleaners and women from the camps working in Israel. With the control of women's freedom of movement seen as essential to maintain the social order, in particular if women worked far away from their kin or community, their respectability was in doubt. Yet such work was often financially advantageous and may also place them in a work environment in which they felt better treated.

If women often point to poverty as the incentive to start working, many of their life stories also relate to some form of loss they had experienced, affecting them both economically and emotionally. They had often lost a parent at a very young age, which was to strongly influence their life courses. Without a father a girl may be raised by her father's brother, who may marry her at a young age, sometimes to his son with virtually no dower or in another disadvantageous marriage. Had she lost her mother, she might be living with her father's new wife, a relation which often led to problems, and again to either an early marriage or a flight into paid labour. Another form of loss was suffered by women who had become widowed; they suddenly had to do without the provider for the household. These widows would often first sell their dower gold and then turn to paid labour.

It was, however, not only these personal losses that counted. For many refugee women, the major loss in their lives was the homeland. Rural and bedouin women lost land and animals and during the first years after the disaster they were often forced to sell their gold in order to survive. Yet not only the economic side of this loss was important. The sense of loss of community this entailed may have insulated women to some extent against the consequences of breaking social norms, such as engaging in wage labour. This is indicated by the story of Imm Jamāl's mother.

The material effects of women's paid employment were quite different for younger girls and widowed mothers. The strong cultural emphasis on the male provider made it difficult for a father to take a girl's full wage, as it would be such an obvious indication of his failure as provider. So, unless they were 'sold in service' girls were often allowed to keep part of the wage themselves, which they commonly used to buy clothes or which they saved for buying gold, while what they handed over to their family at least gave them the sense of 'being able to give'. The influence of employment on their marriage options was ambiguous. On the one hand it was easier for these girls to refuse a husband they did not want, to postpone marriage, and occasionally they even married a co-worker they had met at work (which no doubt, further raised suspicions about the morality of these girls). On the other hand, a father might prevent his daughter from marrying, because he did not want to part with the income she provided him with. In regard to the dower, lower-status employment did not have a positive effect; on the contrary, their dower might well be lower than the average among the poor.

To widowed mothers, income from labour was crucial. Whether it was more than a means of survival depended on the nature of the employment. If they worked in agriculture their wages were usually hardly sufficient for the bare necessities of life. Only the more enterprising, such as the *mu'allima* Imm Sāmir, managed to better their situation. The women working as institutional cleaners, on the other hand, were often able to substantially improve their standard of living. This was not the case only if they worked in Israel; when they were employed in Nablus institutions and had seniority they could also earn relatively well.

Most of these widows spent their money in a way similar to what they would have expected of their late husbands: it was invested in improving the house and occasionally in buying olive trees or goats; it was spent on the wedding of a son, on helping him to start a small business, and, in particular in the camps, also on education. Imm Jamāl managed to expand her house from one very basic, small room to a three-room dwelling with water and electricity installed. Imm Khalīl had helped her youngest son to marry by paying his dower. Imm Hassan, having worked at the local hospital for eighteen years, in the end earning 184 JD a month, had saved a considerable sum of money. With great pride she summed up her achievements: 'We first only had one room, it did not even have a decent door. Every time I had saved some money we built. Now the house has a lower and an upper floor, with a good staircase; it is tiled and has a bathroom inside. We also planted some olive trees, and I registered the land for my sons. Everything from my work.' After having established a base for the household she then helped one of her sons with the costs of marriage and continued to spend most of her money on him. 'His health is very weak, he has a simple job in a local shoe factory and has two sons and one daughter. I want to support him until his children are grown', she said.

For a widow to improve the situation of her sons was very important, as she strongly identified with them and expected to depend on them in her old age. Still, some felt a tension between keeping some money for themselves as security and improving their situation through her sons.

This Imm Khalīl made evident in her hesitation about what to do with the money she would receive as compensation, to keep it in a bank or to help her son build a room. In general, however, widows spent little on themselves. Only about widows without sons was it rumoured that they had considerable sums of money.

Not only sons but also daughters may benefit from their mothers' labour. Just as women stood a greater chance to receive property if they inherited from female testators, employed mothers also supported their daughters in specific ways. Imm Khalīl, for example, intended to buy her divorced daughter some gold, and both Imm Sāmir and Imm Masʿūd paid for the education of their daughters.[9] Yet, whereas some women were able to improve their daughters' future prospects, this was much more difficult for those working very long working hours, such as women working in Israel, who were commonly absent for over twelve hours. As such work was impossible to combine with taking care of children, it was often their older daughters who had to pay the price, being taken out of school at a young age and placed in charge of their younger siblings.

Turning to historical trends, the number of women involved in dry-farming agricultural wage labour and in domestic service has decreased. With the most abject poverty alleviated, women tend to avoid this type of work. Some of them totally refrained from wage labour as their fathers, husbands or sons were in a better position to maintain them. Others managed to finish school and succeeded in finding better work. Those who were really in need of work and had hardly any schooling increasingly found their way either to local urban institutions or to Israel. Yet, with the intifada this process came to a halt, and more women had to turn to domestic work again.

[9] Jansen (1987) writing about 'women without men' in urban Algeria makes two observations which are very similar to widow's strategies in Jabal Nablus. First, some of these widows also prefer to cross gender boundaries (and engage in less respectable forms of employment) as this often means better pay (1987: 245); secondly, they tend to use their income in order to push their daughters towards a more respectable career (1987: 240).

# 8    Gender and garment production

If many women left agricultural labour and domestic service after the occupation, at the same time the sewing trade has attracted a large number of lower-class West Bank women.[1] These women reject the idea of going to work in Israel, even if they could earn there considerably more. Their labour is, however, directly linked to the Israeli economy, as most West Bank clothing producers have become subcontractors to Israeli firms.

Developments in garment production on the West Bank are reminiscent of the global process of restructuring and relocation.[2] As little capital is needed to set up a workshop, the sector is generally characterised by ease of entry and intense competition, with low labour costs and high flexibility crucial for profitability (Rainnie 1984: 146). Historically, the garment sector has been marked by a division between manufacturers who perform all steps of the production process (from designing to marketing) and 'outside shops' sewing ready cut garments received from a jobber and returning the finished product to him (Lamphere 1979: 258). When it became possible to separate designing/marketing and production on a global scale, the most labour intensive parts of the production process were relocated to the South where a more abundant supply of compliant, flexible and low cost labour was at hand (Fröbel et al. 1980; Rhodes et al. 1983; Morokvasic et al. 1986). In most subcontracting firms, the large majority of the workers are women. These women are not preferred as workers because of their innate natural qualities, but rather because existing asymmetries in gender relations define them as highly productive, docile and cheap workers (Phillips and Taylor 1980; Elson 1983). More recently, some garment production has returned to the North, as

---

[1] Part of this chapter has previously been published as Moors (1989). It is largely based on fieldwork conducted in Nablus in 1987. I would like to thank Randa Siniora, who did research on women in the clothing industry on the West Bank, for lending me her unpublished MA thesis (later published as Siniora 1989). The statistical data on women workers are from a survey of ninety female garment workers by the Committee of Working Women in Nablus (CWW) and from my own interviews with twenty women garment workers.

[2] For developments in the Gaza Strip, see Rockwell (1985).

190

with increased unemployment and migration less expensive labour is again available, while quicker changes in fashion and a shorter cycle of trends induce shops to demand very short delivery times and small volume (De la Torre 1984). Production is adapted to flexible demand through subcontracting with homeworkers and small local firms, often run by migrants (Mitter 1986).

Nablus has a long tradition of garment production and is still a centre of the garment trade, yet the structure of Nablus clothing production and the composition of the labour force have fundamentally changed after the Israeli occupation.[3] The labour stories of three women are presented in this chapter. All are involved in the production of clothing but take up very different positions in the production process. Their individual experiences are placed within the context of the structural transformation of the trade and the new gender division of labour. Women's interpretations of these developments vary considerably, depending on their particular background and position. If to some, these changes have meant the demise of a skilled profession, to others industrial sewing is the best option available to gain an income. At the end of the chapter the implications of these shifts for the women-property nexus are drawn.

## 8.1    Producing garments: three labour stories

### Sitt ʿAfāf: artisanal tailoring in decline

When I visited Sitt ʿAfāf she was busy finishing a dress by hand. In her early sixties, she lived together with her aged mother in the somewhat dilapidated family home in the old city of Nablus. Frequently referring to the decline of the sewing trade, she was still very proud of her work as a seamstress and took her time to talk to me at great length about her experiences in the trade.

Born as the eldest of seven children into an old respectable Nablus family of modest means, Sitt ʿAfāf recalled her father, who had worked as a police officer for the British, as a very strict man. After she had finished the seventh grade, he did not allow her to continue her studies although she had been the best student of her class. Still, she did not resent this very much, as she quickly took a liking to sewing after she was apprenticed to Sitt Sukayna A., a well-known seamstress of a prominent Nablus family. 'I was talented and learned very fast', she said, immediately going on to contrast the past with the present-day conditions in the trade. 'Don't

---

[3] In 1983, 47 per cent of all West Bank textile units were located in Nablus and 40 per cent of all West Bank textile unit employees were employed in Nablus (UNIDO 1984: 17).

forget, nowadays they send those girls who fail in school to sit with a seamstress, but previously it was the successful girls, the gifted ones who were apprenticed. Within half a year I had already learned how to do the difficult tasks, how to place a sleeve, how to attach a collar and so on.' They had worked 'according to the ancient system', she recalled. 'The girls, there were usually eight or nine of them, learned through watching and practising. No money changed hands. We were not paid, because we were learning and not really productive, but we also did not have to pay. The seamstresses liked having girls, because they could do more work then. Nowadays if a girl only sweeps the floor you have to pay her . . .'

After having stayed with the same seamstress for over three and a half years, Sitt ʿAfāf opened her own sewing workshop. At that time she may have been ready to start on her own anyway, but she emphasised that the major impetus to do so had been her father's sudden death. 'I felt responsible for my mother and my siblings', she explained. 'I was almost eighteen and they were all younger than me, the smallest girl was only four.' Her workshop was, as she put it, 'successful from the first step'. Although she was of very small stature and, in her words, 'people sometimes did not believe that I was the seamstress', within a few days she herself already had two apprentices.

Having started her workshop in the late mandatory period Sitt ʿAfāf gradually expanded her activities in the 1950s and 1960s. In those days, being a seamstress was a good profession. 'People came to Nablus from all over Jordan and also from Ramallah and Jerusalem', Sitt ʿAfāf recalled. 'Sometimes I had three or four brides a month for whom a complete outfit had to be sewn. I always had work and I was able to work for a large number of clients, because I had many girls working with me.' Indeed, at the apex of her career she had over twenty girl apprentices, and her cousin, a carpenter, had made her three long benches they could sit on. Little had yet changed in workshop organisation from the days she had been an apprentice herself. 'The girls first had to do the finishing and then I gradually taught them the different stages of sewing, mostly by hand, but I had also bought three sewing machines. When I saw the girl was concentrating well, I would give her lessons in cutting; they cannot learn cutting if they do not know how to sew, that does not work.'

This situation changed suddenly and dramatically after the Israeli occupation. With bitterness and barely suppressed disgust, Sitt ʿAfāf summarised her experiences. 'Shortly before the occupation I had sixteen outfits in consignment. The material that I had not yet cut I returned to the owners. Everything was in disarray.' After the situation had 'quietened down', the sewing trade rapidly went into decline. 'Nowadays there are hardly any girls who come to a seamstress to learn how to sew', Sitt ʿAfāf reflected. 'The few girls who wanted to work with me after being employed in a subcontracting workshop I had to send away. If they had sewn something carelessly, they would simply cut off the extra material, and the model would be spoiled . . .' In her view these girls went to the subcontracting workshops, 'because the work is easy, everything arrives there ready-cut, and they only have to stitch it. They can earn money immediately and they like to be amongst the people.' At the same time skilled seamstresses had to face severe marketing problems. 'Everything is brought ready-made from Israel, it is cheaper and the people do not have to wait for it. Maybe nowadays I make one bridal dress a year, if they want something very special that is not available on the market.'

Sitt ʿAfāf herself adamantly rejected the idea of joining the burgeoning subcontracting trade. 'No, I would never want to work in a workshop, you have to guard your dignity, that sort of work is not respectable, absolutely not. Many owners came to ask me to help them with the work, because I know how to sew, but I have always declined their offer. Don't forget there are many families in Nablus, even amongst the poor, who would not allow their daughters to work in a subcontracting workshop and mix with men.' When I asked her whether she had not considered opening a subcontracting workshop herself, she replied half-heartedly: 'I could not open a workshop myself; you need a man, a brother for example, who would go to Israel and arrange for the material, who would take care of the taxes and so on.' Yet it was obvious that she never had considered it seriously and saw it as much below her dignity. Working by herself she still had enough clients, mainly elderly women, some of whom had been coming to her for over thirty years.

Sitt ʿAfāf was a workshop 'owner'. Living in the family home, she had bought some sewing machines and had all the necessary appliances. In Jordanian times her work had provided her with a good income, yet she emphasised that she had neither bought land nor shares and only some gold. Her main impetus had been to take care of the family. 'I was responsible for my mother and seven children; I let them study, I married them and I opened a house', she repeatedly underlined. For the very same reason she herself had not accepted marriage. 'When once a very good man came to ask me in marriage, I sat with him and explained that I was not able to marry, because I had three "responsibilities", my mother, my youngest sister, who had just been appointed as a teacher, and my brother's son, whom I had raised and whose engineering studies I was paying for. Then he asked whether he would be allowed to meet my youngest sister. I told him, "that is possible", and he married her.' Sitt ʿAfāf saw her strategy as a sacrifice for the family and derived great satisfaction from it. 'Had I myself married, my sister would not have been able to marry or my mother would have been placed in an old people's home and my brother's son would not have been able to study. Every morning when my mother thanks me for the coffee I bring her, I feel joy.'

Contemplating her own future, Sitt ʿAfāf emphasised that as long as her mother was alive they would stay in the family home. Her income from sewing was not really sufficient, but she could make do with it. As she put it, 'It is better to be respected by your family, than that you are in need and have to ask them.' She was not planning to move in with her brother's son (whom she had raised). 'Although he says he loves me more than he loves his wife, living in the same house will only create problems', she pointed out. 'My sister's husband is wealthy, he owns four buildings with six apartments each and I may rent one of these; or if need be I might let part of this house to students, but that is always risky with the occupation.'

### Amal: an energetic garment worker

Amal, twenty-eight years old, had been working for over thirteen years as a garment worker when I met her at the garment workers' union, of which she was a member. Born into a virtually landless rural family in a larger village near Nablus, she had gone to school for six years. As her family was needy she then applied for a six-month sewing course offered by social affairs, pretending that she was older, and was accepted. After completion she immediately started working to help her family. 'My brothers were still small', she said. 'There were first five girls and then three boys, we needed the money.'

At the end of the course, several workshop owners had come to interview the girls and had told them about the work they offered. Amal quite liked the medium-sized workshop (S.) where she started sewing. 'The man I went to work for was good. We were there with about 25 girls. If a girl was in difficult social circumstances he would still pay her even if she produced little.' Yet, after six months she had to leave. As her family had been in Kuwait (where her father worked), when Israel occupied the West Bank, they had no residence papers. Through the owner of another sewing workshop (G.) her mother had managed to get these, but in return he had wanted Amal to come and work for him. So it happened. 'There we worked with seven girls, and his brother's son. First, I received a monthly wage, maybe 60 JD, but after six months I asked to work piece-rates, because I was a very fast worker. Then I made up to 120 JD, and he did not even calculate that right!'

Some years later Amal left to work in Kuwait, where her maternal cousins had opened a workshop. She went there because the family was in dire need of money. 'My father had started to build a new house in the village (the old one was of mud-brick), but he was the only earner, a common labourer, making 50 or 60 JD a month . . .', she pointed out. 'So, he had become indebted to the builder, who had even suggested to cancel the debt by taking my sister as his bride . . .' Her relatives in Kuwait had wanted to place Amal as a supervisor, but she did not like that. 'There were over sixty workers, men and women, Indians, Egyptians and Palestinians, and I was a young girl, a relative of the owners. So I preferred to work piece-rates behind the machines, and sometimes I managed to earn 300 JD in one month!' Yet, Amal herself did not spend much. 'Everything was to pay off the debt. My father had also mortgaged land for 500 JD to someone in the village. Most of that amount I earned for him during Ramadan, when we worked day and night.'

Having worked there for over three years Amal returned to the village. The debts had been paid off and she felt she had been away long enough; she wanted to go back home to see her mother, her brothers and sisters. By then in her early twenties, she did not want to remain sitting at home and preferred to return to the first workshop she had worked for. But her father had suddenly decided that he did not like her travelling to Nablus daily, so she started taking in homework from this workshop, earning between 40 and 60 JD a month. Yet she kept trying to convince him to let her go and work at the workshop and in the end she succeeded. 'My father likes money, so I asked him, "what would you say if I went to work in the workshop, I take one month and you will take the other." He agreed.' When she returned to the workshop she started with 80 JD a month. 'The owner had asked me to come back to the workshop because he knew I would produce more there. Every year I received 5 or 10 JD extra. Now I have been working for four years, and I earn 105 JD. And in the summer, when there is much work, he also brings me work at home, but that pays very badly.' Although Amal talked to me about her wages without restraint, the girls in the workshop were not supposed to tell each other how much they were earning. 'That is forbidden, because it would cause problems. Some girls receive a wage they do not really deserve, because they are from villages far away, or from very poor families. But if other girls knew they might complain and say "Don't I work harder than she, why don't I receive more?"'

Amal was proud of her sewing skills and of the support she had been to her family. Her wage also gave her the opportunity to do things she could never have done otherwise. She had bought some gold, and was taking driving lessons, her father did not know about, but the rest of the family approved of. Yet, she was indignant about society's attitude towards garment workers. As she stressed, 'There are people who think that a female workshop worker [bint al-mashghal] is not good, that she mixes with men. But that idea is wrong. Why are they so negative about workshop workers? A secretary might have much more opportunities to do wrong than a workshop worker, who is working in a group. But our society condemns women workers.'

*Imm Ghassān: an exceptional career as subcontractor*

When I talked to Imm Ghassān, who was in her late forties, she had a long history of working in the sewing trade and had become a highly successful subcontractor. Her achievements were embodied in the new building she had constructed in D., a village on the outskirts of Nablus. With pride she showed me the medium-size sewing workshop on the ground floor and the four, spacious apartments on the two floors above.

Imm Ghassān was from a poor, semi-urban background. Her father, originally from D., had been orphaned at a young age and was raised by an elderly single female school director in Nablus. Imm Ghassān had to leave school after four years when her mother started to work as a school concierge and she, the eldest daughter, was to take care of her smaller brothers and sisters. Yet, as her mother wanted her to learn something, a few years later she was allowed to take a short sewing course.

In the mid-1950s, at sixteen, Imm Ghassān was married to a distant paternal relative, a close friend of her father. Her dower was not much, 100 JD prompt and 100 JD deferred, as her husband's family was also poor. 'The house he had rented in Nablus was virtually empty', Imm Ghassān recalled, 'and working as a teacher he did not earn much; part of the wage he had to give to his family, and he also had to pay off the debt he had incurred for the marriage costs.' So, soon after marriage she started to work. As she said, 'I sold the dower gold and bought a sewing machine to help my husband.' A few years later, however, when her husband was sentenced to over two years imprisonment (in a political case), her work was to become the major source of income. For Imm Ghassān this also meant a change from urban to village life. 'Even though I was raised in Nablus, I went to live with his family in the village and started to work the land', Imm Ghassān said. But her major source of income was sewing. 'In the village I was sewing everything the women wanted to wear; at that time there was very little ready-to-wear clothing on the market. Underclothing, wedding outfits, I made everything.' After her husband was released from prison, she continued sewing, as he remained without work for over a year and then went to work in Saudi Arabia only returning to the village once a year.

When Israel occupied the West Bank Imm Ghassān was living in the village with five children, working as a local seamstress and receiving little money from her husband. The situation was difficult. 'In the village if you sew a dress, they keep bringing it back to you, if it is ripped they return it to you, as long as the owner of the dress lives, the dress will come back to you. Most of my time went into mending.' Her sewing activities were, however, to change irreversibly when she met an acquaintance whose husband turned out to be a subcontractor. 'She told me that her husband brought cut material from Israel and asked me whether I did not want to try it', Imm Ghassān said. 'I did want to. First they sent me five dresses without overlock. I finished these and they must have been content with my work, for then they sent me fourteen. And the next time fifty, but these they wanted with overlock. As I did not have an overlock machine, I asked other people to do that while I did the stitching myself.' Encouraged by these positive experiences Imm Ghassān decided to go and look for more sewing machines. She found a man who had closed his small workshop because he did not know much about sewing and she became his partner. Her self-confidence grew rapidly. 'First I did not know how to work these machines, but I learned. There were, however, only four stitching machines and one overlock, that is not enough for two people. I wanted to expand but he did not, so I went to look for another workshop.' When Imm Ghassān met a widow who needed money to raise her children and who also had some machines, they became partners. Yet, this also did not last long because of a disagreement about the rent.

Imm Ghassān's breakthrough as a subcontractor came about in a large village in the northern part of the West Bank. She had chosen this village because it had recently got electricity and there were girls trained in sewing by the social affairs department. When I asked her how she started her workshop there, she said: 'I had given a man half a dinar to announce from the mosque that a woman had come to open a sewing workshop and was looking for girls. They came in large numbers. At that time girls did not go from one village to work in another. I rented a place and started with seven girls, and after one year I had thirty machines and thirty girls working.' But soon there was competition, other subcontractors started to open workshops and girls were attracted by the higher wages paid in Tulkarm, a small town nearby. Then Imm Ghassān repeated the same procedure and started a sewing workshop in a village very close to D., which had recently been linked to the electricity grid. After working there for some years, she managed to open the newly constructed workshop in D.. When I talked to Imm Ghassān she still had about a dozen girls working in A., about twenty-five in the workshop in D. and there were also some girls working at home. Her husband, who had returned from Saudi Arabia in the mid-1970s, and her youngest son were now in charge of the book-keeping, her daughter-in-law was sewing and supervising, while her youngest daughter, a student, kept an eye on the girls working elsewhere in the village, as the university was closed because of the intifada.

Imm Ghassān had relations with a number of Israeli companies and made different types of clothing except jeans, as these required many different specialised machines. If in the beginning Imm Ghassān had taken cut material from other male subcontractors, she soon felt she had to go to Tel-Aviv to arrange for the material herself as this would mean a considerable increase in profits. Recalling those early years she stressed it had been very hard as no other women were going there. 'I would have had problems had I opened my ears to what the people said. If a woman returned after sunset from Tel-Aviv, that was seen as shameful. But I wanted to bring money for the house. Even when my husband was working in Saudi Arabia he did not earn much, and we had to think about the future, about the education of the children.' Her husband's family did not interfere, but her own relatives did. 'They did not want me to come and go, and for five years my mother's brother did not talk to me', Imm Ghassān recalled, adding with pride and satisfaction, 'but that changed when he saw the results of my work.' Her husband had never made problems, but she took care to tell him everything, 'where I have gone, to whom I have spoken, if there was any trouble. So, if someone would say to him, "we saw her there and there", he already knew about it.'

The first times she went to Tel-Aviv was with the man who brought her the material. 'He may not have been a good man', she said, 'but he never talked to me, he respected me. I did not know how to go by myself, he showed me the way to the companies and shops.' Then she took public transportation, travelling with three different share-taxis, from Nablus to Tulkarm, then to Nataniya, and from there to Tel-Aviv. After her husband's return they bought a car and things became easier. He was not, however, a good driver. 'First he did not want to go by car, so I said, it is no problem, I will drive. He did not like the idea, but we went. The first time it was as if every approaching car would hit us, I was very nervous, the second time it went better, the third time I was used to it and I went by myself.' In recent years her son has done most of the driving.

Only girls worked in Imm Ghassān's workshop and, as was common for women workers, in the beginning she paid them a monthly wage. Actually, she had contemplated employing men. 'But in our society you cannot have a boy and a girl working together; you need a separate room', she explained. 'Still I would like to have men, because a man works ten times more than a girl. A girl has no responsibilities, she does not have to bring bread home, she works as much as she likes to. Her family does not put pressure on her, they cannot say she has to spend on herself. But if you have to bring home a bag of rice at the end of the month, or if you want to give your son an education, you will work day and night.' Her husband and son, however, did not want to employ male workers, because that would only cause problems, so Imm Ghassān did the next best thing, she paid the girls piece-rates. 'The problem with monthly wages was that if I was not there, the girls did not work. So I suggested that they do piece-work. First they did not want to, but I asked them to try it for one month, and if they made less, I would pay them extra. But they made a lot more. So, when a new girl comes now, she starts with a very low monthly wage, and once she has learned the work, she is paid piece-rates.' Her best paid girl earned 600 to 800 IS a month (1988). She also had a machine at home and when she had finished in the workshop she continued working at home.

When Imm Ghassān started to work as a subcontractor her children were still small and she had a hard time combining running a workshop and taking care of the children in a village environment. 'I used to work day and night. I went home late in the evening with a driver, he brought me to the village and then I had to walk up to the old centre where we were living. My children were asleep by then. I looked at them, took off their clothes, if these were dirty, while they were asleep. I cooked for them and did the washing. At that time we had neither electricity nor running water. We used to fill four big jerry-cans of water and bring them to our house on a donkey. Later I had a washing machine in the workshop. On Fridays early in the morning, I brought the washing and I took the pots with me to do the cooking. The oven was nearby. I kneaded the dough and made bread. Only when I had learned how to drive and we had a small car things became easier.' Imm Ghassān emphasised that she always took care of her children's education. 'Every two or three weeks I went to the school and asked the teachers how they were doing; the teachers liked that.' All her children have studied, the eldest son in Europe, where he is still living, the other ones at local universities. Only the youngest did not want to learn, so Imm Ghassān sent him to work with her brother in Kuwait. Having recently come back and married, he also became involved in running the workshop.

Obviously Imm Ghassān was the driving force behind the workshops. 'This building is the result of my work', she underlined. 'Had I not been a woman, I would have set up more workshops, not only for sewing.' She had actually asked her brothers to become partners with her in a sesame paste factory, but they were not interested, and her son was afraid of problems with the tax officers. In Imm Ghassān's opinion sewing should have been secondary. Having learned everything through practice she was afraid that without her active participation her son would not be able to run the workshop in the future. 'When a machine broke down the man who came to repair it would take the time to explain everything to me. When we have a new assignment my husband and my son do not know how to set the machines nor are they able to repair them; I do that.' Her eldest son had always stimulated her, but her husband and youngest son 'did not like to take risks'.

Reflecting on her labour history, Imm Ghassān was proud of her achievements, but felt that she had sacrificed a lot and was not sure that she had received much in return. Her work load had been extremely heavy, both taking care of the children and being the main breadwinner. She had built a new workshop and four apartments, registered for her husband and her three sons.[4] One apartment had a separate room for her daughter, whose divorce was becoming final. Yet, when I spoke to her, she was quite annoyed about her son wanting to do things differently and the small amount of money she was given. Actually she had become angry and refused to work for one month. As she aptly pointed out, 'They did not know what to do when two machines broke down and they had to urge me to return to work.' She had done so, but on condition that she received 100 JD a month and that part of the building be registered in her name. She was actually thinking of spending some time with her brothers in Kuwait, if the situation did not improve. They had, after all, offered her money if she stopped working.

## 8.2    From artisanal production to subcontracting

These three labour stories call attention to the very different positions women take up in garment production. Sitt ʿAfāf, a single woman from a reputable urban family started working in the late 1940s and became a successful and respected seamstress with a large number of apprentices. The occupation put an abrupt end to her career, as she found it very difficult to compete with ready-to-wear clothing from Israel and it became increasingly difficult to find girls to help; those with a background similar to hers preferred to attend school rather than become apprenticed. Girls such as Amal, on the other hand, who wanted to work in the sewing trade, were often from a poor rural or refugee background, looking for paid employment because their families needed money. Older, urban skilled seamstresses such as Sitt ʿAfāf did not think much of these girls. Amal and her co-workers were very well aware of the way in which society perceived them, but to them sewing was often the best work they could find. They considered it as much more respectable work than cleaning, which they saw as humiliating, as 'serving' rather than 'working'. If Sitt

---

[4] The land she had already bought when her husband was in still in Saudi Arabia; if at the time it had only cost her 160 JD, she estimated that nowadays she could get 14,000 JD for it because it is near the main road. The building had cost over 20,000 JD.

ʿAfāf's and Amal's cases are fairly conventional, the story of Imm Ghassān, a rural seamstress who was not marginalised after the Israeli occupation, but managed instead to become one of the most successful female subcontractors, is exceptional. True, she had to defy the norms of society, but in the end she also experienced the satisfaction of having managed to build a house and workshop with her own hands, even if it was at great costs.

The divergent options these women had tie in with the great structural transformations in the sewing trade. In Sitt ʿAfāf's heyday, garment production in Nablus was a craft-based industry with clothing mainly produced on demand in small artisanal workshops, where highly skilled tailors worked with a number of apprentices. Garments were produced in two sectors, gender-segregated both in terms of production and marketing. Male tailors worked with male apprentices producing clothing for male customers while female tailors, such as Sitt ʿAfāf, worked for women, assisted by girls learning the trade. Certainly, these male and female sectors were not fully complementary. Male urban tailors generally had a larger clientele, as rural men often had their clothing made in Nablus, while rural women would turn to female tailors in their own villages, such as Imm Ghassān. These worked more often on their own and were involved in simpler clothing production. The internal organisation of the male and female workshops also differed to some extent. For male apprentices the work-career aspect was more emphasised, for female apprentices the learning experience. As Sitt ʿAfāf explained, female assistants usually neither paid a fee nor received a wage, but male assistants did receive something. When girls went to work with experienced female tailors they did not do so to earn a living, but rather to acquire a skill. After all, male and female careers were expected to be different. Men were to set up their own workshop after mastering the trade while women were expected to marry and be provided for. Yet, setting up a sewing workshop was quite acceptable, particularly for single women.

In the late 1950s, cracks started to appear in this division of labour between male and female workshops. A small number of male tailors began producing modern made-to-order clothing for women. In these somewhat larger workshops some elements of a gender division of labour were introduced with girls working as assistants to more experienced male tailors. Such a gender division of labour was already prevalent in the few workshops where ready-to-wear clothing was produced. These were by and large run by male shopkeepers/traders, some of whom also employed female labour. Still, in these workshops a strongly hierarchical gender division of labour had not yet developed. Men were considered better in producing men's wear and women in producing women's wear and, contrary to later developments, in a few cases women were also employed as cutters.

Whereas in the Jordanian period workshops for ready-to-wear clothing were limited in number and artisanal production remained predominant, this situation changed dramatically when, with the Israeli occupation, two strikingly different production systems – Israeli and West Bank – rapidly became integrated.[5] In the West Bank garment sector this led to a sharp decline in the number of skilled tailoring workshops, which were not able to compete with the Israeli ready-to-wear clothing flooding the West Bank markets, while at the same time lowly-paid male tailor apprentices could find better-paid work in the Israeli industry. Skilled seamstresses like Sitt ʿAfāf were also confronted with the problem of Israeli competition.

However, one specific type of garment production has flourished: subcontracting (Awartani 1979: 27; Frisch 1983: 41). Israeli garment producers make use of cheap and less mobile West Bank labour (in particular women) through relocating part of their production to the West Bank. When they came there searching for subcontractors shortly after the occupation, some of the skilled male tailors transformed their independent workshop into a subcontracting unit for the Israeli industry. They receive the cut material from Israeli firms and only perform the labour-intensive parts of the production process, returning the finished garments to these firms at a contracted price per piece. After some time workers who had gained experience in the Israeli or West Bank subcontracting industry also set up their own small subcontracting businesses. This vertical integration of the Nablus clothing production in the Israeli garment industry means that designing, cutting and marketing have largely disappeared from the West Bank. Admittedly, by the end of the 1970s some West Bank subcontractors, often the larger firms where monotonous production with larger production runs (such as jeans) takes place, had become more experienced and a few of these had started to cut the material themselves. Even so, they are the exception rather than the rule. In Nablus there were only a few larger firms (two with over 100 workers), some in turn subcontracting to smaller local firms or home-workers. Then there was a somewhat larger number of medium sized firms (between fifteen and forty workers). But the large majority of production units were very small, with a high turnover.[6]

---

[5] To indicate the gap between the West Bank and the Israeli economy, in 1986 employment in the Israeli clothing industry alone (32,000) was almost twice the employment of all West Bank industry (18,165) (CBS 1987: 382/3; 723).

[6] In 1980, 62 per cent of all Nablus textile firms had less than five employees, 80 per cent less than ten, and 97 per cent less than twenty (UNIDO 1984: 27).

Subcontracting has been accompanied by a particular form of feminisation of the labour force. If in the Jordanian period workshops with women working for men were the exception rather than the rule, this changed after the occupation. In the new 'integrated' industrial workshops the gender division of labour is vertical: the subcontractors are by and large male while most workers are women. As such Amal's experiences in Nablus workshops are fairly representative. Also, male and female workers often have different positions in the labour process, with women exclusively employed as machinists and sometimes as supervisors over women, while only men work as cutters, pressers and in maintenance. Even in machine sewing, men's work is different from that of women. In the smaller workshops women often perform a lot of different tasks, while men are longer in one line of work (standard production). Several entrepreneurs, amongst whom the owner Amal is working for, pointed out that even if they paid men the same wage they would earn in standard production, they would still be very reluctant to perform certain tasks, such as finishing, or a lot of different small tasks. That is seen as women's work and an employer needs either women or children for such work. The few female entrepreneurs often take in cut material from a local subcontractor. Also in this regard Imm Ghassān is exceptional.

In short, highly skilled artisanal production has largely disappeared, a local sewing industry has hardly developed and subcontracting has become the dominant form of garment production. For Israeli garment producers the West Bank is a 'Third World colony' next door: an open market with no competition from outside. As economic integration is accompanied by strong legal, social and residential segregation, labour is very cheap, legal rights are very limited and social security is virtually non-existent. In addition, distances are very short (the distance between Nablus and Tel-Aviv is less than 60 km), there are no time-consuming border formalities, produce is delivered very fast and small lots can also be produced. In this subcontracting industry women find themselves consistently in the lower echelons.

## 8.3    Sewing: a profession in decline

The transformation of garment production from a gender-segregated, skilled profession to a production sector of male subcontractors and female workers has resulted in a loss of status and respectability for the sewing trade and those employed in it. This is the case for both men and women. Although the more successful subcontractors can earn very well, they recognise that they neither have the skill of artisanal tailors nor their previous autonomy, and have instead become fully dependent on their Israeli suppliers. One male subcontractor who had been a very successful skilled tailor with a large number of assistants in the Jordanian period, had difficulty to control his feelings when he showed me his appointment book, his drawing table and his appliances. In the early 1970s he had to give up this line of work and never touched them again. With bitterness he referred to his present position of subcontractor as 'that of a porter, carrying loads [of cut material] for the workers'.

The decline of the profession also has gender-specific consequences. Before the occupation going to a workshop meant learning a skill. Certainly, there were some special sewing courses, where girls paid a fee to learn how to draw patterns, how to cut and how to sew. In Nablus the best known was organised by the Women's Union. Most women, however, learned the trade as apprentices in the artisanal workshops, sometimes taking a special course for additional training, especially to acquire those skills, such as cutting, which not all seamstresses taught their apprentices. In the mandatory period some girls even went to Jaffa to take courses in pattern drawing and cutting, or travelled to Haifa and Jerusalem to learn about the newest models. As Sitt ʿAfāf emphasised, this is very different from working in an industrial (subcontracting) workshop which is not associated with learning a skill. It is true that many female workers had taken a sewing course (varying in length from six months to one year) before being employed, but they pointed out that most of what they had learned there was of little practical use.[7] Rather, they were (re-) trained on the job in guiding material at high speed through the machines, working under great pressure, a skill hardly recognised as such. With training (learning a skill) and work (earning a living) separated, women's work in the garment sector has become linked with low social status and poverty. This is further exacerbated as the workshops are not fully gender segregated. Working long hours under harsh labour conditions, not to learn a skill, but to earn a low wage, under the control of a male entrepreneur and sometimes with male workers, all indicate the failure of men in protecting their female kin and providing adequately for the household. As gender mixing is not seen as problematic amongst the better professions, such as university employees, it is this selective disdain for lower-class working girls about which Amal so strongly expressed her resentment when she stated 'our society condemns women workers'.

This loss of status of the sewing trade has drawn women from a different social background into the garment sector. Previously it was also common for girls from urban, middle-class families to be apprenticed to a skilled seamstress. In some cases these girls themselves had taken a liking

---

[7] Both my data and Siniora's indicate that a little over half of the women workers completed a training course in sewing (Siniora 1989: 59).

to sewing, for others it was the only alternative as their family would not allow them to continue their education. Some of these girls were young, between seven and ten when they were first apprenticed. How they experienced this also depended on the atmosphere in the workshop. When she was almost ten, Sitt Salwā was sent to Khayriyya al-H., 'a very, very clever seamstress, working for the most prominent families of Nablus', but later she went to another seamstress, Karīma Z., because she was living closer by. 'With Sitt Khayriyya we were with about six', she recalled, 'but I was the only young girl, the other ones were older and two women were married. We were not allowed to laugh or to speak or to chew gum, she was very strict. It was different with Sitt Karīma, there we were twelve girls of about the same age. We went together to bring bread, we sat on the wall and ate, we had a very good time together. Sitt Karīma had more girls coming to her because she was living in the old city. We were all from the same neighbourhood, not from here and there. We could talk with each other; we were free.'

In other cases, a woman may only get the opportunity to learn sewing when she was older. Imm Rāᶜida had not been allowed to finish school nor to learn sewing when she was young, because after the earthquake her family moved from Nablus to a nearby village, where they owned large tracts of land. When she was in her late twenties her younger brother invited her and her mother to accompany him to Jaffa, which gave her the opportunity to take a course in pattern drawing and sewing with an Armenian seamstress. As she put it, 'Having been deprived of education I thought I might at least learn something.' She later worked in Nablus and in the early fifties went to Kuwait with her brother, sewing there for the Palestinian women teachers. In those days, being a seamstress was a respectable profession and a number of elderly single Nablus women from better-off families were reputable tailors, often living together with their mother, or with another single sister, who would be either a seamstress herself or a schoolteacher. For village women from shaykhly families, who would not work the land, sewing was the only acceptable work to gain a livelihood if they were widowed. Girls from poor families, on the other hand, would more likely work as domestic servants or agricultural labourers.

More recently sewing has become a trade for non-urban women from a lower-class background with limited education, such as Amal. In my 1987 sample roughly two-thirds of Nablus garment workers were from the camps and the villages. As after occupation subcontracting workshops were also established outside Nablus, in the region as a whole rural garment workers were even more predominant. Statistical data also indicate the 'ruralisation' of garment production. Rural garment workers largely account for the increase in the proportion of industrial workers in the female labour force from 16 per cent to 20 per cent between 1972 and 1984 as the number of urban women has actually declined (CBS 1973: 719; 1986: 908). This ties in with urban women's higher level of education. Even girls from poorer families who have gained their secondary school certificate rarely work in a sewing workshop.[8] A garment worker with only a few years of schooling, for instance, pointed out that her sister who had passed these secondary school exams, was sitting at home and refused to work in a sewing workshop. At the same time, as mentioned before, there has been a particularly sharp decline in the proportion of agricultural wage labourers (from 24 per cent to 11 per cent of the female labour force) (CBS 1973: 719; 1986: 908). It is likely that those rural women who would previously have worked in agricultural wage labour have either given up working for wages or they have entered industrial wage labour. Some sewing workers told me that either their mother or a sister would be still working as an agricultural labourer. That sewing workers usually are from poor families is also visible in the large number of them who had been accepted by the department of social affairs for its sewing courses.

The few female subcontractors like Imm Ghassān are from a similar background as the garment workers, but they had been, or still were, more often married and had children. Usually from the villages or the camps, with only a few years of education, they had started working in the sewing sector as workers or, if they had children, as homeworkers/seamstresses. Realising that there was little future in their jobs, finding their income very limited, and of a particularly enterprising nature they would consider starting their own workshop. If they could get some help from their family, for example, from a brother supplying them with some money or entering in partnership with them or from a sister contributing a sewing machine, or if they had some gold to sell, they might indeed realise their plans.

## 8.4    Gender in the labour process: control and resistance

Whereas most subcontracting workshops employ women, some only employ men and others have both men and women working there. Why are most employees women? Are they cheaper and more docile? If owners have good reasons to employ women, why then do others (also) employ men?

---

[8] About 40 per cent of the women interviewed had not finished primary school, almost 80 per cent had not finished the intermediate level (nine years of education); only two women had acquired the secondary school certificate.

The main reason for subcontractors to employ women is profitability. With the whole production process organised to emphasise non-comparability between men's and women's work, comparing male and female wages is difficult. This is even more so, as men and women are on the whole paid according to different wage systems. Men generally work for piece-rates, while most women earn a monthly wage (in a few cases a basic rate with a premium).[9] Yet, on average, at the end of the month women receive about half what men make and occasionally wage differentials could even be more outspoken. There are in Nablus, for example, two large subcontracting factories producing jeans. Factory A. employs only men, who, in contrast to the usual pattern, work for monthly wages. There is a clear-cut and quickly rising pay scale and mobility chain, and after some training and experience a worker will earn around 150 JD with top wages of about 300 JD. In factory B. mainly women are employed, paid according to the basic rate plus premium system. These women generally make 50 to 60 JD a month with the female supervisors earning around 80 JD. The few men who are employed in this factory (in ironing, maintenance, and the storeroom) earn at least 150 JD.

Entrepreneurs often explained the different payment systems and levels by pointing to men's greater productivity. Referring to the concept of the male breadwinner they argued, as Imm Ghassān did, that men are employed for piece-rates and work long hours because they have to earn a family wage and women do not. This 'male provider argument' is a powerful legitimation of the existing situation. But the wage differentials are too large and the male/female divide is too consistent to be fully explained by differences in productivity. Indeed, employers also acknowledged that women enter the labour market under different conditions from men. Men are able to refuse to work for the low wages women are paid as they have a wider range of opportunities to earn a living. Women's domestic tasks are not the major obstacle; most of them are unmarried and those who were previously married have female relatives taking care of their children.[10] More important is that their mobility is limited as women are culturally defined as needing the protection and control of male kin.

Considering the locational background of the workers, it then seems paradoxical that most of the women workers in the Nablus garment workshops are not from the city of Nablus itself, while the majority of the

[9] Of the women I interviewed, 20 per cent were paid piece-rate; Siniora gives 15 per cent working for piece-rates (1989: 58).
[10] In the CWW survey, 6 per cent of the women was married, 7 per cent divorced and 87 per cent single. Siniora (1989: 49) states that 95 per cent of the women workers were single; of the twenty women I interviewed four were divorced, the others were single.

men are.[11] The point is, however, that rural men who do not work in their own villages often migrate or work in Israel rather than take a low wage job elsewhere on the West Bank. As has been argued in the preceding chapter, very few women follow the same path and those who do so are strongly condemned. Women's options are also more limited in other respects. If men do not like the pay or work conditions, they will try to find another local employer. This is much more difficult for women, as most other sectors are closed to them (such as the construction trade, the wood and metal sectors, and so on) and the pressure of male control makes women reluctant even to switch jobs within the garment sector.[12] If Amal did so several times, this was due to particular circumstances. Furthermore, quite often a male labourer will, after some experience in a subcontracting workshop or in a sewing firm in Israel, buy a few second-hand sewing machines and start his own business. Only a small number of women do this. As Imm Ghassān argued, even though a female owner is not condemned as strongly as a female labourer if she goes to Tel-Aviv, it is still difficult for her to go there by herself and arrange for the delivery of cut material. Imm ʿImād, a successful subcontractor from a camp near Nablus also first engaged in subcontracting from a local subcontractor, then worked in partnership with a man, but in the end went to Israel herself. 'You lose over half of the proceeds if you do not make the arrangements yourself', she said. 'My partner was like a labourer in a workshop, he was the last one to show up and the first one to leave.' As women are much more dependent upon employment in the Nablus garment sector than men, their bargaining power is weaker. Imm ʿImād argued that she never was afraid that her six girls would leave when she was not able to pay their wages on time, for 'a man can always find some work, but where would a girl with little education go? She has no other choice but sewing.'

Labour control is also highly gender-specific. In the case of men, who are generally paid piece-rates, it works basically through market relations. With regard to women the economic side of the relation is downplayed, male employers often taking on the role of a substitute father towards female workers. This 'paternalism' is also reflected in the way in which I heard girls addressing their female employer. Rather than using the term

---

[11] Both the CWW survey and my data indicate that about one-third of the women workers were from the city, one-third from the camps and one-third from the villages. Incidentally, this means that women's net wages are even lower as many of the women who travel from the villages actually spend a large part of their wages (up to one-third) on transport.

[12] More than half the women workers I interviewed were still working with their first employer. Of them over two-thirds had been employed four years or more (the longest period of employment was seventeen years). Siniora reports that 74 per cent of the female workers never changed their jobs (1989: 58).

'my mother's sister' (*khāltī*; the friendly aunt), a common informal yet respectful way of addressing an older woman, they used 'my father's sister' (*ʿammtī*; the strict aunt) as form of address. For women the wage system is obscure, even those who changed jobs were often too shy to ask beforehand what their wages would be, and many worked six days a week for years without ever asking for the vacation they were legally entitled to. As Fatma, an experienced female garment worker and unionist, said, 'A girl accepts anything, but the owner cannot give a man a low wage, he is like himself.' As in Amal's case women workers might also be forbidden to tell each other what they earn. It is true that her employer also took the social circumstances of individual workers into account, yet for other entrepreneurs this was simply another mechanism of labour control. And these employers are not only patronising, but can also be very authoritarian. In one case the union took a large subcontractor to court because he had beaten a female worker. It is because gender is such an important principle of workshop organisation that female entrepreneurs only employ women workers; male workers would be very reluctant to take orders from a woman. Imm Ghassān's wish to employ men only underlines her exceptional position.

Spatial segregation also indicates the working of gendered labour control. If a workshop employs both men and women they are usually working in one or another way segregated from each other, either in a different building, a separate room or in a space closed off by curtains. Yet it is not contact with men which is condemned, as the presence of the male owner or his son is not deemed problematic, but with male workers. One reason to restrict women's contact with male workers is to avoid that women workers would be influenced by men's more market-oriented approach towards work.

On the other hand, women themselves also use gender as a form of resistance. The non-market behaviour of women is not simply an expression of women's subordination, but can also be interpreted as defiance of alienation and resistance to the dictates of the market. For if female labour is so profitable, why then is male labour also employed in the garment sector? If in general owners prefer women as they are cheaper, more docile and have less options to find work elsewhere, the preference of some employers for male workers may indicate that women's docility is fragile. While men tend to express their dissatisfaction about wages and work conditions openly, the form women's resistance takes is different. The same arguments used to underline that male and female labour are non-comparable or rather that women's labour is inferior, women themselves use to create some autonomy. Many women simply refuse to exploit themselves in wage labour like men. Whereas men working for piece-rates often work very intensively and for long hours, employers argue that women are not paid piece-rates because they cannot be pushed and will not push themselves like men. Imm ʿImād pointed out to me that her girls were not able to start work early and remain very late, neither could they do without their one-hour lunch break. Women resist labour pressure through referring to family obligations or to a weak constitution, and they skilfully use relations of patronage to put a certain claim on their employer, emphasising their difficult situation rather than their productivity in the hope of getting a rise. Sometimes they would bring their claims through mediation of their employer's wife or his female relatives. As Fatma pointed out: 'Once we had agreed that we would tell the owner what we wanted. But when I stood up to him, the others all drew back, and I found myself alone. Now I do not talk to him, but I go to his wife, who also comes to the workshop; she tells him what we want.' And if women have considerably less employment opportunities than men, they have one final but difficult option, to withdraw completely from the labour market.

The different forms of labour control and resistance become clear in the divergent employment strategies of the two largest Nablus subcontractors. The owners of the most modern factory of Nablus (factory A.) only employ men, because as they say, they do not want 'the problems women give; women would give a headache'. On the other hand factory B., with mainly female workers, complained of the problems involved in employing men. While in the Jordanian period this firm was a small workshop employing only men, after the occupation it was one of the first workshops to subcontract and employ women. Actually, the owners had first expanded their male work force, but within a few years they gradually replaced these male workers with women, as the men had unionised, demanded higher wages and some of them had brought work from Israel themselves. They considered women as both cheaper and easier to control. This is in sharp contrast to the policy of the owners of factory A. They aim at increasing profitability through raising productivity rather than by exploiting labour through low wages. Starting with a few male workers in the later 1970s, they rapidly expanded production and recently built a new factory. This firm works with a double shift and tries to raise longer-term productivity by creating a stable labour force, through paying relatively high monthly wages and providing a clear-cut wage system and extensive mobility chain. Female subcontractors, like Imm Ghassān, who were not able to employ men but aimed at increasing productivity, did the next best thing, paying women piece-rates. Some women actually preferred that as not all of them employ 'gender difference as resistance' to the same extent. In particular older women with a longer labour history tend to act similarly to men, emphasising their skills and productivity and favouring piece-rates, as this gives them some autonomy. 'If you work piece-rates no one can say anything to you; if you are absent, if you don't work, it is on your own account', one of them underlined.

## 8.5    Women and property: seamstresses, garment workers and subcontractors

What do these transformations in garment production mean for women's access to property? A major change has been the deterioration of the position of highly skilled seamstresses. Previously strict gender segregation had given them a captive female market and had helped to define the profession as respectable and also suitable for the better-off. Some artisanal seamstresses did not start working because of financial need, but rather to have something to do. These women, such as Imm Rāʿida for example, could be heirs to property and would be provided for by their own family. Still, they were pleased not to have to *ask* for money. They might well spend their income on buying a piece of land or investing in some stock or bonds. In other cases, there was a financial impetus, such as in the case of Sitt ʿAfāf, a single woman who took care of her younger siblings. Actually, marital status and a sewing career often influenced each other. Skilled seamstresses were in a stronger position to refuse unwanted suitors because they had a profession and earned fairly well. At the same time, they might take upon themselves financial responsibilities, such as the care of an elderly mother or a brother's son, which in turn stimulated them to continue working and refrain from marriage. As Sitt Salwā, who had taken in one of her brother's sons, said, 'If you marry does that bring you more than a son?' Still, sewing could also be an important source of income for married women who were talented and motivated, and this was all the more so if they were widowed and lacked financial resources.

Although also after the Israeli occupation there are still women who work as independent skilled seamstresses, their situation has generally deteriorated. They often work on their own, as it has become difficult to find girl assistants. Girls prefer to go to school and if they want to learn sewing they take a special sewing course rather than becoming apprenticed to a skilled seamstress. At the same time a considerable number of women have become garment workers in the subcontracting industry. Admittedly, the concept of the male provider is a strong legitimation for the low wages they are paid, yet it also gives them some control over their own income. While they usually start working because of the financial need of the household, they were commonly allowed to keep part of their wages themselves. This is the case both for the younger women, who were still expected to marry, and for the older single or no longer married women, albeit in a different way.[13]

Young women may keep part of their wages to buy clothes and sometimes gold, but they mainly work to help the household until they marry. As daughters they contribute to the costs of living of the household, which may include paying for the education of a brother or sister or, as in the case of Amal, paying off the household debts. They define these contributions in terms of 'gifts'; they are able to give because of their involvement in wage labour. Such 'gifts' could also imply a counterclaim. Wafā', for example, argued that her brother supported her financially when she wanted to start her own sewing workshop, because having worked for years as a garment worker she had lessened his financial obligations by paying for the university study of her sister. A considerable number of these women are working for quite some years. If in some cases it may have been their family blocking their marriage chances, many seem to have refrained from marriage because they did not like the men who had come for them. There is little evidence that having worked as a garment worker influenced their dower.

The second category of garment workers are the older women, or rather women above the ideal marriage age who realise that they might remain single, and previously married women. These women emphasise that an older unmarried woman or a divorcee with children needs money of her own. For them an independent income is very important. In their own terms, 'if nobody pays for you, they cannot give you orders'. They more often spend their income on gold as security for the future, occasionally even save enough to build themselves a separate room with facilities next to their fathers' house, and in some cases buy a sewing machine to start their own small firm or to work as an independent tailor.

The position of the few female subcontractors is very different from that of skilled seamstresses previously. Imm Ghassān and Imm 'Imād, the two most successful ones I interviewed, were shining examples of social mobility. Starting from scratch they had both managed to buy land and to build a new house annex workshop, spending well over 10,000 JD. Yet, to set up a moderately successful workshop they had to flaunt many social norms, such as by going to Tel-Aviv themselves, and with five and four children respectively to take care of, they also had an extremely heavy

[13] There is no strong predominance of very young girls in the subcontracting workshops. Siniora gives 95 per cent between 18 and 29 years (1989: 49), in the CWW survey 43 per cent of the women are twenty-five years or older, in my interviews this is the case with a little over half of the women workers.

work load. Moreover, for every successful female subcontractor there were dozens of women taking in work from male subcontractors, whose situation was not very different from that of women workers.

So, new labour opportunities were created for girls with little education from a poor, non-urban background. For them sewing was often the best work they could get. They preferred sewing to the few other types of work available, such as cleaning or agricultural labour. Urban, middle-class women, however, have shunned the garment sector after the Israeli occupation. As will be argued in the next chapter, they have found other forms of employment.

# 9    Education, professional work and property

If women working in low-status occupations often have to face censure and rebuke, this is not the case if they are employed in the 'better' professions, such as teaching. This chapter addresses women's access to property through such professional work. Since access to (higher) education is a pre-condition for women's entry into the professions, the main trends in women's education will be addressed first. The chapter will then trace the development of professional employment: the opening up of new fields and the professionalisation of other types of work, such as nursing. What such work means for women's access to property ties in with the particular background and position of the women involved. In the mandatory period, professional employment was largely limited to single, urban women from well-known families; gradually, however, some non-urban, married and lower-class women have entered the professions. This change is brought out in the following three labour stories.

## 9.1    Employed in the professions: three labour stories

*Sitt Yusrā, an elderly teacher from Nablus*

When I asked elderly women who had taught them, they often mentioned the name of Sitt Yusrā. Having started her teaching career in the 1930s, she belonged to one of the earliest generations of Nablus teachers still alive. Born in the late 1910s she was the second girl in a prominent, yet impoverished family of five daughters and one son. Her paternal grand-father had held high government positions and had been a wealthy man, but had been forced to leave to Egypt because of his nationalist activities. Her father, a trader, had fallen ill at a young age and the family had spent a lot of money on attempts to cure him. Her mother, of a very well-educated, progressive family of scholars and religious men, was literate; she had been taught reading and writing at a Quran school (*kuttāb*).

Sitt Yusrā's elder sister had also been a teacher, but she was not able to recall much detail about her working life. Sitt Yusrā, on the other hand, both enjoyed recalling past times and was very well able to convey her insights to me. If in some cases women discussed their property only after I had asked them explicitly about it, Sitt Yusrā was proud of what she had managed to acquire and needed little probing to elaborate extensively about her house in Nablus, the second house she had bought in Jericho, the house she had built in Amman, the shares she had acquired, and the savings she had in a bank. Not having inherited much, she emphasised that she had bought all property through her own efforts; her teaching career had been her major source of access to property.

In the 1920s, Sitt Yusrā's family was one of the few living outside the old city, their house very close to that of some Christian nuns with whom her parents had a cordial relationship and who also sometimes instructed the girls after school hours. In those days after completing the fifth and highest grade at the local Aishiyya school, a girl could continue her education only if she was selected for the Teachers Training College for women (*dār muʿallimāt*) in Jerusalem. Eager to study there and supported by her family, Sitt Yusrā took the required exams in arithmetic, Arabic and English and was the only girl of her year admitted.

Like many of the other girls, Sitt Yusrā, about twelve years old at the time, at first found life difficult at the College. It was a strict boarding school, run by an Englishwoman, the inspector of female education. By then her elder sister had already graduated and contact with the family was discouraged. Both culturally and politically the girls found themselves in a very different environment. Sitt Yusrā described to me in great detail how astonished the girls were at the small amount of water they were allotted to wash with. The political tensions in the city also affected them; Sitt Yusrā actually recalled once having been hit on the head by a stone. As in those days the level of education in Nablus was lower than in many other Palestinian cities, girls from Nablus had a particularly hard time. As Sitt Yusrā put it, 'We had only gone to school for five years, while the girls from Jaffa, Nazareth and Safad had finished the first or second year of secondary school in their home towns. Yet, we did manage. Sometimes we even had better grades.'

At that time, the College had a four-year programme with two options, one of which guaranteed a teaching job. 'You could take a registered exam, then you were able to teach, or you could take an easier exam, if you had only come to get an education', Sitt Yusrā explained. 'For us it was necessary to work, so we took the registered exam. We had gone there on the condition that we would become teachers.' More than once Sitt Yusrā emphasised that it was her mother who had paid for their education and had given them the opportunity to learn. After her father had fallen ill, her mother had started to work as a seamstress and soon had become well known in Nablus. After Sitt Yusrā herself became employed, she helped her mother to support the family. She used the argument of financial need to refuse many suitors. 'In those days many teachers refused marriage', she said, 'because as soon as the contract was written, the British authorities fired them. Every time a man came to ask me in marriage, I said no, because I wanted to work. For myself and for our family. Is it not better to work than to need people? My father died when my brother was about ten years old. My mother let all of us learn while my father was ill, and then my eldest sister and I helped her to educate our younger siblings.' Reflecting further on marriage she added: 'and when I was older I was also more critical, my demands had become higher.'

Sitt Yusrā's teaching career started in the late 1930s. Having graduated in 1936, the year the Arab Revolt began, she stayed first at home because of the six-month general strike. By the time she started teaching, primary education for girls in Nablus had been extended up to the seventh grade. There was no specialisation and she taught Arabic to the seventh grade, arithmetic to the sixth, and English to the fifth grade. After three years she was chosen by the director of the Fatimiyya school to become her substitute. Soon thereafter her father died and her mother also fell ill. The family's financial situation deteriorated further and they had to move to another house. So, when in the early 1950s the great demand for teachers in Kuwait reached Nablus, Sitt Yusrā went there because, she explained, 'my brother was still studying medicine, my youngest sisters were in school, and we needed the money'. Yet her time in Kuwait was not a success; she only stayed for one year as she found life there very difficult. In her words, 'even the water was full of sand'.

She returned to the Fatimiyya school, but had another intermezzo abroad from 1956 to 1958 in Saudi Arabia, giving private lessons to one of the daughters of a prince. The pay was very good, and she was living well at the palace, with everything taken care of, but she had to return home when her employer found himself in political trouble and left the country. Again Sitt Yusrā returned to the Fatimiyya school where she worked until the Israeli occupation. Then she stopped teaching. 'I could not accept having an Israeli inspector in the classroom', she said. 'I knew I had to resign or I would end up in prison.' Like the other government teachers appointed before the occupation, she continued to receive her salary from Amman.

Looking back at her teaching career Sitt Yusrā strongly regretted the declining standards of the profession. If previously there had been a very strict selection of girls who wanted to become teachers, 'nowadays', she said, 'everyone can become a teacher and only those whose grades are not high enough to enter university attend Teacher Training Colleges.' The result was that teachers had become less respected: 'If the teacher says something, the pupil will answer her back with a hundred words. In our times they respected their teachers and there was order, nowadays it is chaos.' Yet, on the other hand, she also acknowledged that education had become more accessible, with 'the lower classes even better educated than the higher classes'.

In a very matter-of-fact way Sitt Yusrā told me about her marriage. She had been married in 1961, when she must have been in her early forties. As she first put it, this was just the thing everyone was doing; her elder sister had also married late in life, and her brother had just married. Later she also pointed out that at such an age a woman does not marry for love, but looks after her interests. Sitt Yusrā knew her husband, a high civil servant from Jerusalem, through his sister's daughter, a colleague of hers with whom she had attended Teacher Training College. Yet, she did not seem overly impressed with the marriage, and also attributed her childlessness to her husband: 'He was much, much older than I was, maybe twenty-five years older, but at the time we did not know that. He had registered his age as younger, in order that I would agree. Had I known that there was such a large age difference between us, I may not have married him.' Turning to the wedding, Sitt Yusrā pointed out that the celebrations had been very simple. 'There was no marriage party', she recalled. 'I was old and he was a widower, so I only had a farewell party, there was no singing or playing the drums. Then he came with his family and I went with them to live in his home town.' Her family did not want a dower. They registered 1 JD prompt and 500 JD deferred, 'in case of a divorce', and her husband brought gifts. 'He gave me a bracelet, but I did not want much gold', she said. 'I did not need it, as I already had gold myself.'

In her reply to my question whether he had given her property, she emphasised that she had always remained independent. 'I had nothing from him. Every time he said something about gold, I said that I did not want any. He offered me the gold of his first wife, but I said, "no, that is for her daughter, her children". I did not take any of it, as I did not need it and I was not greedy.' In fact, it was shortly after she had been married that Sitt Yusrā had her first house built. 'I had heard that land was becoming expensive in Amman, that it was a good investment', she explained. 'So I bought half a *dunum* of land for about 1,000 JD.' Her sister's husband, who was living in Amman, built the house, which cost her about 5,000 JD.

After marriage Sitt Yusrā continued to work, but in her husband's home town. When she resigned after the Israeli occupation, she still continued to receive her Jordanian salary from Amman, amounting to about 100 JD. Her husband, on the other hand, lost his job as his department was abolished and only received a very small British pension of 25 JD. 'Of course I had to help my husband pay for our livelihood', Sitt Yusrā said, 'and I did so, but only what was necessary, no more; I never answered him when he said "give me 1,000 JD."'

Around the mid-1970s, Sitt Yusrā started a new project, a house in Nablus, 'for the future', as she put it. Although she did not say so directly, she probably wanted to secure her position as a childless woman with a husband advanced in years. Before marriage she had already bought, together with her elder sister, one *dunum* of land from her mother's brother, her share costing about 250 JD. Building the house amounted to some 15,000 JD. 'It was very cheap', Sitt Yusrā said, 'because my brother built a house next to us, so he could oversee the work, and I was not cheated, as may have been the case otherwise.' It took about three years for the house to be finished. 'It lasted so long because I was a civil servant, receiving only about 100 JD a month. I waited for the money to come, then I gave it to the labourers, we built for some days and waited for the next 100 JD.' In the process Sitt Yusrā had to sell the house in Amman, as she said 'because I needed the money to build here. I wanted to settle in my own country, not in Amman.' Having sold the house in Amman for 37,000 JD she spent a lot on furnishing the new house. 'I bought expensive furniture, had central heating installed and have all the conveniences', she elaborated. 'And I bought a new car. The very same day my husband died, in 1983, I was to bring a new car from the garage. I will never forget that. The remainder of the money I put in the bank and I started to enjoy myself.'

In 1986 Sitt Yusrā bought herself a second house, near Jericho with its pleasant winter climate, so she could escape the cold of Nablus and spend the winter there. Before the occupation the Jordanian and Palestinian elite had their winter quarters there, but after the occupation the Israeli army had taken over the area for some years and the houses had fallen into decay. She bought one of these dilapidated houses and had it renovated: 'Every Monday and Thursday I took the workers to Jericho. First I went together with my brother and his wife, but he has his work, so then I went by myself. Since two years I spend the winter there.' Both the house in Nablus and the one in Jericho were registered in her name.

Looking back at her working life, Sitt Yusrā was quite pleased. 'I am content now I see the result of my work. You only know the value of rest and relaxation if you have tired yourself first. Of my sisters and brother no one is in need, all of them are educated. We all have built our houses. I am not dependent on anyone, I have a house here, a house in Jericho and money in the bank.'

*Latīfa, an unemployed teacher from Balata camp*

Latīfa, in her late thirties, the eldest daughter of Imm Muhammad, was also trained as a teacher, but historical circumstances and a different social background made her labour story very different from Sitt Yusrā's. When I first met her in 1988, she was much more restrained than her younger sisters and had considerable authority at home. Later I understood that she was very careful in confiding in me, as her major aim at the time was to get permission to leave the West Bank, together with her younger brother.

Raised in Balata camp, Latīfa stressed that life had been very difficult when she was small. The whole family, father, mother, five sisters and two brothers, had all lived in two very small rooms. Like her sister Fadwā she had only managed to complete her education by earning money for her school expenses through picking vegetables in the Jordan Valley in the school vacations. Early in life Latīfa had set as her aim to get an education in order to work and to help her family. So she did not mind when, after she graduated from Al-Najah Teacher Training College, her father turned down her maternal cousin, a pharmacist, when he asked for her hand in marriage, claiming that she was to marry a paternal cousin.

Yet her expectations of work and income, which some refugee girls had managed to realise before her, had already become more difficult to fulfil by the time she graduated in the late 1970s. When she registered with the department of education for a teaching job in a government school, there were already many unemployed teachers, often with higher (university) qualifications and better contacts than she had. So, she was only able to work occasionally in different villages as a substitute teacher on a temporary basis. In an attempt to find more permanent employment, she started working as a medical assistant, trained on the job. Yet as she said, 'it only gave me pocket money, I never made more than 20 JD, working from eight in the morning until four or five in the afternoon.'

While she did this work for several years, with her application for a teaching job pending she still hoped to be able to work as a teacher. When someone high-up in the Israeli-led department of education came to where she worked and she heard who he was, she told him her problems and asked him whether he could not help her find a job as a teacher. A few weeks later she was called for an interview. They were, however, not interested in her teaching capacities, but wanted her to work as an informer, regularly providing reports on the other teachers and the students about their political activities. Almost in shock, she told them that she did not really want a job and left the building.

Convinced that there was no chance of a teaching appointment, she applied for a job in Saudi Arabia together with her brother who had recently married and was in need of money to pay off his debts. When they were accepted her brother went to work in a relatively low-paid job, but Latīfa was appointed as a teacher of religion. 'Life was very difficult there', she recalled, 'it was very hot, and I worked in a village without water or electricity, with only mud huts. So, we went to live in the nearest city, which meant that I had to travel 60 km. twice a day. But the pay was very good.'

Her work in Saudi Arabia was a great relief to the family. She sent most of her wages home and, as her mother told me several times, the whole house was built on her contributions. From the money she saved for herself she bought gold and two suitcases full of clothing, so she would not have to spend much when she married. It is this period in her life about which Latīfa enjoyed talking very much. During the long curfews in Balata, she told me many anecdotes about life in Saudi Arabia and about their friends from different nationalities, and showed me the clothing still tucked away in her suitcases, which she had never worn.

After working in Saudi Arabia for four years she had to return home. As their financial situation had improved, her brother's wife no longer accepted her husband's continuous absence. Latīfa was then again faced with the problem of unemployment, as the number of teachers without work had only increased. Yet, she did not have much choice. A woman working in Saudi Arabia needs a *mahram* (a male within the forbidden degrees of marriage) to accompany her, but her father was an old man, unable to travel, and at that time her youngest brother was still in school. When I met her for the first time in 1988, she was considering going abroad again to teach, as her brother had just finished his vocational training. But with the intifada all residents of Balata camp were collectively forbidden to travel abroad and, in fact, she suspected that her brother would probably not be able to travel for at least one year, as he had been imprisoned and still had a suspended sentence.

With such bleak prospects marriage was becoming increasingly important to Latīfa. After graduation she had not minded that her father turned down suitors; at that time she herself wanted to work. But when she returned from Saudi Arabia the situation had become more complex. As she put it: 'Once you are thirty no man comes unless he is considerably older, divorced or widowed.' By then she started to resent the interference of her relatives. 'My brother did not want some of the men I would have married. It is as if he is the one who would marry them! Between my father, my brother and my father's brother no one will be deemed suitable.' Yet she herself turned down the men her brother approved of. One of these was a twenty-four years old, a man whom she refused, suspecting him of wanting to marry her for material reasons. 'He will take me to Saudi Arabia to earn money for him', she said, 'but later he will take a second wife.'

When I talked to her during the second year of the intifada, her prospects had become even more dim. With early marriage becoming more widespread in the camps, no opportunities for work available, and her health deteriorating (she had been shot in the arm by rubber bullets and was very sensitive to tear gas), she was thinking about accepting an elderly widower from a village in the north. 'I told him, I do not know how to work in agriculture, how to harvest, I am a teacher. They said, "no problem, you will do the housework." ' As she put it, there was simply no future. 'My father is an old man. I have saved some money, but it is limited and once it is spent, from where shall I bring then? My elder brother has his wife and children, my younger brother still has to build his own future, he cannot pay for all of us. If there was a job, if I had an income ... But there is no work, there is nothing.'

### Ilhām, a married professional with children

In late 1987, shortly before the intifada I talked extensively with Ilhām, in her late thirties, who was teaching at an institution of higher education. With great openness and enthusiasm she elaborated on her career. Her parents were originally from a large village to the west of Nablus, yet in the early 1940s they had settled in the city, where her father worked for the British army and later opened a shop. The third in a large family, Ilhām first went to school in Nablus and after the 1967 war, when the Nablus schools were closed, in Jordan, where her brother already held a teaching job. After also taking her BA degree there, she returned to the West Bank in the early 1970s and took up her first teaching post in a large village near Nablus. By then her father had already died. As two of her brothers were still studying, she helped in paying for their expenses and she also gave some money to her mother.

A few years later, when she was in her mid-twenties she was married to a man from the village where she was working. She had met him through his sister's daughters, her students. 'I used to visit them and he saw me there', she said. 'It seems he formed a certain idea about me, I had not given it any thought. But when he came and asked for my hand, we sat down together. My family allowed me to sit down with him twice.' He was only a few years older and also worked as a teacher.

As her father had already died, her brother was in charge of arranging the dower. In Ilhām's words, 'At first the family wanted to do it as it is done in this society, a very high sum of money. I said, "why do we have to do it that way, I am not convinced that he can pay. And if I believe that the man is a nice person and we could be happy together, why do we have to make things complicated? As an educated person I should be different from other girls." So I had it my way, the dower was very reasonable. You see, because it was my brother, if it were my father, it would have been different, he would have been more authoritative.' Ilhām pointed out that she did not use her 700 JD prompt dower for clothes or other personal things, but saved the bulk of it, and paid for the refrigerator and other important articles for the house. She also skilfully first postponed the costly party to be held at the engagement to the wedding, and then argued she would rather have a simple wedding and spend the money on something more useful.

As her husband's brothers were all working abroad and his elderly parents had to be taken care of, they went to live near them in the village. 'We did not need to live in the same house', Ilhām said, 'but at least we could be near them, you cannot ask old people to come and live in a place they have not been used to.' Until 1980 Ilhām remained teaching in the village, while her husband taught in Nablus city. Then they sat down to seriously discuss their future. Their salaries as government teachers were low and by then they already had two daughters. 'I earned about 80 JD. No, it never increased, it was always the same, in fact it used to get less, not more. It was paid in Israeli currency and that used to go down quickly.' Her husband earned about the same.

As Ilhām had a brother in the USA it was decided she should go there to get a MA degree. All agreed that she would not be able to take care of her two children, at the time three years and seven months old, and study at the same time. As it would also be much more expensive if the whole family went, her mother and her mother-in-law promised to take care of them. 'To leave the children has been the most difficult decision in my life', Ilhām said. 'My mother-in-law volunteered to take good care of them and my mother also offered to help, so I left the whole family, the husband and two girls. That was a big sacrifice.' Yet Ilhām also emphasised that she always had the ambition to finish her education, and her husband supported her. 'My husband is really a great man, I have to admit, he really encouraged me and gave me the opportunity. He said, "go ahead and do not worry about what will happen in your absence, we will take care of ourselves, it will be a hard and long year but we will manage."'

Ilhām stayed with her brother and his wife for a little over one year. 'It took me exactly one year and three months to get a MA', she said. 'I did it as quickly as possible in order to come back. But in the meantime I did all I could to try to find my husband funding so he could also come and study.' Indeed, by time she graduated she had arranged everything for him, he came with the children, and they moved to the university where he had been accepted for a MA programme. 'The whole thing really was a family project', Ilhām emphasised. 'I sold the gold for the sake of education and only kept the wedding ring and both my brother and his brothers helped us financially.'

Their strategy was successful. Upon returning to the West Bank in the early 1980s they both found professional employment with local institutions, Ilhām herself earning a little over 300 JD, and her husband slightly more. 'We were very lucky', Ilhām said. 'If we had returned two years later, we would not have found employment.' Still, her husband also started to set up a small chicken farm in the village. 'This project is not out of greed', she emphasised, pointing out the insecure political situation. 'The point is, we all feel here that it is risky. Our work depends on so many things that are out of our control. If no money comes from abroad we will not be paid.'

When I talked to her she had three children, all girls, which in more than one way, was not easy. 'As you know in our society it is not sufficient to have three girls, there has to be a boy. Everybody presses so you start feeling yourself that you have to ... but honestly, as for myself, I do not feel that way, three girls should be enough. I am teaching with a full load here, with the responsibility of taking care of the house, taking care of three kids, and nobody can tell you that it is easy, it is not easy. Living in a village makes it even harder, because of the problems with transportation.' Although she still made very long days, Ilhām's work load was lessened to some extent when she found a women to take care of the children and the house while she was working. 'My mother-in-law is getting old, she cannot take care of three children in my absence', Ilhām said. And she was able to afford it, 'We pay her 45 JD a month, and if she still needs some expenses, you know, for her girls, I sometimes help.'

Ilhām emphasised that she and her husband always had one budget. 'We always held our money together; in fact, I am the controller of it', she said laughingly. 'Well, whatever we need we sit down and discuss what we are going to do with the money.' Although she loved to have some fashionable gold, Ilhām had not yet been able to buy any. 'When we came back we were still in need of money. My brother-in-law had built a house in the village, in his father's courtyard, he himself had finished the top floor, and he let us have the middle one; we spent about 5,000 JD on it. And then we were able to buy a piece of land nearby the university. My aim was always to find a place here. We know that living in the village is temporarily because of family reasons, but for our future. We need a place here, so we managed to buy a rather expensive piece of land. It is half a *dunum*, one half for us (our share cost 8,000 JD) and the other for his brother, who lives abroad; for him it is just an investment, but we will build a house on it. So I feel it still is not the time for gold, we still have some debts to pay for that land.'

## 9.2    The first step: getting an education

*The mandatory period: highly selective and urban biased*

To gain access to professional work, getting an education was the first hurdle. In the late Ottoman period there were some government schools in Palestine, but many pupils were taught in private schools. Often these were of the *kuttāb* type, where the Quran was to be memorised and some reading and writing skills were taught. Christian private schools were often set up by foreign institutions; these also provided secondary education, with German, French or English as the languages of instruction.

To the British mandatory authorities education was not a priority. Although the total number of schools increased, the educational budget remained very limited and there were many more pupils applying for admission to elementary schools than there were places available. By 1944 still only about one-third of all Arab children between five and fourteen went either to a private or to a government school and in particular the situation in the villages was difficult (Tibawi 1956: 171). While the earliest section created in the department of education was that of female education (in 1918) and the British opened a boarding training college for women in Jerusalem to facilitate the recruitment of teachers, they did not succeed either in redressing women's lesser access to education. It is true that gradually many more girls went to school, but the gender gap persisted. In 1925/26 18 per cent of the school population was female; this had increased only to 21 per cent in 1944/45. The great divide was between the cities and the rural areas. By the end of the mandatory period, 85 per cent of the boys and 60 per cent of the girls in the city went to elementary school; in the villages, the figures were 63 per cent for boys and only 7.5 per cent for girls (Tibawi 1956: 49, 228). In addition, the educational system was highly selective. Until the early 1930s the Women's Training College in Jerusalem was the only government secondary education available to women in the whole of Palestine. Even in the 1940s some of the women graduating recalled that their matriculation class consisted of eleven girls only. Girls not selected for this college could get secondary education only at private Christian boarding schools, such as the Schmidt's Girls' College (German Catholic) and the Pension at St Joseph (French Catholic), both in Jerusalem, or the (American) Friends Girls' School in Ramallah (Jaussen 1927: 46; Tibawi 1956: 62–3). These institutions demanded a high fee and were accessible only to the well-to-do.

In Jabal Nablus, an area less urbanised than the coastal region and in relative economic decline, girls' access to education was even more limited. In Nablus city up to the early 1940s there was only one elementary school for girls providing seven years of education, the Aishiyya school. As Sitt Yusrā pointed out in her labour story, educational opportunities in Nablus had remained very limited compared with those in other Palestinian cities, such as Jaffa, Nazareth or Safad. In the rural areas there were virtually no girls' schools; a few elderly village women recalled that they had gone one or two years to a *kuttāb* together with the village boys.

Generally, educating boys was given priority, as they were seen to be more in need of literacy; they would have to deal with state institutions, and were to earn a living for their families and for their parents in old age. Girls, on the other hand, were expected to marry, would be provided for, and their labour was needed, if not in agriculture, then in housework. Some also considered that educating girls was morally suspect. In their view, it would be more difficult to control girls who had learned to read and write and a common complaint was that if girls were educated 'boys and girls would write each other love-letters' which would undermine gender segregation and family control over marriage (also Hijab 1988: 65). Even if schools themselves were gender segregated, girls' daily trips to school may be seen as undermining female seclusion and impairing control over girls. But British policy was also a negative factor. To specific requests for girls' education, the mandatory authorities did not respond. In 1930, for example, the demand for boys' and girls' education is recorded in the rural areas and in 1933 the Palestine Arab Women's Congress requested opening girls' schools in the villages (Tibawi 1956: 230). But the mandatory authorities did not react. In addition, the educational programme contained elements of the British concept of a woman's calling. In the village schools there were 'slight variations to allow for the teaching of sewing and embroidery instead of manual work and agriculture' and in the city 'domestic science for girls and workshop work for boys replaced practical agriculture' (Tibawi 1956: 82). In the Rural Women Teacher Training College, there was a 'stress on domestic science and mothercraft' (Tibawi 1956: 52).

It was the daughters of the more prominent, although not always wealthy, progressive learned families in particular, who continued their education after elementary school. Often their father or a close male relative held a high religious position, such as judge (*qādī*) or *muftī* of Nablus. With a long-standing interest in education, these fathers were proud that their daughters had been selected and did not object to them spending four years at the Training College or at a private Christian boarding school in Jerusalem. In the late 1930s, for example, the eldest daughter of the *muftī* of Nablus boarded at the Roman Catholic Schmidt's College in Jerusalem. Referring to the *hadīth* 'Quest for learning is a sacred duty of every Muslim, male or female', these fathers legitimised their stand by arguing that Islam is strongly supportive of women's education (also Tibawi 1956: 228).

With girls' education increasingly common amongst the prominent urban families, those who were prevented from learning strongly resented this. If Sitt Yusrā and her elder sister had been encouraged to achieve at school and to become teachers, in the late 1920s Fadwā Tūqān (later to become a famous poet and writer), who 'preferred school to home' (1990: 46) as she phrased it herself in her autobiography, was sentenced by her brother to 'compulsory confinement to the house till the day of my death' (1990: 48). He had discovered that a boy had been following her on the way to school and that she had been given a jasmine flower. Other women from wealthy families were also much annoyed at not being able to continue their education. Imm Rāʿida, for example, had been a bright student at elementary school, but her eldest brother did not allow her to go to the Training College. 'He did not want girls to be educated', she told me. 'He said "she will fall in love and they will write letters to each other" and that sort of thing.' With some resentment in her voice, she added: 'Later he did allow his own daughters to learn, they even went to university, but he did not want us to go'.

### After 1948: the spread of education

After 1948, educational opportunities increased rapidly for both boys and girls, not only in the city but also in the rural areas. In the 1950s and 1960s the Jordanian government built many new schools to meet the growing demand, while the UNRWA provided nine years of education for refugee children. Education also became attractive to a wider public, as there were more employment opportunities for professionals in the Jordanian administration, with the UNRWA and in the Gulf States, while in the rural areas agriculture was becoming less central as a means of livelihood. The value of education was enhanced because employers based appointments and wage classifications on certificates and length of study, with education virtually guaranteeing a good income (Badran 1980: 58–9). Having lost their land, the refugees had a particular interest in education as a means of social mobility and as a result of the traumatic experience of 1948 Palestinians in general came to regard education as a form of property that could not be taken away. This regard for education continued after 1967 when Israel took over control of all government schools. Although educational standards in government schools are said to have declined and there is a high drop-out rate, children are staying in school longer (Graham-Brown 1984b: 65). It is the specific regard for education among Palestinians which makes the forced closing of schools during the intifada a particular sensitive issue, a frontal attack on Palestinian identity.[1]

If during the Jordanian period teacher training was the fastest growing sector of higher education, in the 1970s and 1980s the main emphasis has been on the development of the universities (Graham-Brown 1984b: 77).[2] Whereas the schools are Israeli-controlled the universities are amongst the few Palestinian national institutions on the West Bank. They were started as local initiatives by a family or groups of influential people in their respective towns and dependent on funding from external sources, mainly in the Arab world (Graham-Brown 1984b: 83). In Nablus, the Al-Najah School, founded in 1918, developed into a teacher-training college in 1965 and became a university in 1977. The number of students rapidly increased and almost quadrupled from 900 students in 1977/8 to 3,500 in 1983/4. Yet, these local universities, symbols of resistance to the Israeli occupation by their sheer existence and one of the few places open to political debate, had to face constant pressure from the Israeli authorities. Like the other universities, Al-Najah has been confronted with book censorship, the refusal of building permits, forced closures and the harassment, imprisonment and expulsion of students and staff members. From the beginning of the intifada all universities on the West Bank were closed by military order.

Although the gender gap in education still persists, it has narrowed and is at a higher level. More girls go to school for a longer period of time. In the Nablus district in 1980/1 the proportion of girl students in primary schools (length of schooling six years) was over 47 per cent, in preparatory schools (three years) it was over 45 per cent and in secondary schools (three years) almost 39 per cent (Graham-Brown 1984b: 69). Yet the spread of female education has not been even. In Nablus city, where schools and, more recently, higher education is available at a short distance and few young girls work for wages, female education has further increased. In the camps with the UNRWA providing schools for both boys and girls and sometimes work opportunities for those finishing their education, girls' school attendance has also grown rapidly. The proportion of girl refugees enrolled in all primary, preparatory and secondary schools increased from 29 per cent in 1950/1, to 36 per cent in 1960/1, 44

---

[1] Primary and secondary schools have been collectively closed by military orders for about nine months in 1988, and for about eight months in 1989 (al-Haq 1988: 311; 1989: 451).

[2] Expansion in the number of places for training teachers has come from the universities, and the Al-Najah Teacher Training College has been incorporated into the university (Graham-Brown 1984b: 78).

per cent in 1970/1, and 48 per cent in 1980/1 (Graham-Brown 1984b: 169).[3] Refugee parents have come to realise that daughters, like Latīfa, may also provide income and security, while sons often need their wages to save for their own marriages.

In the villages, on the other hand, the move of girls into education has come later. In Al-Balad, for example, in 1980 elementary education was common, but there was a definite drop in female school attendance at preparatory level, and only few girls continued to secondary education. A major obstacle to their participation was that they would have to travel to the city daily; actually, the first girls from the village who finished secondary education all had relatives in the city where they could stay overnight. In general, in villages with better facilities, more regular transport to the city and less involvement in agriculture, female school attendance is considerably higher. But in those villages with a great demand for women's work in agriculture, such as in the Jordan Valley where irrigated agriculture, often combined with goat herding, is prevalent, female school attendance could be particularly low and the gender gap was accentuated.[4]

Women have also entered higher education. In the 1950s some women from the prominent families started to study abroad, but this was still exceptional. Sitt Imān, for example, whose father was a religious scholar and for many years had studied in Egypt at the Azhar, told me that her father did not object when she wanted to take her BA in England, but his friends did. 'I was fortunate that he supported me', she said. 'Referring to the hadīth, which urges Muslims to seek knowledge, even unto China, he had argued "if she wants it I will not prevent her. I have raised her and I know how I have raised her."' The development of local universities has broadened the social backgrounds from which students are drawn and has encouraged women's higher education. At Al-Najah University from 1977–1987, an average of 45 per cent of the students were female. Many families may send a son abroad to continue his education, but hesitate to

---

[3] The data for 1950/1 and 1960/1 are for all Jordan, those for 1970/1 and 1980/1 for the West Bank only.

[4] The importance of women's labour becomes visible, for example, in the differences in school attendance between Al-Balad (with only dry-farming agriculture) and Nazlat al-Balad with irrigated land and goat-herding more common. In Al-Balad in the late 1950s a school for girls was built; in 1961 already about 45 per cent of all girls between six and eleven years attended school. In Nazlat al-Balad, on the other hand, the situation was very different; there only 8 per cent of girls in that age category went to school. Although also boys' participation in education was lower there, the gender gap was considerably more pronounced in Nazlat al-Balad. In Al-Balad girls formed 44 per cent of all students, in Nazlat al-Balad only about 25 per cent (calculated from First Census 1963: 28–9, 38–9, 109–10, 118–19). During my fieldwork in the early 1980s, school attendance was lowest amongst girls in families with irrigated land or a large number of goats.

allow a daugther to go abroad by herself or to invest so much in a girl; Israeli statistics indicate that in the period 1984–1987 about 19 per cent of all West Bank students abroad were women (CBS 1990: 725). Especially for rural women going abroad to study could be difficult. In Al-Balad, for example, three girls were enroled in local universities and no boys (as their grades were not high enough), yet about ten boys were studying abroad and no girls.

Not only are about 45 per cent of the students at Al-Najah female, but the subjects they choose are also not strongly gender-specific. In secondary education the proportion of females is roughly the same in the literary and the science stream (Graham-Brown 1984b: 67). It is true that female students at Al-Najah are over-represented in the arts (58 per cent of the total number of students) and under-represented in economics (29 per cent), yet these percentages are not extreme, and in the sciences and in engineering they form 37 per cent and 40 per cent of the total number of students.[5] As universities base their admissions to specific subjects on secondary school exam (*tawjīhī*) scores, girls with a high score are encouraged to study demanding subjects such as science and engineering.

With the recession and growing unemployment among university graduates in the 1980s, enthusiasm for higher education has declined somewhat. After 1983/4 the number of students at Al-Najah has not increased further, and went down in 1987/8. Israeli statistical data indicate that the number of students abroad has declined, in 1988 reaching less than half the number in 1984. The proportion of girls to the total number of students, both in local universities and abroad, has remained roughly the same (45 per cent and 19 per cent respectively), with the exception of 1988, when the percentage of girls abroad suddenly went up to 27 per cent (CBS 1990: 725). This is, however, probably due to a particular decline in the number of male students abroad because of the stricter travel policy of the Israeli authorities towards men. Permission to travel is often denied on such grounds as previous arrests, and if permission is obtained, travel for young males is made conditional on them staying outside the country for considerable periods of time. In particular, boys from poorer families who were previously able to either study with a scholarship in the Arab world or Eastern Europe, are now often refused exit permits for political reasons.

In general, educating girls has been accepted as desirable, in particular if (segregated) education is locally available. Girls tend to resent it very strongly if they are not allowed to complete their education. If previously female education was suspect as it was feared that educated girls would be

---

[5] Calculated for the year 1987/8; data for the previous years are not very different.

more difficult to control, more recently educated girls are seen as in better control of themselves and are given more freedom of movement as they are presumed to know how to behave in 'the public world'. So, education has become another criterium to differentiate between girls. As a rural garment worker said, 'The girls who go to university travel with the same bus to Nablus as we do, but we do not sit together. It is different, if you are a garment worker people talk about you, but they go to study, that is why they are respected.'

### 9.3     Entering the professions: more women, different women

*The growth of female professional employment*

With a larger number of girls going to school and staying in school longer, more women have become involved in professional work. Education has given them both the qualifications for professional employment and this field itself has become an important employer of women professionals.

In the earlier mandatory period, few women in the Nablus region were officially recorded as professionally employed and other types of work were considerably more common. According to the very detailed 1931 census, only 7 per cent of the non-agricultural female labour force could be considered professionals (Mills 1933: 327, 345). By 1961, when the Jordanians took a complete census, professional work had become far more popular among women with the proportion increased to 30 per cent (First Census 1963). Such regionally specific data are not available for later years, but Israeli statistics on West Bank employment indicate a further preponderance of professional work. By 1972, almost 49 per cent of the non-agricultural female labour force were professionals; the proportion of professionals has remained fairly constant thereafter (CBS 1973: 749).

The problem with these data is, however, that women's lower-status work has often gone under-reported; in consequence, the proportion of professionals in the female labour force is exaggerated. Still, the growth of female professional employment is also indicated by the increasing proportion of women in total professional employment. While the 1931 census shows that women formed about 7 per cent of those professionally employed, in 1961 it was 28 per cent and in 1972 it increased to 32 per cent, and amongst non-academic employees (largely teachers) it was almost 40 per cent (CBS 1973: 749); thereafter it only increased slightly. So, the gender gap in professional employment has decreased substantially, even if women are usually employed in the lower professional categories.

While these data are not fully comparable, with the boundaries of the Nablus district not completely identical in the mandatory and Jordanian periods and the data after 1967 referring to the West Bank as a whole, there is no doubt that female professional employment has grown considerably. Who are these women? And in which professional fields are they active?

### Teaching: a respectable profession?

Teaching has become widely accepted as *the* respectable profession for women from various backgrounds. This was, however, not yet so in the earlier mandatory period, when women's education was still suspect and female literacy encountered resistance from those who feared that less control over women would lead to the moral decline of the community. In the early mandatory period many of the teachers in Nablus governmental girls' schools had been Christians. In 1923, however, when the Palestinians were launching a campaign against the imposition of the British mandate, there was a concerted drive in Nablus to appoint Muslim teachers (Jaussen 1927: 49).

This first generation of Muslim teachers in Nablus seems to have had a varied background. Most of them probably only had four years of elementary education themselves, as one of those appointed in 1923, told me. One of the very few women with higher education was al-Hajja Afifa, who had studied with her brother in Beirut and became school director soon after she returned. Gradually the number of better-trained female teachers increased as girls started to attend the Women Training College in Jerusalem and others went to private secondary schools. Yet the number of female teachers remained limited. The British system was not only strongly selective, but British policy also did not allow for the employment of married women in government schools; once the marriage contract was signed they were dismissed.

With more and more women from prominent, respected families employed as teachers the profession itself became more accepted. Teaching was the first major section of state employment open to women. It is true that working as a teacher cuts through the gender division of labour in which men are supposed to be providers, yet its respectability is enhanced as it is a gender-segregated profession and knowledge is highly esteemed in Islam. For those working because of financial need, it was a particularly attractive job as it gave a woman a relatively high and secure income and secondary benefits. As civil servants, teachers benefited from the fixed rules and regulations which, except in regard to dismissal in the event of marriage, did not allow for overt gender discrimination.

Important changes in the profession occurred after 1948. The Jordanian government rapidly extended the number of schools and was in dire need of teachers, while the UNRWA was also recruiting teachers for its refugee schools. At the same time, there was also a rapidly increasing demand for teachers in the Gulf States. From the early 1950s on, a considerable number of teachers went to Kuwait, where already in 1936 two Palestinian women teachers, two sisters, had started the first girls' school (Ghabra 1987: 58). By the late 1950s female teachers also went to Saudi Arabia, when government education for girls' had been started there (Badran 1980: 67). In consequence, there was a great demand for teachers, the educational system became less selective and married women were also allowed to work as teachers in government schools (Hijab 1988: 97).

In those days the background of women teachers became more varied as new categories of women started to enter the teaching profession. The first women teachers going to Kuwait were often young refugee women from an urban, middle-class background, mostly graduates of Palestinian teaching colleges, who went there to support their families after the 1948 disaster (Ghabra 1987: 50). Women from prominent Nablus families also participated in this movement, some, like Sitt Yusrā, because of the much better pay, others because they wanted to see something of the world and were encouraged by the general atmosphere of pan-Arabism prevalent at that time. Gradually refugee girls from poorer families, such as Latīfa, also joined in. With rural girls entering education later, the number of teachers from a rural background remained relatively small.[6]

Although teaching is still seen as a respectable job for women, convenient also for married women because of the favourable working hours, the status of the teaching profession has declined. With the large demand for teachers the requirements were lowered and, as Sitt Yusrā argued, whereas in the mandatory period the brightest girls went to the Training College, later these went to university, leaving Teacher Training to those with lower grades. Work also became more demanding, with young teachers often appointed to the rural areas first. In particular during the Israeli occupation teaching, especially for those employed at government schools, has become an increasingly difficult and poorly paid job. With schools as the focus of resistance against the occupation, teachers are under great pressure; those perceived as politically active (which includes attempts at unionising, which is forbidden) can be demoted, transferred to distant rural areas or even fired. In addition, the pay has become much

---

[6] In the marriage contracts of the sample years in the period 1976–1988, 59 per cent of the women registering their profession as teacher were urban, 25 per cent were rural and 16 per cent were from the camps (n = 155).

worse. Those teachers employed by the Jordanians before 1967 still received their Jordanian salaries in JD, but those employed after 1967 are paid only the Israeli salary in the inflation-prone shekel, which is not index-linked.[7] These developments have made teaching a less attractive profession for those who did not need to work or had other options.

Still, teaching is one of the few local jobs available to university graduates, that is, if they or their family were not too well-known for political activism, for approval of the Israeli administration was needed for all appointments to government teaching posts. By the late 1970s, however, it had become increasingly difficult to find a teaching job; teachers were said to have to pay bribes, or, like Latīfa, were asked to work as informers. With the recession and the rise of unemployment the department of education was said to be more hesitant to employ married female teachers. As the tradition of gender segregation in elementary, preparatory and secondary education did not leave scope for replacing female teachers by male teachers, the discussion centred on whether it was desirable to employ married women as teachers when so many single female teachers were out of work. Although superficially this may seem an attempt to return to the employment policy of the mandatory times, this time it was not so much the propriety of employment for married women which was at stake, but rather the perceived need to relieve men of having to maintain their single female relatives. As such, it can be seen as another indication of the greater centrality of the husband as provider.

### Women in the new professions

During the British mandatory period, there were few other professional opportunities for women except teaching; the higher administrative jobs in the women's educational section were, for instance, held by British women (Tibawi 1956: 34). In the Jordanian period women started to enter other types of professional employment, in particular in government administration and with the UNRWA. Some of those who had been teachers in the mandatory period had received scholarships to study abroad and were appointed to higher administrative positions on return, often in the field of education or social work. As more women were able to acquire a university degree, they also entered professions such as medi-

---

[7] Especially in times of hyperinflation this could have serious consequences. For instance, when in March 1983 a teacher with five years' service received 12,800 IS this was the equivalent of 109 JD, when in March 1984 this had become 48,340 IS this was only worth 80 JD (Graham-Brown 1984b: 77).

cine, dentistry, engineering or pharmacy.[8] In particular, the opening of the local Al-Najah National University in 1977 stimulated women's entry into the professions, both by expanding women's opportunities for higher education and as the university itself became an important employer of professional women. By 1987 women formed about 11 per cent of the academic staff of Al-Najah. Most of these women in the top professions are still from the more prominent urban families.

At the same time other white collar employment grew rapidly, in particular secretarial work.[9] Secretaries, however, cannot be lumped together in one category, because their labour conditions, pay scales, secondary benefits and status vary widely. Privately employed secretaries, such as administrative assistants to doctors or lawyers or those employed by charitable institutions are often paid as little as sewing workers (40 JD a month in 1987) and they have neither job security nor secondary benefits. Those employed in the local administration (such as the municipality) or in national institutions, on the other hand, earn more and are better protected, with fixed pay scales, regulations about secondary benefits and so on. In particular, the university is seen as a very good employer, where secretaries can earn considerably more than government teachers; in 1987 a secretary at Al-Najah with five years' experience, for example, earned about 150 JD. A relatively large number of these secretaries are from a lower-middle-class refugee background, as the UNRWA has been the main institution to set up post-secondary vocational training centres, which provide training in secretarial skills.[10]

In addition, certain types of work have become professionalised. A major example is nursing and midwifery. In the mandatory period, a considerable number of women, who had learned their skills through experience, worked as traditional midwives. Their activities were, however, often not defined as work, and rather than some sort of fixed payment they often received gifts instead. Women working as nurses were

---

[8] Beginning in 1976 a growing number of women registered employment in the higher professions in their marriage contracts. In the sample years from 1976 to 1987 the total number of such registrations was twenty-five, increasing from two in 1976 to thirteen in 1987. The most commonly mentioned higher professions were pharmacist, doctor and engineer. The large majority of women who registered their professions were from the city; in only two cases did village women register.

[9] Whereas in 1972 4 per cent of the female labour force was employed in clerical work (CBS 1973: 740), by 1987 this had increased to about 10 per cent (CBS 1990: 733).

[10] This information is based on interviews with ten married secretaries, that is about 20 per cent of the total number employed at al-Najah. Half of them had been trained at the Al-Tira UNRWA centre in Ramallah. Their fathers were usually self-employed or lower employees, working as carpenter, garage worker, mechanician, driver, lower government employee or teacher. Three of the ten had lost their fathers at an early age. Very few secretaries are from the rural areas.

commonly looked down upon and considered as upgraded servants. In the Jordanian period this started to change slightly as both the government and the UNRWA began to arrange for official training programmes and to hand out certificates. More recently, the educational demands for nurses have further increased, and due to the closure of the local universities with the intifada, many girls whose grades were high enough to be admitted to university, have applied for training as practical nurses. These higher educational requirements have turned nursing into a more respectable profession. Respect for this work has also increased with the intifada, as many nurses work voluntarily for long hours to take care of the intifada casualties.[11] Yet nursing is still by and large a non-urban profession. In the Nablus hospital, for example, where I did research in 1988, about half the nursing students were from the villages and the other half from refugee backgrounds.[12] The women holding higher administrative positions, on the other hand, were more often from urban families.

In short, professional work opportunities for women have increased considerably, and these women are of a much more divergent background. At the same time, however, some types of more informal work have disappeared. This means that in particular for younger educated women work opportunities have increased, while elderly experience-trained women have lost out. The next question is whether professional labour did give women access to property. First I will discuss this for single women, then I will turn to the influence of married women's professional work on the dower and on their husbands' maintenance obligations.

### 9.4    Single women, social class and property

*The prominent families: independent daughters*

Whereas some elderly teachers I interviewed, such as Sitt Yusrā, had married late in life, many of them had refrained from marriage. It was working as a teacher which induced women to remain single, the reverse hardly occurred. For an older single woman to become a teacher later in life was highly unusual, as access to the profession was strictly regulated

---

[11] Hamdan (1991: 34) who interviewed forty-five nurses in four different Nablus hospitals states that thirty regarded society's opinion of their profession as negative, while fifteen saw it as positive; according to forty nurses society's views have improved while five argue that there is no change.

[12] According to Hamdan (1991: 35) of the women nurses in all Nablus hospitals only a good 15 per cent were from the city itself. This percentage includes women from a refugee background living in Nablus city.

through formal educational requirements. As such it was very different from a career as a seamstress.

During the British mandatory period many teachers were from prominent, though not always wealthy, scholarly families. Steeped in a tradition of learning and having managed to get through the highly selective British educational system, these women took great pride in their work. As Sitt Yusrā explained, the British employment policy encouraged many women to postpone marriage, while at the same time their stable and relatively high income made it easier for them to refuse suitors not to their liking. In this period marriages were still strictly arranged and for women from such a family background the number of grooms deemed suitable could be very limited, with only a paternal cousin (*ibn ʿamm*) considered acceptable in more conservative families. If refusing a cousin would mean remaining single, women teachers at least had the advantage that by virtue of their income they would never become fully dependent on their relatives. Even the women from wealthy families strongly stressed the importance of economic independence. Sitt Imān, for instance, who had held a high UNRWA post before retirement, pointed out that in the late 1950s she had contemplated marriage when, in her early thirties, she returned from studying in England. Yet, as she said: 'Maybe because I was higher educated, I had become more critical, I did not like to marry an older wealthy merchant, and my family did not push me. But at that time there was no opportunity to say "that one is more suitable." We did not mix. Abroad I had come into contact with many people, but I did not want to hurt my family by marrying a foreigner. Later that became possible and I saw many girls do so.' In her eyes professional work was very important for women. 'It gives a woman a feeling of self-respect, that she has accomplished something. Work is very important for your dignity, it means that you do not need others. If a woman does not marry or is repudiated, without work she has to depend on her family, then she does not feel free, it is not her own money she spends. There is no dignity if you have to take from others. Everyone likes to be independent.' The labour stories of elderly professional women fit well with Fadwā Tūqān's description of teachers in her autobiography as a particular social group, socially accepted, self-confident and knowing the value of economic independence (Tuqan 1990: 94–5).

Over time, more of these women did marry. As Jordanian policy allowed married women to continue teaching, they were no longer forced to choose between a teaching career or marriage. Gradually also the prominent families became less strict in arranging marriages. Imposing cousin marriage became less common and daughters were allowed some freedom of choice. Yet still quite a few of these women either married late in life, as Sitt Yusrā chose to do, or remained single. Some argued that they preferred their freedom over marriage. Many joined the wave of teachers going abroad, sometimes for financial reasons, such as Sitt Yusrā at her first trip to Kuwait, but also as they liked a change of environment and to see the world. To Sitt Sukayna, a few years younger than Sitt Imān, but from a more conservative background, the latter seemed the most important. In her family of large landowners, at that time only a cousin was deemed eligible. 'We (I and my sister) did not feel our cousin suitable', she told me. 'The family tried to convince us, but we did not accept. And later I thought it is better for me to be free than to marry.' Her great wish of going abroad was finally fulfilled when in 1957 her father allowed her to teach in Aden; she was about thirty then. 'I do not know why he accepted it', she said, recalling that period of her life. 'He had prevented me from going to Kuwait three or four times. Maybe he got tired of me, because every year I asked to go somewhere, seeing so many girls go. But my family used to have some restrictions.' The five years she worked in Aden made a deep impression on her. 'Aden was an excellent experience for me. I liked it very, very much, it changed my personality. For the first time I was independent', Sitt Sukayna explained. 'Here I had worked for eleven years at the Aishiyya school, but I never entered the department of education, my father did not allow it. We went to school by car and we used to have to veil. I dropped the veil in 1957, just before I went to Aden, when there were many demonstrations here. It was very difficult, even if many girls had done so already before me.'

These single women had no access to property through the dower, but earned well. What did they do with their income? Did they use their income from labour to gain property rights? Many of them first emphasised that they had helped their family. Although from prominent families, they pointed out that prominence did not necessarily imply wealth and stressed their responsibility towards their relatives. Some, like Sitt Imān, were supporting their elderly mother or a non-employed sister, others had contributed to the great costs of higher education for a younger sibling. Yet 'helping the family' could also mean, in their eyes, paying (at least partly) for their own upkeep, including sometimes their own higher education abroad.

Their income also allowed for a particular life style, including regular tourist trips abroad, with relatives or as groups of women teachers. Sitt Sukayna, for example, had visited most of the Arab world, Turkey, the USA, the Soviet Union, Kenya, and many countries in Western Europe, sometimes with friends, occasionally with relatives and often with a travelling group. Sitt Nawāl, in her fifties, from a landed family, who had worked as a secretary for a princess in Saudi Arabia and later held a high administrative position at a hospital, was very outspoken about marriage. 'I did not want to marry', she said very directly. 'I loved my freedom, from when I was a small girl.' As a daughter without brothers, she had inherited part of her father's land both in Jordan and in Nablus. When I asked her about property, she stressed the importance of travel to her. In her words: 'I do not like gold and I do not like land, all I need is to travel. Every year I go to Europe, to Cyprus and to other places on vacation. We sold some of the land, and put the money in a bank account to spend it. There are people who like to save money, I do not. I like to go on vacation, to whom would I leave it?'

In the longer term, the most crucial form of property for a single woman would be a house of her own, in order that she would not be forced to live in one household with her brother's wife. Some women did not need to buy or build a house as Sitt Yusrā did. They were already secure, for example, if a father had provided his daughter with a house, or if all brothers had already moved out of the family home. These women would usually put their income in a bank account, buy financial paper, or perhaps a piece of real-estate as security. When Sitt Imān, for example, was living by herself in Amman, holding a high administrative post, she used most of her income on a high standard of living. After returning to Nablus, she spent a lot on the upkeep of the old family home, while she also bought some shares and a piece of building land in Amman as security. Sitt Sukayna was one of the heirs to the house she was living in and had also inherited agricultural land, which gave her a good income in itself. As she said, she was neither very interested in property, nor clever in dealing with it. She had, however bought some shares and a piece of land in Jericho and put some money in a UNRWA investment funds. Other women, however, were very concerned about securing themselves a house or an apartment of their own. Sitt Nawāl, for example, together with her sister had first built a separate apartment on top of the house her elderly half-sister had previously built, before she turned to travelling.

These single women professionals were generally held in high esteem in the city. Al-Hajja Afīfa, one of the very first female school directors, who virtually raised her younger sisters, was much respected amongst the men of religion. Next to her own house she had a mosque built, and the neighbourhood was known as 'al-Hajja Afīfa'. Her sisters showed me the many pictures of her in the midst of a group of religious men. Single women also played a crucial role on the boards of charitable institutions. The Nablus Women's Union had been founded in 1921 by Miryam Hāshim, and one of its best known leaders had been al-Hajja Andalīb al-ʿAmd, after whom a street in Nablus is named. She had set up the well-known sewing courses of the Nablus Women's Union. More recently, in 1976, the poet and writer Fadwā Tūqān and the teacher Yusrā Salāh, served as members of the Deans' Council of Al-Najah College, and in 1984 Dr Muhayya Khilfa became a member of the board of trustees of Al-Najah University, while Sitt Sabʿa ʿArafāt was a member of the board of trustees of Bethlehem University, of Bir Zeit University and of the Council of Higher Education. The acting president of the Women's Union, responsible for a hospital and a girls' orphanage, was also a single professional woman, Sitt Lawāhiz ʿAbdulhādī. If some members on the board of charitable or voluntary organisations were appointed as 'the wife of' certain prominent men, these single women had, even if supported by their family background, acquired a central position in Nablus society through their own stamina.

### The poor: the backbone of the family

From the early 1950s on women from a different background, motivated by other considerations also entered teaching. These were refugee girls who went to teach in order to support their family, which had become destitute after the disaster. If in the first years after 1948, they were usually from urban middle-class background, with the passing of time determined girls from poorer families in the camps also entered the profession, such as Latīfa and her neighbour Laylā, the daughter of Imm ʿAdnān. In their case the relation between income and property was different. If they also kept part of their wages themselves, first and foremost they worked to help their families escape poverty and improve their standard of living. Many of these girls worked for a considerable period of time, often under difficult circumstances in Kuwait or Saudi Arabia, and it was thanks to their efforts that their families in the camps were able to better their living conditions. They were often also instrumental in providing educational opportunities for their younger siblings.

These professionals often postponed marriage. The women themselves commonly felt a heavy responsibility towards their family, and forfeited marriage in order to be able to support their own relatives, sharing emotionally in their improved position.[13] For the very same reason, their family may not encourage marriage either. Laylā, for example, had taught for four years in Saudi Arabia in the late 1970s and then found a job as an UNRWA teacher in Amman. Most of the money she had earned was

[13] Ghabra argues the same about the earlier refugee teachers from urban middle-class background, stating 'to accomplish their mission many of these women decided not to marry' (1987: 51).

spent on the family house in Balata camp (about 3,000 JD) and on the education of her younger siblings. In her own words 'virtually the whole house was my responsibility'. When I talked to her in 1989 she had also bought a house in Amman, and was 'lifting her hands from the Balata house', as she phrased it, because she had her two youngest brothers with her, intending to raise them and to pay for their upkeep and education. She was not interested in gold and had little of it, and when I asked her whether she had bought shares, she answered half jokingly but with a serious undertone 'my shares are in the boys; when they have finished their education and work they will bring me shares'. In her late thirties, she may still contemplate marriage, but also tries to assure her future financially and emotionally through her own work and by raising her younger brothers.

Yet, even the relative success of Laylā was different from that of single women from the prominent Nablus families. If the latter may have contributed to the education of their siblings, this was usually not out of sheer necessity. Laylā's younger sisters and brothers, on the other hand, had been dependent on her to be able to continue their vocational training. Women from a poorer background also found themselves in a much more vulnerable position and the risks involved in postponing marriage were much greater. When there was still a great demand for teachers, these women could find good jobs, and not only greatly improve their own situation, but also that of their family. This could, however, end abruptly due to adverse political or economic circumstances. The labour story of Latīfa indicates how costly this may be for women from a poorer background. Having lost her job and without other sources of income to fall back on, she had again become fully dependent on her own family, with little money and even less space available. In the end considering marriage as the least negative option, she had greatly lowered her demands. In particular with the recession of the 1980s, and even more so during the intifada with its return to early marriage in the camps, some of these women found themselves in a desperate position.

### 9.5     Marriage and property: the dower and the conjugal fund

Whereas few women in lower-status occupations are married, women in the professions more often continue to work after marriage and also after having children. Discussing the specific access of professionally employed *married* women to property I will focus on two areas of debate. To begin with, the impact of professional work on their dower is addressed; then the ways in which these women deal with their dower and income after marriage will be considered.

### Professional women: a better dower?

The relation between professional employment, such as teaching, and the dower raises several questions. Is the registered dower of professional women different from that of non-employed women? Does their registered dower relate in a specific way to what they obtain in practice? Are the gifts they receive particular, either in quality or quantity?

It was not until the 1970s that women had their occupations registered in their marriage contracts and only for the 1980s a sufficiently large number of contracts is available to trace the influence of professional work on the registered dower.[14] To gain insight into the impact of such employment it is not enough to compare these contracts with 'the average dower'. In chapter 5 it was argued that the occupation of the groom influences the nature of the dower notably. As female professionals tend to marry specific categories of men, the husband's occupation rather than that of the wife may influence the nature of the dower. Urban women teachers often marry teachers and men employed in the higher professions (54 per cent versus 16 per cent in the sample); urban women working in the higher professions often marry within their own group (67 per cent versus 12 per cent); rural women teachers tend to marry teachers or employees (52 per cent versus 13 per cent); women teachers from the camps mainly marry teachers, men employed in the higher professions, skilled labourers and the self-employed (73 per cent versus 34 per cent).[15] Only through comparing the dower of women teachers and professionals with that of non-employed women marrying men of the same specific occupational categories is it possible to get an indication of the impact of women's work on the dower.

Table 1 indicates the specific effects of women's professional work on the dower as registered in the marriage contracts. These are most evident in the case of urban women in the higher professions. In their marriage contracts a token dower is most often recorded, the deferred dower is very high, and addenda are hardly ever registered. It is true that such a pattern of registration is also common for their non-employed counterparts, yet it

---

[14] The following statistical data refer to the sample years 1984, 1987 and 1988. Although there are some slight variations between the different years, these are irrelevant, as the focus here is on the comparison between non-employed women and professionals.

[15] The category 'higher professional employment' refers to doctors, dentists, pharmacists, university lecturers and engineers.

Table 1 *Dower according to location, women's profession and men's profession in the 1980s*

| | % token/av. prompt | Av. deferred | % addenda/av. |
|---|---|---|---|
| **Dower of *urban* non-employed women and women in the *higher professions* married to male higher professionals** | | | |
| Sample all contracts | 45 (1,500 JD) | 2,750 JD | 78 (1,190 JD) |
| Non-employed women married to male professionals | 57 | 3,430 JD | 57 |
| Women professionals married to male professionals | 82 | 4,530 JD | 12 |
| **Dower of *urban* non-employed women and *women teachers* married to male teachers** | | | |
| Sample all contracts | 45 (1,500) JD) | 2,750 JD | 78 (1,190 JD) |
| Non-employed women married to male teachers | 40 [1,330 JD] | 2,200 JD | 80 [1,370 JD] |
| Women teachers married to male teachers | 46 (1,810 JD) | 2,730 JD | 77 (980 JD) |
| **Dower of *camp* non-employed women and *women teachers* married to male skilled labourers/self-employed** | | | |
| Sample all contracts | 33 (1,040 JD) | 1,490 JD | 78 (930 JD) |
| Non-employed women married to male skilled labour/self-employed | 48 (1,150 JD) | 1,310 JD | 81 (920 JD) |
| Women teachers married to male skilled labour/self-employed | 44 (1,300 JD) | 1,560 JD | 89 (990 JD) |
| **Dower of *rural* non-employed women and *women teachers* married to male teachers/ employees** | | | |
| Sample all contracts | 36 (1,190 JD) | 2,180 JD | 31 (1,070 JD) |
| Non-employed women married to male teachers/ employees | 58 (1,210 JD) | 2,470 JD | 50 (1,430 JD) |
| Women teachers married to male teachers/ employees | 62 (1,800 JD) | 3,380 JD | 38 (2,200 JD) |

is considerably more outspoken for women in the higher professions, and their dower comes closest to the ideal modern high-status dower of a token prompt dower, a high deferred dower and no addenda.

In fact, professional women have historically been the first to register a token dower. If recording a 1 JD dower only became a trend from the early 1960s on, some teachers marrying in the late 1940s and 1950s (the top female professionals in those years) had already done so. Like Sitt Yusrā they usually had worked for several years and felt they did not need a dower. These women had compelling reasons to support such form of dower registration. Even more than their non-professional counterparts, they regarded themselves as being at the forefront of modernisation. Receiving dower property might be useful as a guarantee to a dependent wife, they told me, but it contradicted a professional woman's self-image as a 'productive member of society'. And they could afford not to register a set amount as they were not only usually from a prominent family background and married better-off husbands, but they also had a good income of their own.

Urban women teachers register a token prompt dower somewhat more often and addenda less frequently than their non-employed counterparts, while both their regular prompt dower and deferred dower are considerably higher. Still, their registered dower is not very different from that of the average dower. This can be read as one more indication of the decline in the status of teaching in the urban context. In the camps, on the other hand, the property rights of women teachers are better secured than those of their non-employed counterparts. They register a token dower a bit less frequently and addenda more often, while the amounts recorded are higher.

Comparing the dower of rural female teachers with that of their non-working counterparts the differences seem similar to those of urban teachers. Yet there are two major divergencies. First, in the rural areas female teachers register addenda more commonly than the average, but compared to their non-employed counterparts they do so considerably less frequently. In fact, they do so even less often than the data in table 1 indicate, as a particularly high proportion of these addenda registrations consists mainly of gold.[16] As was explained in chapter 5, in the rural areas registering household goods implies a very real shift in obligations from the bride to the groom, while in the city and the camps providing household goods is always seen as the task of the groom. It is likely that rural women teachers already copy the higher-status urban model in

---

[16] This was the case in 80 per cent of addenda registrations in the contracts of women teachers marrying male teachers of employees; in the case of non-employed wives of male teachers and employees, it was 24 per cent.

refraining from registering household goods but expecting the husband to bring these. Secondly, comparing the dower of rural women teachers with the rural average, the amounts are considerably higher and a token dower is much more common. This may well indicate that the status of women teachers in the villages is markedly higher than that of urban female teachers.

Yet what do these women receive in practice? For many non-employed women, the dower was important as it could well be their major opportunity to acquire property, mainly gold, but also household goods and an extensive wardrobe. Women teachers and those employed in the higher professions generally had different concerns. To the higher professionals, the registered dower was relatively unimportant. Often from a wealthier family background and marrying a husband of similar background, they would receive valuable gifts both from their own families and from their husbands, while they themselves also earned well. Women teachers are, at least more recently, usually less privileged, yet for them the dower was not so important either. They are often considerably older, between twenty-five and twenty-eight, at marriage. Having worked for some years they would have spent at least part of their wages on buying clothes and some decorative gold. They consider the more traditional types of gold, such as the twenty-one carat bracelets, which are important to non-employed women because of the more stable value, old-fashioned and do not care for it much, as they have their own independent source of income through their work. Many teachers pointed out to me that they were not interested in gold.

Other strategies, although also prevalent among non-employed women, such as attempts to lower the dower for the sake of having the marriage arranged or as an expression of class solidarity, were more frequently encountered among professionally employed women. Both because of their age and their work, women teachers stood a greater chance of already being acquainted with their husbands.[17] To them, companionship in marriage was crucial. This meant that they may actually attempt to lower the prompt dower, often more so in practice than in the contract, in order to prevent their husband going into debt and to save money to, as they put it, 'build up the house together'. Ilhām's labour story shows how she skilfully lowered the dower and limited her husband's costs for the wedding. Ibtisām, a very bright girl from an extremely poor rural family, was even more outspoken in her rejection of dower payments. Very conscious of her background, she had started her

[17] About one-third of women teachers from the city and the camps marry male teachers (while on average respectively 4 per cent and 2 per cent) and over one-quarter of the rural women teachers do so (on average 3 per cent).

labour story with the words 'I am of the poor class, those who have nothing'. Although her grades had been high she only studied for practical nursing in order to be able to support her family as soon as possible. When a maternal relative asked her in marriage she accepted. 'He agrees with what I do', she explained, 'he accepts that I will help my family as long as I live. He is a student at the university and is educated. More important, he is poor, like me, his father died soon after he was born, his mother was an agricultural labourer and his elder brother worked in a restaurant so he could learn. With the university closed now, he works as a labourer in Israel.' Ibtisām did not want to have anything to do with dower payments. 'I said, "I do not want any money", I did not agree. I still do not know how much they wrote, perhaps 650 JD. I said, "it is impossible that I see money."' Neither did Ibtisām want to receive gold. She did recognise that she would not be able to totally forgo it, but wanted to limit it as much as possible.

Thus, female teachers and other lower-paid women professionals, such as nurses, seem to pursue one of two strategies. On the one hand, some of them follow the pattern of those employed in the higher professions on a more modest level. Neither registering a regular prompt dower nor addenda is, however, more risky in their case, as the wages of teachers are lower, and in particular those from a lower class background do not have access to other resources. The deferred dower, however, is always very substantial. It is true that, as has been argued in chapter 6, this often did not mean much in practice. Still, in the case of professionally employed women the high deferred dower registered in their contracts may well give them a stronger bargaining position in the case of divorce, as they are better acquainted with 'the public world' and with an income of their own are less dependent on the goodwill and support of their kin. On the other hand, there are also female teachers who register relatively high sums as prompt dower and as addenda. Even if they do not receive the full amount, having such a comparatively high dower registered means that refraining from claiming it would not go unnoticed. And registering such a dower can be seen as an acknowledgement of their 'greater value'.

### After marriage: income, property and time

Many professional women continue to work after marriage. Even one of the oldest teachers I talked to argued that she would have carried on teaching in the late 1920s if the British had not fired her. What did these women do with their income? Did they indeed keep separate budgets, with the husband as the sole family provider, following Islamic law, or did they give their income to their husbands? Did they keep their dower property or did they sell it? Did they then spend it on the household or did they attempt to find a profitable investment for themselves?

In general, these women used at least part of their income for household expenses. Even those who were reluctant to contribute felt they were not able to withhold completely. When Sahar, in her late twenties and from a lower-middle-class Nablus family, married a teacher in 1985, she had already held a good position in a Nablus hospital for several years. Apparently, the marriage started out with some strains. A stipulation was inserted in the contract to the effect that she would be allowed to do with her wages whatever she wanted. This she had done, she said, 'in order that in the future he will not say, "give me your wage"; as a guarantee that I do not tire myself for nothing, not getting any money in my hand.' When I asked her whether she gave him part of her wages she replied, 'I do not give him money. He spends on the house until his wage is finished, then I spend. Sometimes that is already by the tenth of the month ...' Also amongst the well-to-do professional women many give their husband at least something. Khawla for instance, herself a well-paid professional and her husband a businessman, used to give everything to him. 'But then I found that whenever I wanted to buy something I had to ask him', she said, 'if I finished my money I had to ask him and he said, "be careful, you are really spending much, all of what you are giving me you are spending, what is the use of your work and so on". So I said, "the best thing is your income to yourself and my income to myself and to give a definite amount from my salary to you and keep the rest for me".' She kept about half her salary for herself.

Women did not only often hand over part of their wages to their husbands, but the idea was also current that for some men a major impetus to marry teachers was to lay hands on the income they earned, a fear Latīfa also expressed in her labour story. This is probably the reason that in a sizeable minority of the marriage contracts conditions with regard to work and income were inserted. In the 1970s and 1980s, about 13 per cent of all contracts of urban women teachers contained stipulations about the bride's work.[18] The most extensive stipulation was recorded in 1976 in the contract of a thirty-two year old Nablus woman teacher marrying a considerably younger, twenty-six year old village teacher. The bride made it a condition that her husband 'would house her separately, that she would be *mukhaddara* [lit. secluded; i.e. not having to work in agriculture], that if she wanted she could work as a teacher and continue to do so and that she could do with her wages whatever she

---

[18] Whereas in only about 2 per cent of the contracts of all urban women stipulations of any kind were inserted.

wished.'[19] More common stipulations simply stated that the wife would be allowed to work as a teacher and/or that she could use her wage as she saw fit. As there still is a debate whether a husband can withhold maintenance if his wife works against his wishes, the first condition may strengthen her position, yet the second was superfluous. According to Islamic law a woman always holds full and exclusive control over what she herself earns, without this relieving the husband of his maintenance obligations towards her. That it was deemed necessary to register these rights as conditions in the marriage contract indicates the gap between legal doctrine and social practice.

Inserting such stipulations was largely an urban phenomenon; in the contracts of camp and village women these were rarely recorded. In the few cases it was done, the problematic situation of elderly women teachers is evident. In 1984, a forty-one year old woman teacher from refugee background was married to a forty-seven year old farmer as second wife with a stipulation that 'he would not prevent her from teaching however long she wanted to and that she had complete freedom to do with her wage as she wished'.[20] In 1987, a thirty-three year old repudiated woman teacher from the Balata camp married as second wife to a rural teacher of the same age, inserted the condition that 'she would take half her wage and do with it as she wished'.[21] Apparently it was taken for granted that the husband would take the other half.

Actually, the choice a woman faced was not simply between either keeping (part of) the wage herself or contributing to the household budget, but there was a third interested party, her family of origin. In particular if she was a social climber, from a poor family but having acquired professional skills, employed as a nurse, secretary or teacher, she could well have been the major provider for her own family and may not be able to, or want to, give up this responsibility immediately at marriage. Both Ibtisām and Ilhām still gave part of their wages to their mother. Among the married secretaries at Al-Najah University three out of my sample of ten (all daughters of widows) continued to support their mothers after marriage, often with one-quarter to one-third of their wage. Also in over one-quarter of the urban contracts with labour stipulations it was explicitly stated that the bride would give part (often half) of her wage to her own relatives. In 1976, for example, a twenty-three year old woman teacher from Nablus marrying a twenty-six year old mechanic from Balata camp stipulated that 'half her wage would be for her brother S'.[22] More recently, in 1988, when a twenty-three year old woman teacher living in Nablus married a thirty-year old teacher in Saudi Arabia (both

[19] MN, s. 503 no. 52450, 30/5/1976.      [20] MN, s. 636, no. 122985, 7/11/1984.
[21] MN, s. 676, no. 145184, 6/8/1987.      [22] MN, s. 492, no. 52589, 25/7/1976.

originally from the same West Bank village) the stipulation was inserted that 'half the wage of the wife will be for her father'.[23]

Yet, even if such stipulations had been agreed upon, in practice payment did not always materialise. Rubhiyya, for example, was one of eleven children in a poor refugee family. All her sisters married when they were fourteen or fifteen years old 'in order that they would leave the family', while she managed to graduate in 1971 as staff nurse from an UNRWA training centre. After working for four years in a Nablus hospital she intended to marry a technician also employed there. Yet, her family was against the marriage. 'My father had died before I started working, my brothers were still young, and I had been the main breadwinner', she explained, 'so my mother's brother, who arranged the marriage contract, demanded that after marriage my husband would allow me to give them half my wages. I tried to persuade him by saying "I am convinced of him, money is not everything, I will help them if he agrees to it". And I asked my husband to say that he would indeed be willing to help my family with my salary.' Yet, as Rubhiyya had expected, in practice it did not work out. 'My husband is the eldest son of a refugee family, his father was an old man and he was the main contributor to the household. So I never gave anything to my own family after marriage. At first my relatives were angry and tried to interfere, but then they stopped because they were afraid that there would be problems between me and my husband, which may lead to a divorce. And my brothers started working, so things became a bit easier.'

A woman's income could contribute substantially to the standard of living of the conjugal household, in particular in acquiring a house. If a single woman from a propertied background may have been provided with housing by her own family, married women almost never inherited a house. The oldest teacher I spoke to, who had married in the late 1920s, already told me that she spent the money she had saved from teaching on buying a piece of land and building a house on it. Sitt Yusrā and her elderly sister both saved from their wages in order to build a house. Ilhām and her husband first spent their money on the house near her husband's family and then bought a piece of land, close to the university to later build on. Also to Rubhiyya a house had been a top priority. For two years she had lived with her husband in one of the two rooms of his family's house, then they rented a small house in the camp, and finally, when she already had six children, they were able to build a three-room house for themselves.

Certainly, some non-employed women also contributed to building a house or other longer-term projects. As mentioned previously, they did

[23] MN, s. 709, no. 171564, 3/11/1988.

so by selling their dower gold. Yet, many professional women held a somewhat different perspective on acquiring such property. Non-employed women often considered it self-evident that the house to which they contributed was in their husbands' name. In their view if a woman would record it in her own name this would harm her husband's dignity. Sitt Yusrā may well have been the other extreme, having three houses built and registered in her own name while married. In her case her specific position as an elderly woman without children probably played a role. Still, professional women generally did not disapprove of married women registering such property and it seems to be more common for them to have real estate registered in their own name or to have their name included as co-owner.

Some professional women, like Ilhām or Rubhiyya, did not only contribute their income to acquire the desired house, to pay for education for their children and so on, but also sold their dower gold to do so. Yet it seemed more common for women to hold on to their dower property than to their monthly wages. Sahar, for example, felt obliged to contribute her wage to the daily expenses of the household, but refused to sell her gold to pay off her husband's debts. When she told me he had to pay 60 JD (from his salary of 220 JD) to the bank every month because of the debts he had incurred for the marriage, I asked her whether she had thought about selling her gold to help him. 'No I have not', she answered directly. 'I still have the gold he gave me at marriage, I am free to do with it what I want. I have nothing to do with his debts. He was in a hurry and wanted to do all these things. I also have to think about the future. Even if he asked me to, I would not sell it, you never know what will happen.' Also virtually all secretaries I talked to at the university contributed to the household budget, but they did not sell their dower gold. It seems that they were already able to show their involvement in the new household through their wages, without having to give up the dower.

While married women's professional employment made a higher standard of living possible, the costs involved, in terms of the workload they had to carry, could be high. Rubhiyya, for instance, a staff nurse, worked the first eight years after marriage for six days a week nine hours a day (with a break of three hours in between). Only when she was pregnant with her fifth child did she apply for part-time work (working six hours daily), which she was granted. When I talked to her she had six children between the ages of five and thirteen. Her husband did not help much with the work at home and her eldest was a boy. 'Had it been a girl', Rubhiyya said, 'she could have taken over part of my work. But a boy does not do that. The eldest girl, she is nine, is starting to help me.' Having children and working as a nurse were difficult to combine. 'At first maternity leave was one month, then when there were more of us we demanded it be extended to forty days. But this is all after delivery, you have to work until the last day. Sometimes I had been on duty in the morning and had labour pains in the afternoon. Nor could I breast-feed my children for long. It is forbidden to bring your child to work, so when I had my break I used to go home, feed the baby and then return. But the milk dried up quickly.'

If Rubhiyya was in particularly difficult circumstances because her relatives lived far away, many working women, especially from lower class families, shared her difficulties. Whether women were able to alleviate their work load such as through hiring domestic help or child care was largely a matter of class and affluence. Although many women from poor families avidly used education as a road to social mobility, and within their social environment were seen as highly educated, they often did not quite have the educational qualifications nor the social contacts to enter better-paying professional jobs. Neither did they have the other resources available to their better off colleagues, such as financial support from their own kin or their in-laws or a husband with a well-paying job. It is true that their work gives them status and they like the independence of earning money, yet there are many demands on their income, and even more on their time.

## A note on women, paid employment, and property

Part III indicates that women's access to income from paid labour is restricted. The definition of men as providers in itself discourages female wage labour, while the cultural importance attached to the control of women's freedom of movement, undermines women's bargaining position *vis-à-vis* their employers, resulting in low female wages in the private sector.

Yet women are not simply passive victims of local constructions of gender. Some actually appeal to gender constructs to withdraw from the labour market altogether. Employers looking for female sewing workers, nurses or cleaners told me time and again that there were many men applying for jobs, but they had a hard time finding women. Few married women actually work in lower-status occupations, not because their husbands would not allow them to work, but rather as they themselves opt to refrain from paid employment; in their eyes it is not worth it. Single women are more often found in lower-status employment, precisely because their claim on their male provider is weaker, in particular after their father's death. And the most active in these jobs are poor widows, who have no one to provide for them and whose appeal to other central values, such as household autonomy, is strongest.

The very same elements which restrict women's options also leave them some room for manoeuvre on the labour market. Gender segregation does not only exclude women from certain occupations, but it also protects their employment in teaching, nursing and even to some extent in institutional cleaning (for instance in the women's wings in the hospital and in girls' schools). Segregated education has always provided women with career prospects. Gender integration can, in fact, be detrimental to women's position on the labour market, as is evident in the case of the sewing trade, where successful artisanal seamstresses have virtually disappeared and the best positions have been taken up by male subcontractors with female workers employed in the lower echelons. As has been argued for younger sewing workers, also in the labour process itself women may employ gender constructs and appeal to their femininity to counterbalance the strong pressures and exploitation at work.

Women's access to property through paid labour ties in both with existing gender constructs and processes of economic and political change. While the concept of the male provider legitimises large male–female wage differentials, the emphasis on men as providers also gives women a claim to their own income. If they support the household this is never taken as self-evident but recognised as a sacrifice. Whether women have potential access to property depends on whether relatively well-paid and stable employment is available to them. In the British mandatory period, this was largely limited to sewing and teaching. Seamstresses had a protected (female) market, while teaching had also the great advantage of formal public employment with one pay scale for men and women. After 1948 with the expansion of the (Jordanian) state and of education, there was increasing demand for women in (semi-)public employment, be it as teachers, medical staff, administrative workers, or cleaners. After occupation one more option, however controversial it may be, became available, work in Israel.

Yet, the meaning of paid employment for women's access to property also depends on the particular position of the women involved. Two quite divergent patterns are evident. On the one hand some poor, often illiterate widows have managed to greatly improve their material situation; rural widows have entered institutional cleaning in Nablus, while widows from the camps have also worked in Israel. Their income was crucial to 'build up the house', which refers both to improving the house itself, and to supporting their children, included investing in productive property for them. Yet, they do so at great costs, having to deal with criticism of the community and a very heavy work load. At the other side of the spectre the single and occasionally married women from the well-to-do families, employed in respectable higher professional work, have largely invested in themselves, if necessary in a house of their own and various forms of security, such as real estate. Other women relate in various ways to these social opposites. Poorer refugee women who have managed to become teachers started out with investing in their household of origin, but, if they remained single and successful, they also turned to life style spending. Married women from (lower-)middle class families often invest in their house and husbands to improve the household situation and in the future of their children.

# 10    Women and property revisited

The previous chapters discuss the different perspectives expressed by women in the Jabal Nablus region in regard to property and the various strategies they follow. Over time, a major trend has been the partial transition from dower to paid labour as a central mechanism for women to gain access to property. This trend ties in with the greater emphasis on the conjugal bond, rather than on kinship (the natal family) as a main source of women's socio-economic security. At the same time, this study qualifies such generalisations by pointing to the importance of focusing on the situated meanings of women and property, and to the mutiple positions women take up with regard to property. In these last pages I will bring together two lines of argument on women, power, and property. First I will discuss how changes in the construction of the gendered person may both be the effect of power relations and have consequences for women's access to property. Then I will shift the focus to the lived experiences of individual women, linking the multiplicity of their positions to the way in which these are infused with power. Finally, I will briefly return to some issues raised in the introduction.

## 10.1    Commoditisation and the male provider: constructing gender

In the literature on women and property the focus has often been on the nature of the property concerned. This study has started from another angle and has concentrated on how the positions of the women involved have influenced their access to property. One central concern has been to avoid taking 'women' as a given, but rather to discuss the various ways in which shifts in the meanings of manhood and womanhood have an impact on women's property ownership. At the same time, an attempt has been made to understand the context within which such meanings have been produced.

Whereas in the mandatory period many peasant households in the Jabal

253

Nablus region still directed production towards subsistence, by the 1950s labour migration had become a trend. It did not take long for agriculture to become subsidiary to various forms of male wage labour, often outside the West Bank, both in the Gulf States and later in Israel. Although few rural women themselves have turned to wage labour, these developments have affected them substantially. When productive property, in the form of access to land and livestock, was still central in social organisation, kinship relations were of paramount importance and women, active in agriculture, were regarded as productive. The marginalisation of agriculture and the greater access of younger men to wage labour has had a double effect, kinship has become less important and women's labour has become less valued. As a result, rural women who were previously first and foremost seen as productive daughters have become increasingly defined as unproductive wives, dependent on their husbands.

Yet, while changes in the political economy of the area have had a great impact, the greater emphasis on men as providers was not simply the result of processes of commoditisation and changes in the international division of labour. It was rather the effect of the interaction of such factors with existing local constructions of gender. Both in the legal system and in locally held views, women were defined as 'protected dependents', with male kin and husbands seen as responsible for their maintenance. The rapid growth of male migration and wage labour created the context in which these concepts turned into social practice. Husbands were not only increasingly seen as, but also became, providers, while state attempts at modernisation have led to legal reforms, further emphasising the conjugal tie.

In the rural areas these shifts in definitions of womanhood have affected women's access to and control over property, especially dower property. Once a village woman has become defined as a dependent wife, finding a husband who is a good provider is of central importance. Fathers are happy to leave the dower to their daughters if such a groom is available; they may even contribute to it. For, after all, compared to what the groom and his kin are to spend on housing the value of the dower has decreased. The greater popularity of the token dower also indicates the more central position of the groom; then even women's willingness to forego some of the prompt dower becomes invisible. And once regarded as dependent wives, few women are inclined to buy productive property from their dower; they rather sell their gold and invest it in their husband or his house. Furthermore, the ascendency of the deferred dower does not only emphasise the marital tie, but also emphasises that women need property once they lose their husband, rather than when they marry.

Whereas in the rural areas this process only gained momentum in the late 1950s, in the city conjugality was already underlined earlier. Among the poor, many were not able to support their kin, while in the case of the better-off the combined effects of the growth of education, professional employment, and modernisation led to a greater emphasis on the conjugal household. In the city, there also was a much longer standing tradition of women being seen as non-productive. Even if women were active in the segregated women's world, this work was hardly recognised as such. As urban women in the mandatory period were defined as dependent wives, their relation to dower property was different from their rural counterparts. Urban fathers commonly did not take from their daughters' dower; amongst the poor they may even allow a man to pay less for the sake of the marriage, while amongst the wealthy a father may well spend lavishly on his daughter. Married women regularly invested their dower in their husbands' endeavours or in his house, and already by the mandatory period the deferred dower was widely registered and sometimes more important than the prompt.

The direction of historical change in the city has been different from the rural areas. It was in the city that female education first became available and accepted, and that professional employment opportunities for women developed. In consequence, for specific categories of urban women the definition of women as consumers was modified to some extent. Through their entry into professional labour, these women became increasingly seen as 'productive members of society', while their income could give them access to considerable property. If this was at first only the case for upper-class single women, more recently also married and lower-class women have become involved in such employment. Especially to the women from a wealthier background, the greater emphasis on their 'productivity' only made the dower less important to them. As heirs to their fathers' property, married to better-off men, their income already gave them considerable personal economic autonomy.

It was the refugee women who experienced the most rapid and dramatic changes. Driven from their homeland, they lost all access to inherited property and often also had to sell their dower gold. Simultaneously, their dependence on fathers and husbands was undermined by poverty. The older generation of women turned to all types of low status work for the survival of the household, while some of the younger women succeeded in becoming involved in professional work, often to support their own families; as such they became defined as 'valuable daughters'. To many of these women the dower has remained relatively important, but they also tend to use it to support their husbands and children.

## 10.2    Women, property and power: acquiescence and subversion

Conventional explanations for women's diminishing access to property would consider women first and foremost as victims, either of 'Muslim social structure', 'male dominance', or 'the structure of dependency'. But such perspectives are not very useful in gaining insight into why women themselves acquiesce in, or even support, their reduced control over property. Women's topical life stories, on the other hand, indicate that women may well see advantages in 'giving up property', for property does not necessarily mean power.

To understand how women have participated in the process of losing control over dower property we have to turn to the lived experiences of actual women. In the first place, although the dower could be an important source of property for women who had very little economic security themselves, it was also, and is, part and parcel of the process of marriage. While women generally have less access to dower property, they have gained more influence in marriage arrangements. In particular, women from the more conservative wealthy families have seen great changes. If previously their marital options were severely limited, more recently, being educated and sometimes professionally employed, they have gained a considerable say in their own marriages. And even rural girls with little schooling are more often able to refuse unattractive suitors, such as elderly widowers and so on. Many women interpret the process of historical change with a focus on the person of the groom, including his capacities at providing, rather than by concentrating on the material assets they themselves acquire at marriage. In fact, it is not unusual for women to attempt to bargain down the dower in order to marry a man they are convinced of. In addition, losing in terms of gender may mean a gain in terms of social hierarchy. Both among the elite and later also among the lower classes, refraining from registering dower obligations indicates a rise in social status. Some lower-class women, on the other hand, identifying with their male counterparts, prefer to register a token dower, as they regard this as a means to subvert class reproduction.

Women in the rural areas have another reason to acquiesce in their declining control over property. Owning property, and in particular productive property, coincided for them with being defined as productive members of the household, which implied a very heavy workload rather than control over their own labour. In a system in which refraining from agricultural labour becomes an indicator of higher social status, women see their loss of control in terms of gender as compensated for both by a lighter work load and a higher social status.

In short, women give up their property rights as other issues are more important to them. They care more for the person of the groom than for the property they may receive, defined as a 'dependent wife' their work load is less than that of a 'productive daughter', and they experience a rise in social status. And once a husband has become the provider it makes sense to invest in him after marriage. Rather than striving for immediate material benefits for themselves, by investing in their husbands they put a moral claim on them and also may expect to gain materially on the longer term.

Still, women have also developed countervailing strategies, subverting the definition of husbands as providers. Under certain circumstances holding on to existing traditions can be interpreted as a counterpractice. In the case of dower property, poor and rural women still often register a regular amount as prompt dower, indicating some distrust in their husbands' future success as provider, while they also prefer the 'better' types of gold. They may in practice not always receive the full amount registered, yet at least if they refrain from claiming it this is visible and acknowledged. In addition, a new strategy has developed, the registering of household goods as addenda in the marriage contracts. While the middle classes still publicly reject it, registering household goods has become increasingly common.

Holding on to existing traditions has been of particular importance in the case of inheritance practices, with most women still refraining from claiming their share in their father's estate. Conventionally this has been seen as yet another indication of their 'subordinated' status. Yet, in a sense, with the stronger emphasis on *husbands* as providers, the lack of change in inheritance practices may be seen as a countervailing strategy. Admittedly, women argue that they do not claim their share as their brothers have to provide for their own households, yet they also point out that they prefer not to take it, as then they can still call upon the support of their kin *vis-à-vis* their husbands. If they really had gone for conjugality they would take their share in their father's estate and hand it over to their husbands. In fact, some of the women who claim their share do so as they are pressured by their husbands; their access to property is in no way an indication of gendered power, but places them in a more vulnerable position.

It is in the field of paid employment that women have developed new and highly visible, countervailing strategies. For if men are supposed to be providers, female paid labour in itself is anathema. In various ways women have transgressed these gender boundaries. Poor women are not only working for wages but have purposely turned to better-paying labour, be it as cleaners in urban institutions or by working in Israel. They do so by emphasising other central values, such as household autonomy and use the income from such work by and large to improve the material situation of the household. As these women usually are not married, they do not undermine the concept of the husband as provider, but the more general definition of men as providers. This reflects both the lesser preparedness or ability of men to take care of their female kin and points to women's unwillingness to remain dependent on their male kin.

Whereas lower-status employment still caries a stigma, women's professional employment, which also goes against the grain of the system of the male provider, has increasingly become socially accepted. Single women from the better-off progressive families have a long tradition of employment in the professions. If in the beginning such employment was not immediately seen as suitable to women it did not take long for it to become approved of and positively valued with their income contributing to greater personal autonomy. Gradually also lower-class and married women have become involved in this type of employment; they have first and foremost used their income to improve the standard of living of the household.

These various strategies bring us back to some issues raised in the beginning of this study. A contrast has become evident between the views of well-educated, usually urban, women and those holding respectable jobs on the one hand, and poorer non-employed women on the other. The former tend to support women claiming their inheritance rights, to be critical of the dower and to be strongly in favour of women entering paid labour. Such a point of view does not fit well with the concrete experiences of many poor and rural women, to whom paid labour means a very heavy work load, who cannot afford to lose their kin's support by claiming their inheritance share, and continue to see the dower as an important source of property, even if they give it to their husbands. Still, to all of them access to property (or the recognition of their rights to it) helps to strengthen their dignity and self-respect.

### 10.3     Different positions, various strategies

Besides my fieldwork experiences, another urgent reason to concentrate on women's access to property was to counter the predominant emphasis on a culturalist perspective in Middle Eastern studies, with women first and foremost defined in terms of Islam, and constructed as essentially different and particularly subordinated. Still, in the process of doing fieldwork and writing up this study, 'Islam, difference and power' have come up time and again as topics of discussion. In this last paragraph I will return briefly to the ways in which I have attempted to deal with these issues, which may point readers to some wider implications of this study and to questions left to be addressed.

Placing property at the centre of this study invites a focus on processes of socio-economic change, in particular on the way in which colonisation, commoditisation, and economic dependency tie in with existing property and gender relations. The marginalisation of agriculture and the rapid growth of male migration and wage labour have had a decisive impact on women's access to property. Yet, discussing property also makes paying attention to certain aspects of institutionalised Islam imperative. At various moments in this study the gendered discourse of personal status law has been discussed, which regulates major mechanisms for women to gain access to property (that is inheritance, marriage and divorce), and works with such centrally important notions as the male provider, the dower, and the absence of conjugal property. From there I have turned to the concrete interactions of the Jabal Nablus population with the court system, such as in marriage and divorce registrations and court cases, which can be seen as moments at which legal and local concepts and practices interact with each other. Social practices often are at variance with the discourse of the law: women commonly renounce their inheritance rights, they may well give their dower to their husbands, and part of their income is regularly pooled and functions as a conjugal fund. Even so, a general awareness of women's rights under the law is important; if women renounce their rights in property, the very notion that they are giving something up may strengthen their position.

Such a focus on local traditions does not need to regress into exoticising the inhabitants of Jabal Nablus or regarding them as essentially different from 'us'. Rather, the argument is that paying attention to the ways in which people conceptualise and deal with property asks for specificity, be it historical, cultural, or whatever. This would at the same time avoid an equally problematic one-sided emphasis on sameness or commonalities, and a perspective that addresses only cultural homogenisation and greater global uniformity. For instance, whereas initially the concept of the male provider caught my attention because of its commonness and the similarities with such Western notions, it did not take long to discover that even if only discussing this concept for Jabal Nablus its meanings are multiple and its effects on women's access to property vary. It is true that there is a partial shift from male kin to husbands as main source of economic support for women, a development also seen elsewhere. Yet the meaning of such a transition and its impact on women's relation to property differs greatly, depending on the context discussed and the positions women take up. Again, a few examples suffice to illustrate the argument. Whereas the greater emphasis on husbands as providers has had a very limited impact on the way in which women deal with their inheritance share (with brotherless, elderly single, and wealthier women still most likely to receive their share), it has had a substantial influence on rural women's dealings with dower property (who have increasingly lost control over it). Whereas in discussing inheritance, women point to their emotional attachment to their brothers and their dependence on them in times of hardship, and widows happily renounce their share for the sake of their sons, in regard to paid labour, they stress their limited trust in their brothers' and occasionally sons' ability to provide for them.

Focusing on property also undermines the notion of the homogeneity of women in the Middle East, and places issues of power asymmetry, not only between men and women, but also amongst women on the agenda. Although for heuristic reasons rough divisions have been made in this study between poor and wealthy urban women, rural women, and women in the camps, I have attempted not to discuss these and other differentiations as bounded stable categories. For dividing women into a number of categories with certain characteristics is problematic. Empirically, it easily leads to an endless subdivision of categories with in the end difference losing all meaning. Theoretically, it assumes that certain background characteristics impell women to act in a certain way, leaving little space for women's agency. Instead, the focus has been on the various positions women take up within specific situations, and how these are infused with power. Individual women may find themselves in divergent positions depending on which aspect of their person is 'at stake'. Acknowledging that women may take up partial, ambiguous and sometimes contradictory positions, leaves open the possibility that women themselves can both be implicated in and resist such regimes of power. Taking women's multiple positions as point of departure requires attention to the multiple points or the different kinds of resistance women employ.

# References

Abu-Lughod, Janet, 1971, 'The demographic transformation of Palestine', in Ibrahim Abu-Lughod (ed.), *The tranformation of Palestine*. Evanston, Ill.: Northwestern University Press.

Abu-Lughod, Lila, 1990, 'Anthropology's Orient: the boundaries of theory on the Arab world', in Hisham Sharabi (ed.), *Theory, politics and the Arab world: critical responses*. New York and London: Routledge, pp. 81–132.

Ahmed, Leila, 1992, *Women and gender in Islam*. Berkeley: University of California Press.

Alcoff, Linda, 1988, 'Cultural feminism versus post-structuralism: the identity crisis in feminist theory', *Signs* 13, 1: 405–37.

Altorki, Soraya and Camillia El-Solh (eds.), 1988, *Studying your own society: Arab women in the field*. Syracuse: Syracuse University Press.

Ammons, Linda, 1978, 'West Bank Arab villagers: an administered people'. Harvard University, unpublished PhD thesis.

Amos, Valerie and Pratibha Parmar, 1984, 'Challenging imperial feminism', *Feminist Review* 17: 3–19.

Anderson, J., 1951a, 'Recent developments in shariʿa law III: the contract of marriage', *The Muslim World* 41, 2: 113–26.

1951b, 'Recent developments in shariʿa law IV: further points concerning marriage', *The Muslim World* 41, 3: 186–98.

1951c, 'Recent developments in shariʿa law V: the dissolution of marriage', *The Muslim World* 41, 4: 271–88.

1952, 'Recent developments in shariʿa law VIII: the Jordanian law of family rights 1951', *The Muslim World* 42, 3: 190–206.

Antoun, Richard, 1972, *Arab village: a social structural study of a trans-Jordan peasant community*. Bloomingdale: Indiana University Press.

1990, 'Litigant strategies in an Islamic court in Jordan', in Daisy Dwyer (ed.), *Law and Islam in the Middle East*. New York: Bergin and Garvey Publishers, pp. 35–61.

Appadurai, Arjun, 1986, 'Introduction: commodities and the politics of value', in Arjun Appadurai (ed.), *The social life of things: commodities in cultural perspective*. Cambridge: Cambridge University Press, pp. 3–64.

Asad, Talal, 1976, 'Class formation under the mandate', *MERIP-Reports* 6, 10: 3–8.

Aswad, Barbara, 1967, 'Key and peripheral roles of noblewomen in a Middle eastern plains village', *Anthropological Quarterly* 40: 139–52.

Awartani, Hisham, 1979, *A survey of industries in the West Bank and Gaza Strip.* Bir Zeit: Bir Zeit University Publications.

ʿAyyush, D., 1985, 'Ahwāl al-zawāj wa l-talāq fī l-diffa al-gharbiyya al-muhtalla', *Majallat Jāmiʿat Bayt Lahm* 4: 71–97.

Badran, N., 1980, 'The means of survival: education and the Palestinian community, 1948–1967', *Journal of Palestine Studies* 9, 4: 44–74.

Beneria, Lourdes and Gita Sen, 1981, 'Accumulation, reproduction and women's role in economic development: Boserup revisited', *Signs* 7, 2: 279–98.

Benvenisti, Meron, 1986, *Report 1986: economic, legal, social and political developments in the West Bank.* Jerusalem: The West Bank Data Base Project.

Bertaux, Daniel, 1980, 'From the life-history approach to the transformation of sociological practice', in Daniel Bertaux (ed.), *Biography and society: the life history approach in the social sciences.* London: Sage. Pp. 29–46.

Bisharat, George, 1989, *Palestinian lawyers and Israeli rule: law and disorder in the West Bank.* Austin: University of Texas Press.

Böhl, F., 1927, *De opgraving van Sichem: bericht over de voorjaarscampagne en de zomercampagne in 1926.* Zeist: G.J.A. Ruys' Uitgevers.

Boserup, Ester, 1970, *Woman's role in economic development.* New York: St Martin's Press.

Bourdieu, Pierre, 1979, 'Les trois états du capital culturel', *Actes de la recherche en sciences sociales* 30: 3–6.

1980, 'Le capital social: notes provisoires', *Actes de la recherche en sciences sociales* 31: 2–3.

Canaan, Tawfiq, 1931, 'Unwritten laws affecting the Arab women of Palestine', *Journal of the Palestine Oriental Society* XI: 172–203.

Caplan, Pat, 1984, 'Cognatic descent, Islamic law and women's property on the East Africa coast', in Renée Hirshon (ed.), *Women and property, women as property.* London: Croom Helm, pp. 23–43.

CBS (Central Bureau of Statistics), *Statistical Abstracts of Israel.* Jerusalem: CBS (1973; 1986; 1987; 1989; 1990).

1967, *Census of population 1967. West Bank of Jordan, Gaza Strip and Northern Sinai, Golan Heights.* Jerusalem: CBS.

Cohen, Abner, 1965, *Arab border villages in Israel: a study of community and change in a social organization.* Manchester: Manchester University Press.

*Critique of Anthropology* 3 (1977) 7 & 8.

Dalman, Gustav, 1964 (1928–42), *Arbeit und Sitte in Palästina I-VII.* Hildesheim: Georg Olms.

De la Torre. José, 1984, *Clothing-industry adjustment in developed countries.* London: Macmillan.

Doumani, Beshara, 1985, 'The Islamic court records of Palestine', *Bir Zeit Research Review* 2: 3–30.

1995, *Rediscovering Palestine: merchants and peasants in Jabal Nablus, 1700–1900.* Berkeley: University of California Press (forthcoming).

Eickelman, Dale, 1989 (1981), *The Middle East: an anthropological approach.* Englewood Cliffs, NJ: Prentice Hall.

El-Khatib, Adib, 1985, Housing in Nablus: socioeconomic characteristics and housing satisfaction of three Palestinian sub-groups. City University of New York, PhD thesis.

Elson, Diane, 1983, 'Nimble fingers and other fables', in Wendy Chapkis and Cynthia Enloe (eds.), *Of common cloth: women in the global textile industry.* Amsterdam: TNI, pp. 5–15.

Engels, F., 1972 (1884), *The origin of the family, private property, and the state.* New York: Pathfinder Press.

Fabian, Johannes, 1983, *Time and the other: how anthropology makes its object.* New York: Columbia University Press.

First Census, 1963, *First census of population and housing as of 18th November 1961.* Interim report no. 8 Nablus. Amman: Department of Statistics Press.

Flax, Jane, 1987, 'Postmodernism and gender relations in feminist theory', *Signs* 12, 4: 621–43.

Frisch, Hillel, 1983, *Stagnation and frontier: Arab and Jewish labour in the West Bank.* Jerusalem: West Bank Data Base Project.

Fröbel, Folker, Jurgen Heinrichs, and Otto Kreye, 1980, *The new international division of labour.* Cambridge: Cambridge University Press.

Gerber, Haim, 1980, 'Social and economic position of women in an Ottoman city, Bursa', *International Journal of Middle East Studies* 12: 231–44.

Ghabra, Shafeeq, 1987, *Palestinians in Kuwait: the family and the politics of survival.* Boulder (Colorado) and London: Westview Press.

Goody, Jack, 1973, 'Bridewealth and dowry in Africa and Eurasia', in Jack Goody and S. Tambiah, *Bridewealth and dowry.* Cambridge: Cambridge University Press, pp. 1–59.

1976, *Production and reproduction.* Cambridge: Cambridge University Press.

1990, *The oriental, the ancient and the primitive: systems of marriage and the family in the pre-industrial societies of Eurasia.* Cambridge: Cambridge University Press.

Graham-Brown, Sarah, 1980, *Palestinians and their society, 1880–1946.* London: Quartet Books.

1982, 'The political economy of the Jabal Nablus, 1920–48', in R. Owen (ed.), *Studies in the economic and social history of Palestine in the nineteenth and twentieth centuries.* London: Macmillan, pp. 88–176.

1984a, 'The economic consequences of the occupation', in N. Aruri (ed.), *Occupation. Israel over Palestine.* London: Zed Press, pp. 167–223.

1984b, *Education, repression and liberation: Palestinians.* London: World University Service.

Granott, Abraham, 1952, *The land system in Palestine: history and structure.* London: Eire and Spottiswoode.

Granqvist, Hilma 1931. *Marriage Conditions in a Palestinian Village I.* Helsingfors: Akademische Buchhandlung.

1935. *Marriage Conditions in a Palestinian Village II.* Helsingfors: Akademische Buchhandlung.

Hamdan, Nadia, 1991, ʿAl-ʿāmilāt fī mustashfayāt madīnat Nāblus', *Shuʾūn al-Marʾa.* Nablus: Jamʿiyyat Shuʾūn al-Marʾa, pp. 20–41.

Hammam, Mona, 1986, 'Capitalist development, family division of labor, and migration in the Middle East', in E. Leacock and H. Safa (eds.), *Women's work: development and the division of labor by gender.* South Hadley (UK): Bergin and Garvey Publishers, pp. 158–74.

Harlow, Barbara, 1990, 'Prison text, resistance culture', *MERIP-Reports* 20,

3&4: 67–9.

Harris, Olivia and Kate Young, 1981, 'Engendered structures: some problems in the analysis of reproduction', in Joel Kahn and Joseph Llobera (eds.), *The anthropology of pre-capitalist societies*. London: Macmillan, pp. 109–147.

Haq, al-, 1988, *Punishing a nation: human rights violations during the Palestinian uprising, December 1987 – December 1988*. Ramallah: Al-Haq/Law in the Service of Man.

1989, *A nation under siege*. Ramallah: Al-Haq.

Hijab, Nadia, 1988, *Womanpower: the Arab debate on women at work*. Cambridge: Cambridge University Press.

Hiltermann, Joost, 1991a, *Behind the intifada: Labour and women's movements in the occupied territories*. Princeton: Princeton University Press.

1991b, 'Work and action: The role of the working class in the uprising', in Jamal Nassar and Roger Heacock (eds.), *Intifada: Palestine at the crossroads*. New York: Birzeit University and Praeger Publishers, pp. 143–159.

Hindiyyeh, Suha, A. Ghazawneh and S. Idris (Women's Study Centre, Jerusalem), 1991, 'Zāhirat al-bastāt fī l-iqtisād al-filastīnī ghayr al-rasmī'. *Afaq Filistiniyya Series*. Bir Zeit University. Working Paper no. 1, 5.

Hirshon, Renée (ed.), 1984, *Women and property, women as property*. London: Croom Helm.

hooks, bell, 1982, *Ain't I a woman? Black women and feminism*. London: Pluto Press.

Hull, Gloria, Patricia Scott and Barbara Smith (eds.), 1982, *All the women are white, all the blacks are men, but some of us are brave*. New York: Feminist Press.

Issawi, Charles, 1982, *An economic history of the Middle East and North Africa*. New York: Columbia University Press.

Jansen, Willy, 1987, *Women without men: gender and marginality in an Algerian town*. Leiden: Brill.

Jaussen, J., 1927, *Coutumes Palestiniennes. Naplouse et son district*. Paris: Geuthner.

Jennings, Ronald, 1975, 'Women in early 17th century Ottoman judicial records – the Sharia court of Anatolian Kayseri', *Journal of the Economic and Social History of the Orient* 18: 53–114.

JMCC (Jerusalem Media and Communications Centre), 1991, *No exit: Israel's curfew policy in the occupied Palestinian territories*. Jerusalem: JMCC.

Joseph, Suad, 1986, 'Study of Middle Eastern women: investments, passions and problems', *International Journal of Middle East Studies* 18: 501–9.

Keddie, Nikkie, 1979, 'Problems in the study of Middle Eastern women', *International Journal of Middle East Studies* 10, 2: 225–40.

Keesing, Roger, 1989, 'Exotic Readings of Cultural Texts', *Current Anthropology* 30, 4: 459–69.

Khalifa, Sahar, 1976, *Al-Subbār*. Jerusalem.

1980, *'Abbād al-Shams*. Jerusalem: Dār al-Kātib.

1990, *Bāb al-Sāha*. Beirut: Dār al-Adab.

Kressel, Gideon, 1977, 'Bride-price reconsidered', *Current Anthropology* 18, 3: 441–58.

Kuttab, Eilleen, 1989, 'Community development under occupation: an alternative strategy', *Journal of Refugee Studies* 2, 1: 131–8.

Lamphere, Louise, 1979, 'Fighting the piece-rate system: new dimensions of an old struggle in the apparel industry', in Andrew Zimbalist (ed.), *Case studies in the labour process*. London: Monthly Review Press, pp. 257–77.

Layish, Aharon, 1973, 'Women and succession in the Muslim family in Israel', *Asian and African Studies* 9, 1: 23–62.

1975, *Women and Islamic law in a non-Muslim state*. New York: Wiley.

Lazreg, Marnia, 1988, 'Feminism and difference – the perils of writing as a woman in Algeria', *Feminist Studies* 14, 1: 81–108.

Leacock, Eleanor, 1978, 'Women's status in egalitarian society: implications for social evolution', *Current Anthropology* 19, 2: 247–75.

Leacock, Eleanor, and Helen Safa, 1986, *Women's work: development and the division of labor by gender*. South Hadley: Bergin and Garvey Publishers.

MacCormack, Carol, 1980, 'Nature, culture and gender: a critique', in Carol MacCormack and Marilyn Strathern (eds.), *Nature, culture and gender*. Cambridge: Cambridge University Press, pp. 1–24.

MacCormack, Carol and Marilyn Strathern (eds.), 1980, *Nature, culture and gender*. Cambridge: Cambridge University Press.

Mansour, Antoine, 1988, 'The West Bank economy: 1948–1984'. In George Abed (ed.), *The Palestinian economy: studies in development under prolonged occupation*. London: Routledge.

Marcus, Abraham, 1983, 'Men, women and property: dealers in real estate in 18th century Aleppo', *Journal of the Economic and Social History of the Orient* 26: 137–63.

1985, 'Real property and social structure in the premodern Middle East: a case study', in A. Mayer (ed.), *Property, social structure and the law in the modern Middle East*. New York: State University of New York Press, pp. 109–129.

Migdal, Joel (ed.), 1980, *Palestinian society and politics*. Princeton: Princeton University Press.

Mills, E., 1933, *Census of Palestine 1931*. Alexandria.

Mitter, Swasti, 1986, 'Industrial restructuring and manufacture homework: Immigrant women in the UK clothing industry', *Capital and Class* 27: 37–80.

Moors, Annelies, 1989, 'Restructuring and gender: garment production in Nablus', *MERA Occasional Paper Series*, Amsterdam: MERA.

1991a, 'Women and the Orient: a note on difference', in Lorraine Nencel and Peter Pels (eds.), *Constructing knowledge. Authority and critique in social sciences*. London, Newbury Park, New Delhi: Sage, pp. 114–23.

1991b, 'Gender, property and power: *Mahr* and marriage in a Palestinian village', in Kathy Davis, Monique Leijenaar and Jantine Oldersma (eds.), *The Gender of Power*. London, Newbury Park, New Delhi: Sage, pp. 111–28.

1994, 'Women and dower property in twentieth-century Palestine. The case of Jabal Nablus', *Islamic Law and Society* 1, 3: 301–31.

Morokvasic, Mirjana, Annie Phizacklea and H. Rudolph, 1986, 'Small firms and minority groups: contradictory trends in the French, German and British clothing industry', *International Sociology* 1, 4: 397–419.

Morris, Benny, 1987, *The birth of the Palestinian refugee problem 1947–1949*. Cambridge: Cambridge University Press.

Mundy, Martha, 1979, 'Women's inheritance of land in Highland Yemen', *Arabian Studies* 5: 161–87.

1988, 'The family, inheritance, and Islam: a re-examination of the sociology of faraaʾid law', in Aziz al-Azmeh (ed.), *Islamic law: social and historical contexts*. London and New York: Routledge.

Nassar, Jamal and Roger Heacock, 1991, 'The future in light of the past', in Jamel Nassar and Roger Heacock (eds.), *Intifada: Palestine at the crossroads*. New York: Birzeit University and Praeger Publishers, pp. 309–17.

Nimr, Ihsan, 1975 (1938), *Tārīkh Jabal Nablus wa l-Balqaʾ* (I-IV). Nablus: Matbaʿat Jamʿiyyat ʿUmmāl al-Matābiʿ al-Taʿāwuniyya.

Ortner, Sherry, 1984, 'Theory in anthropology since the sixties', *Comparative Studies in Society and History* 26: 126–66.

Ortner, Sherry and Harriet Whitehead (eds.), 1981, *Sexual meanings: the cultural construction of gender and sexuality*. Cambridge: Cambridge University Press.

Owen, E.R., 1981, *The Middle East in the world economy*. London: Methuen.

Owen, Roger, 1988, 'Economic development in mandatory Palestine: 1918–1948', in George Abed (ed.), *The Palestinian economy: studies in development under prolonged occupation*. London: Routledge, pp. 13–37.

Pastner, Carroll., 1980, 'Access to property and the status of women in Islam', in Jane Smith (ed.), *Women in contemporary Muslim societies*. Lewisbury: Bucknell University Press, pp. 146–86.

Pels, Dick, 1986, Property or power? A study in intellectual rivalry. University of Amsterdam, PhD thesis.

Peters, Emrys, 1978, 'The status of women in four Middle Eastern communities', in Lois Beck and Nikkie Keddie (eds.), *Women in the Muslim world*. Cambridge: Harvard University Press, pp. 311–51.

Phillips, Anne and Barbara Taylor, 1980, 'Sex and skill: notes towards a feminist economics', *Feminist Review* 6: 79–88.

Pollock, Alex, 1988, 'Society and change in the Northern Jordan Valley', in George Abed (ed.), *The Palestinian economy: studies in development under prolonged occupation*. London: Routledge, pp. 245–59.

Rainnie, A., 1984, 'Combined and uneven development in the clothing industry: the effects of competition and accumulation', *Capital and Class* 22: 141–56.

Rhodes, E., D. Wield and Noel Heyzer, 1983, *Clothing the world: first world markets, third world labour*. Milton Keynes: Open University.

Rockwell, Susan, 1985, 'Palestinian women workers in the Israeli-occupied Gaza Strip', *Journal of Palestine Studies* 14, 2: 114–36.

Rosenfeld, Henry, 1960, 'On the determinants of the status of Arab village women', *Man* 40: 66–74.

1980, 'Men and women in Arab peasant to proletariat transformation', in S. Diamond (ed.), *Theory and practice: essays presented to Gene Weltfish*. The Hague: Mouton, pp. 195–219.

Said, Edward, 1978, *Orientalism*. New York: Random Books.

Samed, Amal, 1976, 'The proletarianization of Palestinian women in Israel', *MERIP Reports*, 50: 10–26.

Sayers, Janet, Mary Evans and Nanneke Redclift (eds.), 1987, *Engels revisited: new feminist essays*. London: Tavistock.

Sayigh, Rosemary, 1981, 'Roles and functions of Arab women: a reappraisal', *Arab Studies Quarterly* 3, 3: 258–74.

Schlegel, Alice and Rohn Eloul, 1988, 'Marriage transactions: labor, property, status', *American Anthropologist* 90, 2: 291–309.

Schölch, Alexander, 1982, 'European penetration and the economic development of Palestine, 1856–82', in Roger Owen (ed.), *Studies in the economic and social history of Palestine in the nineteenth and twentieth centuries*. London: Macmillan, pp. 10–87.

Simpson, John Hope, 1930, *Report on immigration, land settlement and development*. London: His Majesty's Stationary Office.

Siniora, Randa, 1989, 'Palestinian labor in a dependent economy: women workers in the West Bank clothing industry', *Cairo Papers in Social Science* 12, 3. Cairo: The American University in Cairo Press.

Smith, Pamela Ann, 1984, *Palestine and the Palestinians, 1976–1983*. London and Sydney: Croom Helm.

Strathern, Marilyn, 1984, 'Subject or object? Women and the circulation of valuables in Highlands New Guinea', in Renée Hirshon (ed.), *Women and property, women as property*. London and Canberra: Croom Helm, pp. 158–76.

Tamari, Salim, 1981, 'Building other people's homes: the Palestinian peasant household and work in Israel', *Journal of Palestine Studies* 11, 1: 31–67.

Tamari, Salim and Rita Giacaman, 1980, *Zbeidat. The social impact of drip irrigation on a Palestinian peasant community in the Jordan Valley*. Bir Zeit: Bir Zeit University.

Taqqu, Rachelle, 1977, 'Arab labor in mandatory Palestine, 1920–1948', Columbia University, unpublished PhD thesis.

Tibawi, Abd al-Latif, 1956, *Arab education in mandatory Palestine: a study of three decades of British administration*. London: Luzac.

Tucker, Judith, 1983, 'Problems in the historiography of women in the Middle East: the case of 19th century Egypt', *International Journal of Middle East Studies* 15: 321–36.

1985, *Women in nineteenth-century Egypt*. Cambridge: Cambridge University Press.

1988, 'Marriage and family in Nablus, 1720–1856: towards a history of Arab marriage', *Journal of Family History* 13, 2: 165–79.

Tuqan, Fadwa, 1990. *A mountainous journey: the life of Palestine's outstanding woman poet*. London: The Women's Press (transl. of *Rihla saʿba rihla jabaliyya*. Akka, 1985: Dār al-Aswār).

UNIDO, 1984, *Survey of the manufacturing industry in the West Bank and Gaza Strip*. Vienna: UNIDO.

Van Arkadie, Brian, 1977, *Benefits and burdens: a report on the West Bank and Gaza Strip economies since 1967*. Washington: Carnegie Endowment for International Peace.

Waines, David, 1982, 'Through a veil darkly: the study of women in Muslim societies', *Comparative Studies in Society and History* 24, 4: 624–59.

Warnock, Kitty, 1990, *Land before honour: Palestinian women in the occupied territories*. London: Macmillan.

Weir, Shelagh, 1989, *Palestinian Costume*. London: British Museum.

Welchman, Lynn, 1988, 'The development of Islamic family law in the legal system of Jordan', *The International and Comparative Law Quarterly* 37: 868–86.

1990, 'Family law under occupation: Islamic law and the shariʿa courts in the West Bank'. in Chibli Mallat and Jane Connors (eds.), *Islamic family law*. London, Dordrecht, Boston: Graham and Trotman, pp. 93–119.

Whitehead, Ann, 1984, 'Men and women, kinship and property: some general issues', in Renee Hirshon (ed.), *Women and property, women as property*. London and Canberra: Croom Helm, pp. 176–93.

Yahya, Adil, 1991, "The role of the refugee camps", in Jamel Nassar and Roger Heacock (eds.), *Intifada: Palestine at the crossroads*. New York: Bir Zeit University and Praeger, pp. 91–107.

# Index